The Nashville Musician's Survival Guide

Eric Normand

The Nashville Musician's Survival Guide

by Eric Normand

Just Ducky Publishing
7051 HWY 70 S
PMB # 330
Nashville, TN 37221-2207

www.SurviveNashville.com

ISBN: 978-0-578-08367-4

Cover design by Kelly Normand
Interior design by Eric Normand
Photography: Eric and Kelly Normand (unless otherwise noted)
Copy Editors: Kelly Jacobs and Kelly Normand
Proofreaders: Donna Harmon, Peter Speliotis
Production Consultant: Sonja Chapman
Website design by www.JustDuckyDesigns.com

Acknowledgements

Many people donated their expertise and time to this project by way of interviews, expert chapter reviews, feedback, photographs, and much-needed advice. You all went the extra mile for me and this project and I am eternally grateful. I would like to thank you for your invaluable contributions:

Rhett Akins: Artist, Vocalist, Songwriter — www.rhettakins.net

Brittany Alyn: Artist, Vocalist, Songwriter — www.brittanyallyn.com

Polly B: Artist, Musician

Brian Beihl: Nashville Touring/Session Drummer

EJ Bernas: Senior Director Southwest Region - Universal Music Group

Bob Bullock: Producer, Engineer — www.bobbullock.net

Bart Busch: Engineer — www.stationwest.com

Mike Chapman: Bassist, Producer — www.myspace.com/mikechapmanmusic

Sonja Chapman: Production Editor — www.heinemann.com

Brenda Collady: Grand Ole Opry Museum & Photograph Curator

Michael Elsner: Guitarist, Composer, Songwriter — www.michaelelsner.com

Serona Elton: Assistant Professor, Music Business and Entertainment Industries, University of Miami Frost School of Music

Jim Elyea: Author of "Vox Amplifiers, The JMI Years" — www.voxguidebook.com

Greg Fogie: Sound Engineer, Recording Engineer, Tour Manager

Colt Ford: Artist, Songwriter — www.coltford.com

Giovanni: Producer, Engineer — www.therecordshopnashville.com

Donna Harmon: Mother Hen

Mike Holmes: Keyboardist, owner of Hot Haus Recording Studios

Shannon Houchins: CEO Average Joes Ent. and President AVJ Records — www.averagejoesent.com

Brad Hochstetler: VOX Product Manager — www.voxamps.com

Acknowledgements cont'd

Clint Jacobs: Bassist, Teacher

Kelly Jacobs: Teacher

Mikey Jaeger: Sound Engineer, Cartage Technician

Lee Kelley: Nashville Touring Drummer

Dan Kimpel: Author, Speaker — www.dankimpel.com

Denise Mattox: Page Designer, Blogger — www.musicianswidow.com

Ebie McFarland: Publicist — www.ebmediapr.com

Danny Milliner: Bassist, Band Leader

Logan Moore: Singer, Songwriter — www.loganmooremusic.com

Ronan Chris Murphy: Producer, Mixer, Artist — www.venetowest.com

Kevin Neal: President BLA Nashville — www.buddyleeattractions.com

Steve Pope: Bus Driver, Team Leader, Bus Mechanic

Rich Redmond: Drummer, Producer, Speaker, Author — www.richredmond.com

Judy Rodman: Vocal Coach, Recording Artist, Stage & Television Performer, Hit Songwriter, Session Singer, Producer & Vocal Consultant — www.judyrodman.com

Derek Sivers: Founder of CD Baby, Entrepreneur, Advisor — sivers.org

Randy Smith: Nashville Touring/Session Bassist/Vocalist — www.nashvillemusicpros.com/profile/RandySmith

Jason Somerville, Amy Woolf, Michelle Bernadsky: Roberts Brothers Coach Leasing — www.robertsbrotherscoach.com

Peter Speliotis: Chef, Restaurateur, Advisor

Tim Teague: Guitarist, Vocalist — www.myspace.com/teagueguitar

Scott Tweten: Nashville Touring Guitarist

Ben Vaughn: EVP & GM EMI Music Publishing

Luke Williams: Singer, Songwriter, Guitarist — lukewilliams.net

James Wood: Cellist, Recording Engineer, BMI, Inc.

Dedication - A Special Thank You

Writing this book has been a journey, a journey that began long before I ever set foot in Nashville. Throughout my life I have been fortunate to have had countless opportunities to learn from many great teachers. And in my mind, teaching does not always take place in a classroom. I dedicate this book to all the great teachers of the world, and to:

my wonderful wife, Kelly, you are my inspiration and guiding light. I could not have done this without you, thank you for your great patience and tireless work.

my wonderful son Josh, you've taught me much about life and music, thank you.

my good friend and mentor "D", thanks for helping to show me the way, it was your words that helped this book come to be.

my Mom and Dad, thanks for always supporting my musical ambitions (and for providing room and board for the first 27 years of my life).

my good friend Peter Speliotis - thanks for exploring music with me, teaching me the "art" of vibrato, and encouraging me to follow my dreams. You were always there for me.

my good friend Bill Blaine – you also taught me much, thank you.

Rob and Jody Gourlay - you guys were the best role models I could have ever asked for - thanks for giving me a chance when I needed it.

all of the great Nashville artists who gave me a chance and welcomed me into their families – Vern Gosdin, Toby Keith, Rhett Akins, Daryle Singletary, Jeff Carson, Chad Brock, David Kirsch, Jamey Johnson, Ronnie Pittman, Frank Taylor, Mindy Ellis, Angela Hurt, The Watercolor Project, and countless others.

all the great bands and musicians I've played with over the years, you're all part of my extended family.

all of my guitar students, you taught me selflessness and patience, and your passion also helped me to keep the fire burning.

Libby Knight wherever you are, thanks for giving me a gig when I needed it most.

the Fiddle and Steel - thank you for helping me get my start in Nashville.

the rest of my family, friends, and coworkers past and present - In life, each person is the sum of all of their relationships and experiences. We are all teachers and students. Together we can find the answers.

Contents

Foreword: About This Book

Nashville, or Music City, is a truly unique, always interesting, and often mysterious place. It is a place of yearning, a place for learning, and a place for craftsmen and dreamers alike. This place, that some also refer to as the country music capital of the world, is also the world's second largest music production city, and a place where dreams can come true or be crushed. Every day, from all over the world, aspiring musicians, artists, songwriters, engineers, producers, and music enthusiasts move to Nashville to pursue their lifelong ambitions and dreams of making it in the music biz. Once they get here, some of them become successful, but many find out that the music industry of Nashville is not what they thought and are unable to achieve their dreams and aspirations, often resulting in a premature and hasty exit.

Before my arrival to Music City in 2002, I had already spent 15 years working as a professional musician and guitar instructor in New England. During those formative years most of my musical activity was spent in working bands - rock bands, top 40 bands, blues bands, original projects, basically a little bit of everything. While I did get by, I earned as much of my living from teaching as I did from playing and never really achieved the success I had envisioned as a performer. By the time I got to Nashville, my attitude was "I'm going to do whatever it takes to make a living from playing music." I didn't care about becoming a star; I just wanted to earn a living solely from music, something I wasn't able to do in New England. My approach to working in Nashville was that of a "hired gun" - "I don't care about being your business partner, I'm here to play guitar for you!"

What is a hired gun? Hired guns make up the bulk of the professional music world. If you go to a concert and see your favorite artist or "band", the players backing that artist are essentially hired guns. Even though they might *seem* like a band entity, most recording and touring artists are the sole proprietor of their businesses, and their bands are comprised of hired guns. When you hear a song on the radio or that CD you just bought, 9 times out of 10 the music was recorded by professional studio musicians, also essentially hired guns.

Becoming a hired gun in Nashville is what I set out to do, and, as I have learned, working as a hired gun on the tours based out of Nashville is the most practical way to earn a living as a player in this town. This book provides all the pertinent info needed to succeed in Nashville in that regard. And, if you are interested in building your success as a songwriter or artist, you *will* need to understand this dynamic, as hired guns will be playing on your demos, albums, showcases, tours, and if you do well enough, award shows.

So by the time I pulled into town with my family in a rented Ryder truck full of everything we owned, I was hungry and eager to dig in to my new career as a freelance musician, but like every newcomer, I hadn't a clue about where to begin digging. Unlike most musician immigrants to Nashville fresh off the boat, I was extremely fortunate to be armed with a secret weapon, my good friend and mentor "D". D is a guitar player friend of mine that I knew and jammed with back in New England, and in the early nineties he moved to Nashville and began his own journey into the big music industry centered here.

D became my Nashville mentor and guided me with some great direction that helped me to find my own path. I had an endless supply of questions and grilled him heavily during my Nashville infancy. He graciously took me under his wing, taking me to his hangouts, introducing me to his industry friends, teaching me some Nashville chops; he even gave me one of his guitars and helped me land one of my first road gigs. He taught me how to network and go about building the relationships I would need to survive. When he spoke, I hung on every word, and his advice proved invaluable.

Since those early days, my career has taken me down many roads, some good ones, and some bad ones too. All in all it has been a massive growth experience providing me with much insight into the world of big music business. Along the way I have met many great people - players, singers, writers, engineers, producers, all with their own story. Often these fellow journeymen have offered advice and insight, and sometimes they have asked for mine. At some point a while back it occurred to me that the Nashville music scene could benefit from a book designed to help musicians better understand how this scene is structured, and how to go about finding work. A book that would provide the details and insight that could help musicians and artists on a practical, day to day street level. I searched for books and articles and found many geared towards songwriters, but very few writings geared towards helping the musicians, technicians, and aspiring artists. Ultimately, it was my quest for this knowledge that led me to write this book.

The Nashville Musician's Survival Guide is an outline of concepts, strategies, and tips that can help musicians find paying jobs that will allow them to earn a living from their craft in Nashville and beyond. The first section of this book, **Music Related Jobs within the Nashville Music Industry**, covers three separate, but often overlapping categories: the Nashville Nightclub Industry, the Nashville Touring Industry, and the Nashville Recording Industry. The details about job requirements, pay structures, and the networking required to land gigs will be outlined in great detail. Also explored are some of the other music related support roles and industries: techs, cartage, rehearsal studios, repair technicians, production companies, music retail, music teachers, administrative personnel and more.

The second part of the book, **Touring Life**, goes into great detail about the different aspects of touring: what it's like to live with a band, to live and sleep on a bus, dealing with fans, fly dates, eating on the road, and the impact that long-term touring can have on relationships. Also within this part of the book is a section called tour diaries - personal accounts of interesting and often funny scenarios that can only happen on the road.

The third section, **Interviews**, features candid one-on-one interviews with Nashville music industry veterans from every corner of the community. Country artist and hit songwriter Rhett Akins, senior director of marketing Southwest region for UMG EJ Bernas, ace recording engineer Bob Bullock, A-list session bassist Mike Chapman, indie artist Colt Ford, and others provide deep perspective from their experiences in Nashville.

The fourth section, **Nashville Institutions**, explores some long-standing entities that are at the core of music city. The Grand Ole Opry, the A-Team, the Musicians Union, BMI and ASCAP, and the good ol' boy network have all been here since just about the dawn of time, and an understanding of these institutions is essential to all aspiring music professionals in Nashville.

The fifth part of the book, **Nashville Specifics**, talks about the culture shock of relocation, Tennessee climate, cost of living, where to live, getting around, non-music related employment, and a few other helpful things specific to living and working in middle Tennessee.

Sustainability, the sixth and final section of the book, explores some of the long-term problems and potential solutions of being a career musician in Nashville and beyond. Issues like repetitive motion injuries, self-marketing, home recording, wearing a lot of hats, and overall mindset and character will be discussed.

Interspersed throughout the book are some real-life accounts from my experiences and travels as well. Although many of these situations and stories are specific to the Nashville music industry, many of the concepts put forth are universal to all who desire a career in music. If you are considering moving to Nashville or another big music business metropolis to pursue your career in music, this book can give you some idea of what to expect. If you are new to town, this book could be a valuable tool in helping you get off the ground. If you have been here a while and are struggling, it might inspire you to try some different approaches. If you already enjoy a successful career, it might help re-enforce what you already know or give you a different perspective. This book only scratches the surface of the possibilities that exist in this place, and one can only truly comprehend this scene by experiencing it firsthand. However, I believe the knowledge on these pages can potentially save you some time, money, frustration, and maybe a few embarrassing moments.

I don't consider myself an expert on the Nashville music scene; certainly there are many others here with greater credentials and differing opinions. I don't claim to have all the answers either; I simply want to share what I know, based on my life experiences, from my perspective, as well as the perspectives of some of my friends and peers. The concepts and strategies I am putting forth are a set of guidelines that stem from my knowledge and have worked for me. If you talk to others here in Nashville, you will certainly hear about alternate approaches to earning a living from music in this town. Everyone's path is different, and at the end of the day it is up to you to determine your own path.

After living my first 35 years in small town America, relocating to Nashville was a wakeup call of epic proportions. There are so many supremely talented individuals here, and I feel truly blessed to be a small part of a place so rich in music culture and tradition. It is my goal that this book will offer assistance and inspiration to those who quest knowledge and insight to the Nashville Music Scene and desire a career in music here and everywhere. It's a strange and mysterious world; the tour starts now.

One last thing: While my experiences and adventures in Nashville over the past decade have been a journey in and of themselves, the writing of this book has been its own journey, one that has not only helped me better understand the totality of my experiences here, but one that has also yielded me a new skill, writing, an activity that presents a whole new set of problems that need solutions. One of the issues I had to deal with as an author involved gender, as I had to decide which pronoun to use throughout the book, "he" or "she." To make things simple, I went with "he," in most cases. I'm not sure of the ratio between males and females in the Nashville music community; there are obviously thousands of men ***and*** *women pursuing their dreams here in Music City. I hope no one is offended by this detail; this book applies to ALL musicians.*

Craftsmen and Dreamers

> *"A man who works with his hands is a laborer; a man who works with his hands and his brain is a craftsman; but a man who works with his hands and his brain and his heart is an artist."* – Louis Nizer

To succeed in the music industry you need to first understand how the business works, but more importantly, you need to understand yourself. Why are you here? What are you trying to accomplish? Are you trying to make a good living from your craft or become rich from it? Do you want to be a superstar, or would you be just as happy to be a sideman? How important is it to you to "make it" in the music business? What is your definition of "making it"? Do you feel that you need to be in the public spotlight, or do you think you could be happy working behind the scenes? Are you a craftsman or a dreamer?

The concept of the craftsman and the dreamer is a way of looking at the music industry I have devised to help clarify the bigger picture and to help you decide how and where you fit in. So, what is the difference between a craftsman and a dreamer, and into which category do you think you fit? No matter which side you tend to lean towards, it is likely that you have some elements of both, and one is not necessarily better than the other.

Craftsmen are musicians, singers, engineers, songwriters, technicians, and other music industry related workers that approach their careers from the practical standpoint of earning a living from their craft. If you are a craftsman, you are interested in jobs, gigs, recording sessions, and anything that will pay you for your services on a regular basis, both short and long term. Skilled craftsmen are good at what they do and approach their career in music in the same manner that carpenters, factory workers, and other service and manufacturing industry professionals approach theirs. Find work, do the work, get paid for the work, and do what you must to have plenty of work. You are goal oriented and work at honing and perfecting your skills. You view each job as a challenge to be conquered and see each gig, session, or tour as an opportunity that might create more opportunities. You approach your career systematically and work at building relationships that will ensure your survival long-term. In the world of the craftsman, your desire to earn a consistent living from your craft will often make it necessary for you to put your personal and artistic preferences aside, as your employer's wants and needs will usually take precedence. A good craftsman understands his role, enjoys his work, and is willing to do what is necessary for the bigger picture and long term goals.

Dreamers are musicians, singers, engineers, songwriters, technicians, and other music industry related people that view their career destinations in a more immediate manner. If you are a dreamer, you are likely interested in becoming a popular recording and touring artist, a hit songwriter, or maybe a Grammy winner. The success you are envisioning is one in which you are on top of the pile as the artist, writer, or producer that creates the product that will ultimately command the attention and adulation of the masses. You are trying to "make it" in the music biz and will do so at all costs. You feel compelled to put yourself out there and make things happen. You are sure of your talents and certain that you are on the verge of being discovered and getting a deal soon. Your next gig, tour, or recording is your biggest priority and goal, and seeing it through will ensure your success. A dreamer might or might not be a skilled craftsman, but in most cases, you are definitely in search of being something beyond a regular working musician or craftsman.

There are extremely important elements that lie within both the craftsman and the dreamer, and most successful people have traits from both. Within the dreamer there is ambition, desire, passion, and an incentive to keep moving forward. The dreamer dreams of being more than he already is and going places he has never been. Within the craftsman lie the skills, knowledge, and practicality that will enable the dreamer to pursue and achieve his or her dreams.

If you are a dreamer, try to look past your immediate goal and desire of "making it", and maybe ask yourself, what is it that you want to make? How do *you* define making it? Once you can determine that, use the practical skills of the craftsman in you to get there. No matter what "making it" means to you, there will forever be more steps to be taken, so get used to walking. A continued education of your own nature and the potential roads that lie ahead will help enable you to choose the best steps possible. If you are leaning more towards the craftsman side of the fence, you are already in a good position to continue moving forward, as are most journeymen; just remain aware of the path.

Regardless of where you fall within this spectrum, the life of a career musician is comprised of a series of steps on a ladder to be climbed, relationships to be nurtured and developed, thresholds to cross, and doors to be opened. Don't expect the music industry to be the system that makes your career happen, for in reality, it is you that creates the system. So take a little time out and ask yourself, are you a craftsman, a dreamer, or a little of both?

Chapter I

Music Related Jobs In Nashville; Connecting The Dots

"I had been on the road for a long time and was not really getting anywhere. Bob Johnston, a friend of mine, had taken over Colombia in Nashville. He asked me if I wanted to come down. I did - thank God I did."
— Charlie Daniels

If you are a musician or entrepreneur living in Nashville, thinking about moving to Nashville, or just curious to understand how the world's second largest music production city conducts its business, the first thing you will need to understand is the hierarchy of things - how this place works. If you are interested in navigating these waters, it will be to your advantage to understand the industries within the industry: what the potential music related jobs are, how they are interconnected, and how these jobs can be acquired.

A Changing Landscape

First of all, the Nashville music industry, like all music industry at this point in time, is going through a change. Under the old model, a major label would sign a promising artist, finance an album project, help organize touring, provide the marketing and financial means for that artist to achieve radio airplay, and essentially put that artist on the map. In many cases, the label would also help artists develop a lasting career.

Now, this is happening on a much smaller scale and with less frequency than it was in the booming 90s, a time many consider the heyday of the modern Nashville era. It's no secret that radio is dying a slow and painful death as the masses have gravitated to the Internet to hear and obtain music. The online digital revolution has taken away much of the power and impact of the major record labels and their future is uncertain. In the past, an artist toured to promote album sales. Presently, recorded music sales are a smaller percentage of many artists' incomes than they were just a short time ago, and in many cases, new music is released to help promote an artist's tour.

Social networking sites like MySpace, Facebook, Twitter, and a host of others have helped level the playing field for many independent artists, making it now possible to achieve a music career that was previously unattainable. As many music business journalists have written, these changing trends are midstream, and while many make predictions, no one knows for certain what the new model, or models, will be. Regardless of all these changes, there are still some likely certainties within the Nashville music industry.

The Nashville Recording Industry

Nashville is home for many world-class recording studios, and combined with a small town feel, it has been, and continues to be, a destination for artists and groups from all over the world. There are also hundreds of major recording and touring artists living in middle Tennessee that continue to record new music and literally thousands of songwriters recording demos here on an ongoing basis. Nashville is also home to a great number of independent artists and bands trying to make their mark in the world and many of them record regularly as well. Although some of the big million-dollar studios are struggling with a few even closing their doors, one of the new trends has been an explosion in the number of home-based project studios, enabling many musicians, producers, engineers, and studio owners to obtain or create previously unattainable work.

The Nashville Touring Industry

Hundreds of Nashville-based artists (mostly in the country music genre, but also in pop, Christian, and other genres) who built their success on the old model still have a strong fan base and continue to tour nationally, providing thousands of jobs for musicians, techs, managers, bus drivers, etc. Many artists are now earning more of their income from touring than from album sales, and this is good news for everyone that enjoys riding around on a tour bus.

The Nashville Nightclub Industry

Nashville is a year-round tourist destination with visitors coming in droves from every corner of the globe to see the world-famous Ryman or maybe catch a glimpse of their favorite stars around town (it isn't that uncommon to see artists like Toby Keith, Joe Nichols, or Kid Rock hanging out or sitting in at Nashville nightclubs on occasion). This tourism industry helps to create a nightclub industry where live music is featured seven nights a week, year-round. Although the level of musicianship and pay can vary greatly, if a musician or singer knows how and where to apply themselves, supplemental to full-time work can be had in this industry as well.

Additionally, the nightclub industry provides thousands of jobs to wait staff, cooks, door men, PA techs, etc. many of whom are musicians working towards a full-time career in their field. The clubs and bars of Nashville are also an important networking tool for many in Music City.

These three major components of the Nashville music industry create an additional sector of support industries including rehearsal facilities, cartage companies, music stores, musical instrument manufacturers, instrument repair, production companies, management companies, accountant firms, music educators, and pawn shops.

View of downtown Nashville from the Shelby Street foot bridge

Plugging In

"The snow falls, each flake in its appropriate place." — Zen saying

So, how are all the music related industries and jobs in Nashville interconnected and where do you fit in? Let's start with the recording industry.

The Nashville Recording Industry

This sector regularly provides work for recording studios, producers, recording engineers, session players, cartage companies, and administrative personnel. As there is a seemingly endless supply of songwriters in this town, songwriter demos are a large portion of what is recorded in the Nashville studios. If a songwriter has a publishing deal, in most cases, the publishing company requires a minimum amount of songs to be turned in monthly, and will finance these professionally recorded demos, quite often at a studio they work with regularly. There are also many songwriters without publishing deals that regularly employ studios and studio musicians to record their demos, financing these projects themselves.

When major artists record their album projects, for the most part, the producer will employ "A-Team" session players. It is fairly uncommon for a musician who is not a member of the A-Team to get to record on a major album project, although there have been more exceptions to this in recent years as major artists like Tim McGraw and Jamey Johnson have used musicians from their touring bands on their recordings. The A-Team players also do some, but not all, of the demo work, and it is the recording of songwriter demos that is perhaps the best opportunity for non-A-Team players to obtain paying work and experience as a session player. Ultimately, it is the songwriters and artists that create most of the paying recording session work in Nashville.

Additionally, Nashville recording studios continue to record album projects for artists and bands from all over the world as well as various TV and film scoring projects providing an additional sector of work for many studios, engineers, producers, and musicians.

Touring

With somewhere between 500 and 1000 touring entities based out of Nashville (this estimate is based on conversations I've had with several different booking agents), this makes the touring industry a substantial source of employment for thousands of music industry workers. These tours range from mid-level artists traveling on one or two buses with a band and crew of usually 8 to 12, to lower-level artists with three or four piece bands traveling by van, to mega stars traveling with an entourage of 50 or more on half a dozen busses or more, carrying full production in several semis with their own catering in tow. Most tours fall into the first two categories.

The essential employees on a typical mid-level tour would consist of the artist, a 3 to 6 piece band, bus driver, sound engineer, merchandise person, and possibly a road manager and monitor engineer (on many tours, a band or crew member does double duty as road manager). An entourage of this size can easily travel on one bus. One step up from this would include all of the previously mentioned jobs plus a monitor engineer, instrument tech, backline tech, and lighting designer, and would travel with two buses and maybe a trailer or separate truck for equipment and the occasionally annoying crew member.

The biggest tours often carry full production in several semis and would have large crews in addition to the artist and band. A large-scale operation as this would probably have a designated tour manager, road manager, and stage manager, 1 or 2 instrument techs, a backline tech, an audio crew of 4 or 5, a lighting crew of 3 or 4, a video crew of 3 or 4, a rigger or two, 10 or more drivers, and possibly a catering staff of 3 or 4. Most band and crew members on small to midsize tours are independent contractors working directly for the artist. On larger tours carrying their own production, many of the crew members are employees of the various production companies supporting the tour, and will work exclusively for that artist for the duration of a touring season. For many music industry workers in Nashville, landing a job as a band or crew member on a national tour is more easily attainable than the long-term endeavor of acquiring or creating regular studio work.

Nightclub Industry

The Nashville nightclub industry plays a unique role as it provides both income and networking opportunities for many Nashville music industry workers. Most newcomers to Nashville discover the Broadway scene first, as it is the most obvious grouping of clubs downtown. For musicians and singers that are good at hustling and armed with a large repertoire of country, rock, and pop standards, there is some work to be found in this freelance scene whose audience is primarily tourists and a few hustling music entrepreneurs. It can be a hard pace, and if you don't educate yourself about how and where to work, the pay and morale can be low. Approached in the right manner, you will earn a supplemental income while honing your chops and building relationships that will lead to other work. (Just remember, if you're going to gig regularly on Broadway, you'd better know the intro to "Working Man Blues" and "Ramblin' Fever".)

There are many other pockets of clubs around the city - on Second Avenue, Printers Alley, Demonbreun Street (between I40 and "the roundabout"), The Gulch, West End, Belmont, East Nashville, and many more. The freelance factor applies to many of these as well, and the pay varies greatly. Many connected musicians and industry workers frequent some of these clubs regularly, and it takes some research and exploring to determine the best networking opportunities within them. It is within some of these nightclubs that songwriter and artist showcases often take place, and this can bring in additional musicians attempting to network with whatever industry personnel might happen to be in attendance.

Finding Your Niche

These three separate industries overlap in many ways and at the same time there is a definite inaccessibility from one scene to the others for many. Many workers in the different areas of these three industries remain loyal to whatever clique they are a part of, often at the exclusion of outsiders. Obtaining regular paying work in the recording industry, while extremely desirable for many, is possibly the hardest nut to crack, and is most commonly attained through personal relationships built over a long period of time. This makes touring work a big goal and main focus for a large percentage of music industry workers in Nashville. While extremely competitive, touring work can be more immediately attainable, and it is through networking in the Nashville nightclubs that many a player or tech has landed his first road gig. Songwriters looking to gain exposure and make contacts will also frequent some of these clubs, in addition to making the rounds at songwriter nights at places like the Bluebird Café or the Commodore Grille.

Earning income from your craft within the Nashville music industry is all about longevity. There are more workers here than there is work for them, and this makes for a high level of competition. You need to understand this and apply yourself in ways that make sense for you. Many folks will say that Nashville is a five-year town. That you've got to put in at least five years of hustling and working the scene if you expect to succeed here. I think a better way of looking at it is that if you move to Nashville, you'd better be in it for the long haul. It's a job. Approach your music career in Nashville like any other career - start from the bottom, dig in hard, build strong and lasting relationships, and slowly work your way up. Just be sure to arm yourself with knowledge and *dig* in the right places. The relationships and connections you will need to succeed in your chosen field in music are all here. All of the music industry jobs in Nashville are available to those who possess enough drive, perseverance, knowledge, and people skills to achieve those ambitions. Are you one of those people? It's now time for the craftsman in you to go to work.

Top: Lower Broadway as seen from entrance to The Stage (Robert's in foreground)
Middle left: Tootsies Orchid Lounge - Middle right: rear entrance to the Stage
Bottom left to right: Legends Corner, Printers Alley, 12th and Porter

Chapter I.I

Nashville Nightclub Industry

> *"No single style or performance can typify all of country music. But one strain of country is something old and new called honkytonk. It is both a style and a place, and of the place it used to be said that "honky-tonks were where a white man could get killed by his own kind while listening to country music."* — from a Time Magazine article published on September 27, 1976

The live music scene in Nashville covers a lot of ground. There are hundreds of nightclubs and bars in and around the city that feature live music, many of them seven days a week, year round. The types of venues and styles of music and bands vary greatly. Also varying greatly is the quality of performers and the pay rate. There is one whole part of the live music scene that is somewhat tied to the country or country/pop market, and many of the musicians and singers working in these clubs are also connected to the touring and recording industry. This scene is largely tourist driven. A secondary side to that world is the singer-songwriter scene, centered on singers and songwriters usually backed by a lone acoustic guitar and performing in venues that cater to them. There is also a handful of blues clubs, and a blues and R&B scene connected to that. There are some (not many) jazz clubs and a smaller scene that works within that world. There are also some jam bands and funky improv groups that play at some of the college bars and other trendy venues. And there is also kind of an underground power pop/ punk / metal scene here as well.

We've got honky tonks, concert clubs, biker bars, and clubs for stars (John Rich of Big and Rich fame has his own members-only bar called The Spot). Karaoke bars, hip-hop and dance clubs - whatever you're looking for, you can probably find it somewhere here in Music City.

One part of this club scene that has some crossover to the Nashville based touring industry is a tourist-driven stretch of clubs downtown on lower Broadway. While not always the most musically rewarding scene to be involved with, there are many musicians working on the strip that are also employed by national acts (there are also many, if not more, that are not). Broadway may lack style for the musical purist, but it does serve a practical purpose with the connections that can be made there. It's kind of a breeding ground for newbies and veterans alike where relationships can be formed that can lead to touring work and other more lucrative gigs.

If you don't have the stomach or patience for Broadway, there are many other possible routes to take, many of which might offer a more musical setting; they are just not as obvious or concentrated as "the strip". Figure out what you're trying to accomplish, educate yourself about the different nightclub niches within the city, and then determine what part of this scene you want to plug yourself into to accomplish your goals.

Front room of Tootsies

Nightclub Musicians

"We're just a bar band, that's all we are." — Kurt Cobain

If you are a musician, songwriter, or music entrepreneur trying to build your music career in Nashville, you will probably be spending some time in the bars and clubs around town, especially at first. Unless you already have a good job in your chosen field, you will need to make new connections, and it is in the clubs that many of these connections can be made. (It is very unlikely that you are going to land a good road gig or pub deal from an ad on craigslist.)

Performers at the Stage on Broadway

First of all, regardless of what some jaded players around town might say, playing music in the Nashville nightclubs is both practical and essential for the career minded musician, serving many different purposes for many players. I believe that at the core of many a great player is a nightclub musician. Nightclubs are the places that most professional musicians and singers have spent the most time performing. Unless you went straight from music school to a national tour, there's a good chance that you spent some time in a local band grinding it out on a local or regional club circuit before you thought about moving to Nashville. Once you are here, it is often a nonstop barrage of nightclub activity that will lead to either your advancement or premature exit. So don't be put off by the term; it is at the core of many a great player.

One important thing to understand about the Nashville club scene is that many of the "bands" playing around the city are actually comprised of freelance musicians, often with varying levels of commitment to any given project or gig. In many situations, a singer will have a weekly time slot at a club and a core group of their favorite regular players that he or she will try to get commitments from for a weekly gig or gigs. As many players in this town are involved in several projects at once, quite often a singer's favorite players aren't available. Sometimes players will also bail at the last minute for something more lucrative, for instance, a paid recording session, or an out-of-town gig. If a singer's first call player isn't available or cancels, they will call their second and third choices, etc. As singers are sometimes booked for gigs at the last minute, their regular players might not be available on such short notice, and this can result in complete strangers filling in, usually by a referral.

Because of this basic element within the Nashville night club scene, many of these "bands" don't rehearse and might only come together as a band for a weekly gig or two. There are, of course, some bands comprised of groups of musicians that are exclusively committed to their band projects, rehearsing regularly and performing in the clubs around town and elsewhere in middle Tennessee, but from my experience, the freelance groupings are more commonly found.

Instrumentation

Although lead singers are an essential component for most bands, their unique role puts them in a different position than most other players; therefore, an entire chapter has been dedicated to them (see page 25).

Drummers, bassists, and guitarists are by far the most in demand and commonly used musicians in most live band situations. And, as you might guess, there are far more drummers and guitarists here than needed, and never enough good bass players (especially ones that can sing harmony). In addition to the classic trio instrumentation, if another player is added to an ensemble, it is quite often a keyboardist. In many situations, it could also be a second electric guitar, steel guitar, fiddle, or mandolin.

In some situations, the fourth or fifth member of an ensemble might be a "utility player" who might play a range of different instruments at different points of a performance, such as electric and acoustic guitar, mandolin, fiddle, dobro, lap steel, etc. Some steel guitarists also play lap steel and/or dobro. There is also a demand for strong harmony singers that can play acoustic guitar.

Banjo players are fairly uncommon but can occasionally be found in some settings. There's an old joke that goes *"What is something you never hear said in Nashville? - Can someone ask the banjo player to move his Porsche?"* Also worthy of mention would be that there is some demand for horn players in the blues and jazz scene, although the amount of paying gigs around town is minimal in those genres.

Styles And Genres

The range of genres played in the nightclubs and music venues of Nashville vary greatly, but country music and country music hybrids make up a large part of what is regularly performed. Many clubs around town, especially the ones that cater to the tourists, feature singers and bands that can play a full night of cover material consisting of a mix of classic country, modern country, southern rock, classic rock, pop, and R&B. There are a few clubs that regularly feature bands that play only classic rock, and there are a few blues clubs around town also. Scattered throughout the city and its surrounding communities are a plethora of venues geared towards many different niches including bluegrass, jazz, indie-rock, folk, jam bands, singer songwriters, and others. The ratio of cover material to original music can vary greatly within these niches, especially outside of the tourist driven part of the scene.

Onstage at Layla's Bluegrass Inn on Broadway, and yes, that is chicken wire!

Different Types Of Paying Nightclub Work In Nashville

» Broadway gigs

» In town gigs (non Broadway)

» Gigs on the outskirts of town

» Showcases

Suggestions For Nightclub Musicians In Nashville

Here are some concepts that I have found helpful in becoming an active freelance musician in the Nashville nightclub scene.

» Be friendly and courteous. This should be a no-brainer, but you would be surprised at how many competent players don't get called back because they were perceived to be stiff, dry, boring, or even rude. Be objective about your social skills and learn how to turn on the charm.

» Know a lot of songs, in a lot of different genres. Having a big repertoire will give you an advantage over the players that don't. *(See the Nashville 100 chapter)*

» Know your material. Don't just wing it. Make it a point to obtain recordings and learn the material of the band or artist you are working with whenever possible. Even if it is just one gig, this could make the difference of a callback or not, *and* save potential embarrassment.

» Know traditional country music. Being able to play country music with an authentic feel will set you apart from the players who don't, especially if you're trying to obtain work with a country artist.

» Know the Nashville number system. This system of assigning numbers to chords will help you survive songs you don't know, either by the use of charts or hand signals.

» Be punctual or early for your gigs.

» Have good, reliable gear.

» Look presentable. This will not only help you please the singer you are working with, but it will also help your appeal to anyone that might be eying you for another gig.

» Become a lead singer. Many singers want to be able to take a rest mid-set during the long hours of club gigs and will often ask another player in the band to sing a couple of songs. Developing your lead singing ability is not essential, but can help you to work more.

» Be able to sing harmonies. There are more players here than there is work for them. Being a good harmony singer gives you a big advantage over the players that aren't.

» Be ready to jump at a moment's notice. If it is your goal to play a lot of gigs, you need to expect some calls to come in at the last minute, sometimes an hour or so before a gig.

Freelancers - Ships At Sea

"Once you've decided what aspect of your field to freelance, take the time to establish yourself. The biggest misconception people have is that they're going to jump right into it and start making money, ... Not true. Just because you build it doesn't mean they'll come." — Laurie Rozakis

What is it like to work as a freelance musician in Nashville? In a recent conversation I had with a young drummer considering relocating to Nashville, I was asked this very question. It seemed like such a simple question, yet it's answer was difficult to easily explain to someone that had never been here. After giving this question much thought, I realized this was because the career of a freelance musician in Nashville can cover a lot of different ground and go in many different directions at once. There are a lot of freelancers or "hired guns" working in every aspect of the Nashville music industry, and the experience can vary greatly depending on each individual's unique circumstances and relationships.

The term "freelance musician" implies that you are an independent contractor, and that all employment is temporary, even if it is temporary for a long period of time. If you are working as a hired gun in the nightclubs around town, you will probably never join a band, but you might play in many. If you are hired to play in the road band of a touring artist, you will be working for artist X Inc., and while you may be traveling, performing, and living with a "band" you are, nevertheless, an independent contractor employed by the artist. This same basic principle holds true in the world of paid recording sessions as well. You don't belong to any one group, but you try to get your fingers into everything that you can. Throw yourself to the wind, and see where the wind takes you.

One way to look at it is to compare it to the career of a lone professional assassin (think CIA, James Bond movies, etc.). A call comes in the middle of the night with instructions about a job that needs to be carried out. You decide to accept this job, make the necessary preparations, and proceed to carry out the mission. You "execute" the job to the best of your ability to please your temporary employer so that he or she will want to call you again for more work. You receive payment for successfully completing this mission and return home to wait for the next call. The next call might come in a day or two, or it might not come for six weeks. While waiting for the next call, you'll use your resources, and circulate through whatever channels are available to you to land more work. Sometimes the work might be steady, and sometimes there will be big gaps in between jobs. If you are good at what you do and make the right connections, your reputation will precede you, putting you on a short call list, but that doesn't mean there will always be work. You're like a ship at sea that will never reach its port. Alone, always searching, waiting for that next call. Okay, enough of the spy novel stuff, but you get the point.

Do you need to be a freelance musician to earn a living in the Nashville music industry? Not necessarily, but in general, yes, you do, at least at this point in time. There are, of course, exceptions to every rule, like the occasional band that becomes successful or a recording studio owned by a group of partners. But these are few and far between. In general, the Nashville music industry is comprised of professional freelancers, often working within a collective group, or several collective groups of individuals, in the worlds of songwriting, recording, performing, etc., and it has been this way for a long time. That's not to say that there aren't some good "bands" or groups of players firmly committed to their projects in Nashville. Those kinds of situations do exist here, but most of them don't earn a living directly from their band project.

So, how do you become a professional freelance musician in Nashville? There are four basic ingredients you'll need to reach a point that you will be called on a regular basis for your services as a hired gun: time, money, a good reputation, and relationships with the right people. Being proficient at your craft will help too.

1. **Time:** To build the reputation and relationships you'll need to get those calls requires an upfront investment of time. You'll need to make the rounds to the clubs regularly to establish a reputation and build connections (weekly would be a good start, nightly would be better), and this takes time.

2. **Money:** It could take anywhere from a couple of months to even a year or more to get off the ground, so you'll need to figure out how to support yourself financially in the meantime. You should plan on working a day job along the way (or find a spouse with a really good job).

3. **Reputation:** Establishing a good reputation also takes time; you can't force your projection on others. You need to establish yourself as a good person, as well as a good player if you want people to call you.

4. **Relationships:** Building relationships that will lead to work also takes time. You can't force friendships to happen; they just happen on their own. You can, however, try to put yourself in situations that tend to have more "connected" people around.

So, back to the original question, what is it like to be a freelance musician in Nashville? Let's assume that you have invested the time, built a solid reputation, and have established enough relationships that you are getting some paying gigs around town regularly. What kind of gigging situations might those be?

When I first moved to Nashville, I aggressively went after as much in-town work as I could, and after about six months of working at it, I had networked my way into several different situations (all of which were paying gigs). The following overview of some of my activities at that point in time should give you some idea about what it can be like to work as a hired gun in the Nashville nightclubs.

One of my first weekly shifts was at the Second Fiddle on Broadway where I played every Tuesday from 6:00 to 9:30 P.M. with a singer named Mindy Ellis. I landed this gig by the way of a referral (word-of-mouth) and received a CD of most of the obscure tunes in advance. The drummer and bassist were the same two guys about 80% of the time, and they each "subbed out" the gig occasionally when another commitment conflicted. We played a song list that consisted of mostly classic female country standards combined with some modern country radio hits, a few R&B tunes, a little bit of classic rock, and some of her originals. This particular gig allowed us to take breaks, and we usually took at least one 20 minute break per gig. The size of the audience varied week to week and so did our pay, as we received a base pay of $20 each plus tips. The average was probably $50-$60 per player per night.

Around that same point in time, I worked my way into a weekly Saturday night shift at the Fiddle and Steel Guitar Bar with Frank Taylor. Once again, the other rhythm section players were usually the same players, but occasionally subbed out their shift, as did I. We played a mix of classic and modern country, classic rock and blues, and a handful of "Margaritaville" type dance floor classics for the tourists. Our shift ran from 10:00 to 2:30, and our pay was also a base plus tips, averaging usually between $50 and $80 per player.

Aside from these regular weekly shifts, I would get random calls to fill in for somebody else's "subbed out" gig. The gigs ranged from other clubs on Broadway to different clubs around the city, and the material and pay varied. For many of these random fill-ins, the initial call and notice of the gig was last-minute, often coming the day before, and sometimes the day of the show. Literally all of these gigs came with no rehearsal, and in many cases I found myself playing with complete strangers, or maybe having a connection to only one of the other players.

On some of these last-minute gigs, I came knowing a lot of material being played; on others, very little. In situations where I didn't know the material, other musicians in the band would assist me via the number system, either holding up fingers, or mouthing the numbers of the chords (one, four, etc.). This fly by the seat of your pants approach can be both exciting and nerve-racking. It's very satisfying when you play something that you've never played before and it comes out great. On the other hand, it's quite nerve-racking when you play something that you've never played before and it's a train wreck. Overall, I found that doing this on a regular basis made me a better player, as this approach requires deep concentration and hard listening.

Occasionally, a call would come for me to play on some aspiring artist's "showcase." For a typical showcase, a CD, sometimes accompanied with Nashville number style charts, is given to the players a few days or weeks in advance. Sometimes there might be a paid rehearsal or two (usually $50 or so per player); other times not. These showcases would take place in nightclubs, on weeknights, and usually paid $50-$75 for a 45 minute set.

During this period of time, I was also getting occasional calls to play club and casino gigs out of town, usually, van and trailer type situations. These calls would come from either singers I had worked with, or players I had previously worked with. Song lists varied from classic to modern country, to classic rock and blues and the pay usually averaged around $150 per night.

If this kind of routine sounds chaotic and unpredictable, that's because it is. The combination of my 2 to 3 regular weekly shifts with the random last-minute calls never really paid all of my bills, and I was regularly engaged in eBay and pawn shop activity to try to bridge the gap financially. For me, all this nightclub activity served a higher purpose, as every gig provided me with more experience and new relationships *in addition* to supplemental income. In time, the relationships I made in the clubs led to the more lucrative and prestigious world of touring.

Some players don't mind the kind of frenzied existence inherent to freelancing in the clubs on a long-term basis, and I personally know of a couple of musicians that have been earning over $40,000 a year working solely on Broadway. They invested the time, built their reputations, nurtured relationships, and went to work. Meanwhile, some are still waiting for their first call.

Like a ship at sea that never reaches its port.

Gigging In Nashville

"Honky Tonk: a usually tawdry nightclub or dance hall; ***especially*** *one that features country music."* — Webster Dictionary

Lower Broadway has probably the biggest concentration of nightclubs featuring live music in the city. It is a truly unique place and deserves its own category. First and foremost, Broadway is a 3 block stretch of a dozen or so clubs lining both sides of the street that provides a year round destination for tourists, many whom travel from around the globe to visit some of the more famous spots on the strip such as Tootsies, Roberts or the world famous Ryman right around the corner. Most of the clubs on Broadway have an old western honky tonk feel to them and feature live music 7 nights a week. If you take a drive down Broadway with your windows open, you will hear the sound of a dozen bands booming out the open doors of clubs in tight proximity, creating a hellish cacophony of drums, guitars and twang infested vocals that can be heard nowhere else.

The music (and occasional slaughtering of music) can seem almost non-stop. This fact helps make it the most obvious place for someone new to town without any contacts to start meeting some players and singers and attempt to insert themselves into the scene. When I first moved to town I hit these spots nightly to break myself in. In general, there are 2 shifts that bands and singers can play 7 nights a week year round: 6:00 to 10:00 and 10:00 to 2:00. During the meat of the tourist season, which is April thru November, many clubs add on an afternoon shift from 2:00 to 6:00 that gives a few more slots to bands and solo performers. In recent years, a few of these clubs have moved to a schedule of three daily shifts year-round. Tootsies and a couple others actually have four shifts beginning with an 11:00 AM to 2:00 PM slot that features acoustic solo performers.

The pay for most of these clubs is $20 to $50 base pay per player plus tips with a few places offering slightly more. If your front man knows how to work the crowd you might make upwards of $100 per man; if he doesn't, you might make only $25. $60 is considered a pretty good average. Relying on the tip jar for pay is one reason why there are minimal breaks. If you take a break you might lose your crowd as there are so many clubs in walking distance, or so it's thought. It is also important to note that there is often a cap on base pay at the clubs in Nashville, for instance $20 per player up to 5 players. You can still have a 7 piece band but you will only get $100 total base pay to split among the 7 players. It is also common for players to work "doubles" or even the occasional "triple." Just like it sounds, a double is usually 2 back to back shifts and might equate to 8 hours of nonstop playing, other than the 20 minutes between shifts in which you will be moving your gear to the next club.

The music played by these singers and musicians are a mixture of old Country standards (see Nashville 100 song list), newer top 40 country, classic rock, pop, and blues. The biggest hits by the biggest artists of all time are regularly beaten to death; songs by Merle Haggard, George Jones, George Strait, Hank, Waylon, Travis Tritt, Keith Urban, Toby Keith, Lynyrd Skynyrd, Journey, Guns and Roses, and Jimmy Buffett, to name a few, are performed daily with varying degrees of efficiency. The audience is here to drink and sing along with familiar classics, so this typically keeps the song lists to well known and well worn tunes, with some exceptions of course.

The Players that work on Broadway often work at a grueling pace, and these gigs serve different purposes for many of them. If you start talking to players on breaks (if they have one) or between shifts, you will find some are Broadway regulars trying to hustle a living, some are road guys playing for fun, some are networking and honing their chops, some are newbies to town trying to make contacts, while others have been squeaking out a living by playing solely on Broadway for years and even sometimes decades. Just start talking to people and many will be happy to tell you their story. On any given night, you might be hearing an unknown singer backed by players that work for artists like Rascal Flatts, Keith Urban, Brad Paisley or many other major acts. Of course this won't be obvious if you don't already know who these players are.

Players on stage in front room of Tootsies

Hangin' out and sittin' in is the tried and true approach to obtaining work on the strip. As I noted earlier, what appears to be a band is quite often a group of freelance players who were called at the last minute, and this fly-by-night approach can equate to opportunities for many. If you want to be able to work regularly on the strip you will need to know the standards, or the Nashville 100 as I call it. Knowing these tunes will also give you some common ground when it comes to sitting in.

Pick a club with a band playing and just hang out for a bit. If and when they take a break, try to engage in conversation. If you're a drummer, chat with the drummer; if you're a guitarist chat with the guitarist etc. Try to talk to as many folks in the band as you can (without wearing them out). Be friendly, complimentary, and be sure to tell them that you're a player. Don't necessarily ask to sit-in on your first encounter, but don't be afraid to ask if you feel you are prepared and getting a warm reception. Find out if this band or singer has a regular shift and when they are playing again. If you can slowly build some friendships with a handful of singers and players this way, they will eventually ask you to sit-in. Sitting in around town on a regular basis will increase your contacts, increase your visibility, and quite often lead to gigs. This basic approach can also apply to getting work at clubs outside of Broadway.

FYI - You don't need to bring your own ax to sit in as most players will let you play on their gear. Except for some writers nights and blues jams, it is actually inappropriate to use anything other than the house bands gear as it not necessary and only slows things down.

A Few Other Things To Know About Working On Broadway

Parking can be a nuisance especially during tourist season. Quite often you will need to double park to load in your gear, and then if you want to save a $10 parking charge, spend 10 to 20 minutes driving around to find a free spot. There is no cover charge at most clubs on Broadway, and the clubs on "The Stage" side of the street are non-smoking while the clubs on the other side are smoking. The bands play long and loud thru less than great PA systems, quite often spanning 3½ to 4 hours with a minimal break (sometimes pee breaks for players are provided by the singer playing a couple of songs solo). Most of the clubs in Nashville that have live music also have house PA systems, some of which even sound good. It is also noteworthy to mention that many of the bands play songs considerably faster than the record, sometimes called "Broadway Tempos." And if you plan on gigging regularly on Broadway, know the Nashville Number System, it is absolutely essential!

Nashville is oversaturated with people trying to get ahead in the biz. There are simply more players and singers than there is work for them. This high level of competitiveness makes for some shark infested waters. While there are a lot of genuinely nice people that will go out of their way to help you, there are others that are less than helpful or sincere who might show you some interest but have ulterior motives in mind. There is also an element of territoriality, as many musicians are trying to protect their gig. Of course this is true everywhere, just be forewarned.

There is life outside of Broadway. There are many other paying gigs in Nashville outside of Broadway that are less obvious to find. Right up the hill you'll find the somewhat hidden historic Printers Alley right off of Church Street. Printers Alley has been home to many a club since the 1940s and has a great old town feel to it with elegant Victorian style architecture and a cobblestone street. In the early sixties an unknown guitar player worked nightly at clubs in the alley years before the world knew him as Jimi Hendrix.

Many clubs have come and gone in "the alley," but since 1996 **The Fiddle and Steel Guitar Bar** has been a staple, and at times a great hang for many of Nashville's road musicians when they're not on tour. Often called the "Cheers" of Nashville, the club has a great vibe to it, a decent stage with a house drum kit, and a good PA system with a house engineer. Over the years, the Steel has been known to be "sit-in friendly" frequently allowing guest performers to show their stuff. I used to hang out at the Steel often when I first moved to town, and this ultimately led to my first road gig. Before Rascal Flatts was a household name they were one of the house bands at the Steel for quite some time.

The Bourbon Street Blues and Boogie Bar, right next door, has also been a long-standing staple of the alley, featuring live blues and R&B bands nightly. And Lonnie's Western Room, just a few doors down, has been a prime destination for the Karaoke crowd for many years.

Second Avenue is home to several clubs that feature live music, among them, BB Kings and the world famous Wildhorse Saloon, both which feature local, regional, and national acts nightly.

If you go down Demonbreun Street to the roundabout, there are a handful of pub style bars, some of which have live music regularly. Places like the Tin Roof and Dan McGuinness have been popular hangouts for years and feature bands that play everything from country to Motown, to classic rock and original music.

Take James Robertson parkway across the river to East Nashville and you will find another cluster of trendy college and indie bars. This area is somewhat unknown to tourists and is home to some cool hangouts that feature a variety of live music like the Five Spot, the Foobar and the Family Wash. In general, gigs at these clubs are tips only, or play for the door scenarios.

At the time of this writing, these are the biggest clusters of nightclubs that feature live music in the city. There are many more worthy of mention that are scattered throughout the city and its outskirts each with its own unique vibe and type of clientele. Here is a little more on some of these stand alone music emporiums.

The Exit Inn is a great concert club with a great stage and top notch production and is a stop for many national acts coming thru Nashville. Third and Lindsley is another stop for nationals, regionals, and local acts and is a popular place for industry showcases, as is 12th and Porter and The Rutledge. The Mercy Lounge (birthplace of the MuzikMafia) is housed in an old mill building off of Eighth Avenue, and Douglas Corner is a great listening room with a diverse array of bands and performers a little further down 8th avenue. There is the world famous Bluebird Café, king of the singer songwriter night, and the Commodore Grille which is also a popular destination for that crowd. The Basement (right below Grimeys) is a great club for the indie scene and the Tap Room and Café Coco are good places for the jam band types. A few others worthy of mention would be the Listening Room, Spring Water, The End, The Station Inn, The Rock Bar, and Sambuca.

The pay rate for these venues runs the gamut from pay to play to upwards of $100 per night per player and everything in between. Most clubs in the city are tips only or a $20 to $50 base pay plus tips. Be aware that there are a few pay to play clubs here as well, as some clubs require performers to pay a "production fee" for use of their PA and sound engineer. The audiences range from tourists to locals, college kids to music row execs, but the biggest draw in general (excluding the tourist laden Broadway) is musicians, singers, writers, and music industry wannabes. This is good for those who are out networking but bad for the players who are playing for tips, as most musicians in this town are broke.

This information about the Nashville clubs is based on my personal experiences of gigging and exploring Music City over the past decade. I am sure I have left out some useful venues; however I wanted to write about the venues in which I have firsthand knowledge. There are far too many to address each one individually, but if you perform an internet search on Nashville nightclubs you will find plenty more to check out.

Gigs on the outskirts of town are more likely to be outside of the microscope of the Nashville music industry. While there are some clubs outside of Nashville proper that do hire singers and bands that frequently play the in-town scene, these venues are lower on the radar. Beyond the downtown area is a plethora of sports bars, biker hangouts, and other venues similar to the neighborhood bars found in small towns across the country. Many of the bands that play in these clubs are comprised of locals who are often not connected to the Nashville music biz' and just play with their buddies on the weekends for fun. There are of course some pros mixed into this scene as well. Anything from classic rock to blues to country to metal can be heard. The pay ranges from free to $75 per player per night on the high side.

This scene might be similar to the same kind of scene that you experienced in your hometown, and may or may not pay as well. These lower profile gigs might offer some good opportunities, as the fact that they are off the radar might make them a little less likely to be found by the throngs of hungry performers frequenting the in-town clubs. These gigs can also be a good way for some Nashville musicians to enjoy some music for the soul without the pretenses and pressures of the in-town gigs.

The Fillin' Station, located in Kingston Springs, is one of my favorites of these "outside the microscope" clubs and housed in an old garage stall right out of yesteryear. The place is intimate, loaded with character and owned by former member of the band "War", Patrick Weickenand, a great harp player who often sits in with bands in between tending bar. Featuring live music weekly, it is a favorite watering hole for many on the west side of town.

Showcases for aspiring artists mostly happen in nightclubs (although some take place in rehearsal halls). An artist showcase is typically a 30 to 45 set of non standard material that is performed by a rehearsed band in front of some music industry professionals, usually with the goal of obtaining a record or publishing deal.

The singer, with or without the help of some kind of management, will typically choose some material that fits their vocal style and ability. Whether the material is original or not is irrelevant, as most of these showcases are intended to highlight the singers' performance and vocal abilities. Typically, the songs are either their own originals or songs that have been written by an outside writer that have not been cut yet. If the singer wants to have a strong performance, they will usually have at least one if not several paid rehearsals with the band they have put together for this showcase. A paid rehearsal in Nashville for any singer who is taking his career seriously should pay nothing less than $50 to $75 per player, and the showcase itself should pay similarly.

It is not uncommon for some singers to hire professional session players to play on their showcases, although they will usually require a higher level of pay. A typical showcase will consist of 8 to 12 songs that need to be learned by the players, and charts are often used to insure a flawless execution. Most showcases happen on weekdays between 6:00 and 8:00 PM, as this is when the 9 to 5 music industry workers from the Row are done in the office and on their way home. If somebody tells you they are playing a showcase at 10:00 PM on a Saturday night it is almost definitely NOT a real showcase. Part of the appeal of a showcase to some industry pros (in addition to the prospect of discovering an undiscovered talent) is free drinks and hors d'oeuvres with their cohorts on the way home from work and *this* is one reason why legitimate showcases are typically held on weekdays around 6:00 PM.

Singers

"I have a simple life. I mean, you just give me a drum roll, they announce my name, and I come out and sing. In my job I have a contract that says I'm a singer. So I sing." — Tony Bennett

Every year, thousands of singers and aspiring artists that arrive in Nashville are vying for a handful of performance opportunities, and this makes for some stiff competition. As there is a limited amount of paying work, and many newcomers will literally play for free just to be seen or heard, the singer will need more than just musical ability to succeed. While this is true for all musicians, there are a few factors that make their role a little different than that of the other players working in the clubs of Nashville.

The goals of singers who move to Nashville vary greatly. Many are aspiring to be recording and touring artists, some fall more into the songwriter category, and others are interested in more immediate paying work, be it nightclub performances, demo singing, or working on a tour as a harmony singer. The lines often blur, and many singers often have career aspirations that encompass most or all of the above. Regardless of a singer's long-term goals, working as a nightclub performer in Nashville is usually the first step, as it can provide experience, contacts, and supplemental income.

Landing gigs is a little different for singers than it is for players. Where the players can network their way into a gig by meeting other musicians and sitting in, the singer needs to create the gig by getting hired by a nightclub owner. Hanging out and sitting in is a good way to start building a name for yourself. Ultimately, you will need to figure out who hires the talent and try to make it a point to sit in while they are in the room, possibly speaking with them about your intentions in advance.

If the singer is part of a band that moved to or formed in Nashville, this dynamic can work a little differently as someone else in the band might be in charge of booking. However, at the present time there seem to be more groups comprised of freelance players in Nashville then there are "bands", and it has been this way for at least the last decade. Perhaps this is because it is easier for a single person to relocate than it is for an entire group.

So let's assume that you are a singer that has moved to Nashville with little to no connections and would like to start performing in the clubs to start building a name for yourself while getting paid for your services. You are ultimately in search of two entities: gigs at which you can perform, and players to back your performances. Here are a few avenues you could pursue.

Solo Acoustic

If you can sing a whole night of cover material *and* provide your own accompaniment, either by acoustic guitar or keyboards, then you have eliminated the need to hire other players to start playing gigs and earning income. While performing solo may lack some of the energy and fun of a band, there are many plus sides to this niche.

As solo performers are self-contained, they can accept literally any gig that is offered without worrying about the availability of other players. With many clubs offering a base pay plus tips for compensation, the solo performer, in many situations, can earn more than one could in a band, as there is no splitting of the tip jar. They can also sing any song from their repertoire without worrying about other band members knowing the material. Perhaps the biggest selling point for performing solo in Nashville is that it is a way for singers to start performing live even if they don't yet know many other musicians.

There are plenty of clubs all over the city that hire solo performers and the styles and genres can vary greatly from one performer to the next. If you are looking for paying work, a mix of easily recognizable country, pop, rock, and R&B covers are the norm. Many of the clubs on Broadway hire soloists for afternoon shifts, typically from 2:00 PM to 6:00 PM, and during tourist season a couple of them add an additional shift from 11:00 AM to 2:00 PM. Other areas that the solo performer might obtain work would be at some of the clubs and restaurants on the avenues around Broadway, the Fiddle and Steel in Printers Alley, restaurants and clubs at Gaylord Opryland, and clubs on Demonbreun Street near the roundabout, among others.

Singing With A Band

If you can't provide your own accompaniment, you will be looking for nightclub gigs that require full band accompaniment, and this means you will need players to back your performances. This doesn't mean you need to have an entire band waiting in the wings to get booked for a gig. If you are friends with, or have some connection with another musician that knows most of your material and has shown an interest in working with you, you have a good starting point. When you are talking to a nightclub owner, speak with confidence and sell yourself. If you can book the gig, musicians will follow. Once you are hired for the gig, enlist the help of your musician friend, or any other players you know for that matter. If they aren't available for your gig, ask them if they can help you find some players that are available. At the absolute least, they can probably provide you with some phone numbers. This town is full of players looking for gigs, and most players know a lot of other players. This approach won't work for all of the nightclub niches in Nashville, but it can work on Broadway and other tourist driven parts of the scene.

If you're going to attempt to work regularly at the in-town nightclubs, especially if you have minimal contacts with other players, it is essential to have a large repertoire of standard cover material. Tourists like to hear songs they recognize, and freelance players are more likely to know these songs. Being able to call out the key in which you sing each song is helpful, especially if you do it in any key other than the original.

The singers that have the best results performing in the Nashville nightclubs are the ones that are the best front people, not necessarily the best vocalists. Many of these clubs only provide a minimal base pay, so it is up to you as the singer to hustle for the rest with the tip jar. Running a successful tip jar operation is an art form (see the chapter "How To Run A Good Tip Jar"). Just hang around on busy nights at the clubs on Broadway and make some mental notes about the singers and bands that seem to have it going on. In many situations a singer with only mediocre vocal abilities might be a great front person with a natural ability to lead a nightclub party. This kind of singer will typically earn better pay, and therefore have no problem finding players to back them.

If you can't or don't want to perform a night of cover material, there are still other avenues to be found; you just have to be creative and find your niche. If you desire to perform mainly original or obscure material, you probably won't be earning any income to speak of, at least initially. You will also have to find players that are willing to commit themselves to your project, or pay out of your own pocket to hire freelance players to back your performances. If you use some hired guns to play this kind of material, they will expect to receive the material in advance, and you should expect that they will more than likely be reading from charts at the gig. A paid rehearsal or two can be helpful, but not essential with the right players. In Nashville, this is all commonplace.

So, it all comes back to you, the singer. You have to decide what kind of gigs you want to go after, whether or not you want to get paid for your performances, and what your long-term goals are. Do your best to understand the competitive nature of your chosen profession, it's no different than being an actor in Hollywood. Put yourself out there, dig in hard, and try to have some fun along the way.

Shockwave - circa 1994 *Photo by David Petty Photography*

Bands

"Band: 1.) a unit of social organization especially among hunter-gatherers, consisting of a usually small number of families living together cooperatively. 2.) something that constrains or binds morally or legally." — free dictionary.com

Regional Touring Cover Bands, Casino Bands, Unsigned Bands, Bands For Fun

There are many different kinds of bands in and around Nashville; random groupings of freelance players backing singers performing covers around town, original bands featuring a regular lineup of committed players, weekend warrior cover bands that moved from their small town to Nashville and attempt to work in the clubs regularly, blues bands, Nashville-based traveling top 40 bands, and just about any other kind of band that you can think of. Some are paid for their performances and many are not. Some perform live regularly and some never make it out of the practice hall. With the exception of Nashville based casino bands and regional touring cover or top-40 bands, most bands that are living and working in Nashville make very little money on a consistent basis. There's nothing wrong with being involved in a committed original or cover band project that's working toward some long-term common goals. As this writing is geared towards those who desire to earn income from their craft as quickly as possible, the emphasis here will be geared more towards the immediate and practical side of being a craftsman.

Regional Touring Cover Bands and Casino Bands

As it is so difficult for musicians living in Nashville to make a living in town, quite often players find that by going out of town with a band they can earn the missing piece of income they couldn't find in town. There are many levels and variations of these situations and often the lines between them can blur.

Many Nashville based regional touring cover bands and casino bands travel by van and trailer and stay within about a 500 mile radius of Nashville. Some might have an RV and even fewer might have a used tour bus like the dreaded 79 Eagle. There are casinos in virtually every state, and this provides a lot of work within a 10 hour drive of Nashville. There are bands doing this that have had the same lineup of players for years, while there are also some singers that hire freelance players to back them on weekends out of town. These gigs are similar to bar gigs you may have done before you came to Nashville, and a casino show for an unknown band is basically a bar gig. You will probably play 3 to 4 sets of dance oriented cover material to an audience that is there to drink, dance, gamble, and escape the daily grind of life. These audiences don't care that you're from Nashville; they are just there to party.

The goals of these unknown Nashville-based touring entities vary greatly as well. Many of these bands exist purely for financial reasons as this is one of the only ways for some Nashville musicians to earn any real income from their craft. Some of these bands are also working towards the goal of building a long-term fan base and name for themselves. A plus side to joining one of these bands would be some financial stability. A downside would be that you are now out of town as often as a national act but without the clout or perks that go with that territory. You will also be taking yourself out of the loop to a certain extent, as you won't be in town very often to network.

Job Requirements For Musicians In Regional Touring Bands And Casino Bands

» All the same requirements of nightclub musicians

» *And*, you must be able to sit upright in a van or car seat for up to 10 hours at a time.

How to get hired by one of these groups is not as easily defined as some of the other performance related jobs in Nashville. The same kind of networking for in-town club gigs and road bands can apply here as well, especially for the bands that hire some freelancers. Unlike most in-town work and national level tours, some of these bands will put ads looking for players in online classifieds such as Craigslist, although it is ultimately word of mouth that lands these gigs as well.

The pay range for these kinds of bands varies. Many out of town club and casino gigs (that require any extensive travel) pay around $150 per player per night, and most casinos and some clubs also provide meals for the band. Some bands will pay you a set fee and cover transportation costs while some will require everyone to pitch in for gas out of their own pocket. There are also some touring top 40 style dance bands based out of

Nashville that travel extensively and even pay a salary. Many of these situations only hire players that make a firm commitment, but as I mentioned earlier there are some freelance situations in this market as well.

Out Of Sight, Out Of Mind

A couple of months after I arrived in Nashville I did a gig on Broadway. On a break I was chatting with the drummer who was more than a competent player and seemed to know a lot about the town. He told me that he had moved to Nashville 2 years earlier, and shortly after his arrival joined a touring top 40 band, which kept him on the road for a majority of the next year and a half. While he was working with a good group of players and making decent money, he found that in spite of living in Nashville for almost 2 years he had very few connections and no in-town work as he was rarely around. He had moved to Nashville to work towards his goal of playing professionally on a national level tour, and while he was making a living from playing music, the van and trailer thing was getting old and keeping him out of the loop. Recently freed from his top 40 captivity, he said he felt like he had wasted the last year and a half and it was like his career in Nashville was just now beginning. If you're out of sight, you are out of mind.

Original Bands and Indie Bands

While this is a broad category encompassing many different kinds of bands and mindsets, I am referring to the bands that perform mostly original material and are working towards goals like touring on a regional and national level, building an international fan base, selling their songs and merchandise online and at shows, becoming signed to an indie or major record label, and/or achieving international radio airplay.

What is a band? The word "band" to most people implies a collective group of musicians that are bound by a common purpose or set of goals (at least initially) and build their careers together. For many, the word "band" brings to mind groups like the Beatles, the Rolling Stones, Metallica, Aerosmith, Fleetwood Mac, etc. How many bands can you name in the Country or Country Pop genres? Not many, with the exception of a rare few like Alabama or Trick Pony. And in reality, Trick Pony wasn't even a real band. The three front people had the record contract and the other players were hired guns.

The very nature of the Nashville music industry discourages the true concept of a band, and here are a couple of reasons why. If you are firmly committed to a band project and make that your priority, you are limiting your possibilities for other work and connections. Simply put by my mentor D when I first moved to Nashville; "Whatever you do, don't join a band. Bands starve." He said that if I wanted to make a living in Nashville as a musician, joining a band would limit my availability for other work and my options in general. If you are part of a band working towards some lofty goals, you are probably putting a lot of time into that project while more than likely working a full time job. There are only so many hours in a week and now you have put all of your eggs into one band basket. Because it is so hard for most people to make any real money from the industry here, players usually take good paying gigs when offered, and this fact eventually puts the band concept in the back seat for many.

Historically, record companies, especially in the country market in Nashville, have signed individuals not bands, and the individual they always sign, is the lead singer or front person, not the other players of a given band. Signing an individual is much safer and simpler: only one person to deal with, one person to control, and one person to potentially "let go." By signing a group of individuals collectively as a band they are putting themselves in a weaker position; they have a more complicated situation legally, and they run the risk of the whole deal falling apart if a band member leaves. Even though the major labels no longer have the clout they once did, this concept still can apply. If a band is trying to achieve success without the help of a record company, in many situations, the singer still holds most of the cards. If you are involved with or firmly committed to a band, it is worth considering these basic facts.

That said, let's assume that you are a part of an unknown Nashville-based band. You understand these facts and are willing to tough it out. Your band wants to play some in town gigs for some local exposure. If you want to get paid for your performances, keep in mind that the same tourist driven club scene that hires singers with freelance players might also hire your band, providing you can and will play a full night of covers. Throwing in the occasional original can work, but in general, playing an obscure original in the middle of a set of covers to a bunch of tourists can be like farting in church. Depending on the venue, the pay will vary from a base of $20 to $50 per player plus tips, to tips only, or even pay to play.

If you can't or don't play covers and want to build your success solely around your original material, this fact will unfortunately take many of the paying in-town gigs off the table for you. There are still plenty of places to play: they will just be tips only or pay to play. Some other options might be booking some double or triple bills with other more established bands that have a similar style and larger followings. You could also set up showcases and invite your friends and whatever industry contacts you might have.

As an unknown band trying to become successful in Nashville, you are basically in the same boat as any aspiring artist; there is no right or wrong approach and the odds might be slightly worse for bands than individual artists. This doesn't mean that being involved in a band project isn't right for some. Many professional musicians in Nashville that make their living from the commercial side of the industry are also involved in side band projects. Many day-jobbers not involved in the Nashville music industry also enjoy being involved with original bands and side projects. A good band project can provide a healthy creative outlet as well as give the individuals involved an additional platform in which to showcase their abilities. And as Nashville is so driven by the freelance mentality, sometimes it just feels good to be a part of something. There is nothing wrong with following your dreams, just be a realist, understand the business, and move forward with cautious optimism.

Bands For Fun

My favorite kind of band is a band that plays music simply for the sheer joy of it. Nashville is so full of people that are desperate to "make it" at all costs that many lose sight of this basic principal. Just put aside all your career goals for an evening and get out with some friends and play! Many Nashville musicians, professional or not, have side projects with their musician friends and sometimes these are the most rewarding bands to be a part of. There are many variations on these bands but the concept is simple. Just play music you like to play, with people you like playing with, and don't worry about getting called back, the tip jar, or who might be watching. Let the music be the star!

The "North Ely Opry" bluegrass band, performing at "Old Threshers," Shelbina, MO, 2010

Bartenders at the Fiddle & Steel *Photos courtesy Denise Mattox*

Nightclub Jobs: Non-Performance Related

"I'd probably be famous now if I wasn't such a good waitress."
— Jane Siberry

Within the nightclub industry of Nashville is a variety of supporting roles that can offer regular employment and income for many musicians and music industry workers. For musicians and singers trying to establish new connections, getting a job in a nightclub that features live music can help create some short-term financial stability while putting them in daily contact with other musicians and music industry types. Some of the potential jobs to be had in this industry would include bartenders, wait staff, doormen, sound engineers, PA techs, managers, bar backs, hawkers, cooks, and maintenance people.

Many nightclubs and music venues around town have house PA systems that require regular attention. Some clubs have a simple set up that requires a PA tech to come in once every week or so and give the system a quick run through, fixing broken cables and gear. Other clubs with a more elaborate system require good sound engineers to mix bands on a nightly basis. Some clubs fall somewhere in between, requiring a minimally qualified engineer to help a band during set up, give them a basic mix, and then leave once things are up and running. The pay for these sound engineering jobs can vary greatly, anywhere between $20 and $100 per night depending on the club. $50 per show or shift is somewhat average. In most situations, the sound engineer or PA tech receives a fixed pay with no tips, with most of these jobs paying under the table.

Bartenders and wait staff personnel working the right shift at the right club can earn decent money. The pay for these jobs is largely dependent on tips, so those who know how to hustle typically earn better.

It is common in many of the Nashville night clubs for some of the employees to be talented singers, musicians, songwriters, etc., and for them to sit in with bands nightly. More than once, I have seen someone working as a bartender or door man at a club eventually wind up as one of the regular performers at that venue.

PREVOST

Chapter I.2

Nashville Touring Industry

"I've seen every highway in the United States, and they all look alike to me." — Loretta Lynn

Working as a musician or crew member for a national act based out of Nashville is a realistic and attainable goal for competent and easy to get along with musicians and techs. Touring is all about the hang, or the downtime. To work in the touring industry, it's a given that you will be competent enough to do your job when it's show-time. The real unknown for many musicians new to touring, and perhaps a bigger variable, is attitude. For the most part, people that get fired from tours lose their job because of bad attitudes and personality conflicts, not lack of musicianship.

That being said, if you can learn 20 songs note for note, are easy to get along with, enjoy living in close proximity of your coworkers 24-7, and would like to see the country while slowly building connections in the music industry, you are a perfect candidate to work on a tour. This section of the book will outline many of the most common touring jobs and provide an overview of basic job requirements, pay scales, and how to go about the networking required to land those jobs.

Keep in mind that in Nashville, most of the tours reside in the country or country/pop genres. As most in Nashville know, the term "country music" is broadly used, and in many cases an artist categorized in the country genre has just as many, if not more elements, of rock, pop, and R&B. This is good news for all the musicians in Nashville who lack roots in traditional country music (which are many). If you are in this category, it wouldn't hurt to learn a little Merle Hagard and Hank Sr. anyway.

If and when you do get a job with a national act, in most cases you will be working for an artist, not a band. Although you will be playing with a band on stage and spending more time with the band members than the artist, the artist is usually the ultimate CEO of the tour. Whether the artist is currently on top of the heap, somewhere in the middle, or a one hit wonder from 10 years ago, never forget that it's the artist's show, and that the artist is the boss.

Crowd before a Rhett Akins concert in Bristol, TN - 2009 *Photo courtesy Clint Jacobs*

Artists

"I don't know anything about music, in my line you don't have to."
— Elvis Presley

If a singer or aspiring artist works towards their goals hard enough, long enough, knows the right people, and/or has a great streak of luck, he or she might become successful enough to earn a real living as an "artist". The term artist implies one who makes art, and in reality many musicians are artists on some level. However, in Nashville, "artist" usually refers to a singer that has become commercially successful enough, or has enough financial backing to warrant touring, hire musicians, managers, and a crew, and has or at one time had a record deal. For musicians that don't want to squeak out a meager living playing on Broadway forever, landing an artist gig can be a great way to establish yourself, earn a living, and gain some clout that will help elevate your status as a musician in Nashville. Here is some perspective that might help you understand the world of the artist.

Most great artists usually possess some unique and less than obvious characteristics that helped to get them where they are. Perhaps they have a certain intangible aura or charisma that turns heads when they walk into a room or that commands attention during performances, or maybe it's as the French would say, "a certain kind of I don't know what". To be a successful artist, one must be a great politician onstage and off, knowing how to say the right thing at the right moment and knowing when to say nothing at all. They must be a great salesperson selling songs, ideals, merchandise, and ultimately themselves. They must be willing to live within a strange, media driven world that often deprives them of privacy. They must be willing and able to handle an unspoken, yet relentless pressure that will last for most of, if not their entire career. Many artists enjoy being the center of attention, and some also possess some narcissistic-like tendencies.

Not all great singers have what it takes to be a successful artist. Just because someone is a brilliant vocalist doesn't mean he or she will be an exciting performer or transfer well to tape. How many times have you seen a show where you thought, "Great voice, but I'm bored to tears"?

Not all great artists are great singers. Some of the biggest names in modern country music (and other genres) sing live and in the studio through pitch correction software such as the

Antares auto tuner (some artists may never have had a career if it weren't for the invention of this magic little box). This is commonly known throughout the industry, and virtually unknown to the masses. It is the artist's total package that sells the song.

Not all artists write their own material. Some do, but many do not. This doesn't really matter to the audience either, as most are unaware of this fact. The artists that do write their own material often have more control over their career and earn more money, but not always. Most of Elvis's hits were not written by him, as is also the case with George Straitt, Shania Twain, and many other mega stars. This obviously didn't stop them from becoming successful.

There are different levels of success for artists, with some having long strings of hits and decades of touring, some having a more moderate success, and others only having a brief moment in the sun. The level and duration of success they achieve isn't always within their control, but artists that have a lot of drive and/or great management seem to fare better.

A newly emerging artist will more than likely be touring on a small budget. This means that he or she will probably be traveling and living with a band and crew on the same bus or van. This might also be true for mid level artists, artists with minimal airplay, or artists that simply choose to keep touring costs at a minimum. Touring on this level, in close proximity of the artist, can be great or not so great, depending on the artist. Some artists are great to be around - personable, fun, easy going, and these situations can be ideal, with a family like atmosphere. Of course some artists might be better off to have their own bus as they can create a "walking on eggshells vibe."

Most mega-stars like George Straitt, Toby Keith, Faith Hill, etc; travel on their own bus with only a driver and small entourage consisting of possibly a manager and assistant, while the band and crew travel on another bus or busses. On this level, there is often a sense of disconnect between the artist and band/crew. It is not uncommon for the band and crew to rarely see or have any contact with the artist except for on stage during performances.

No matter how friendly or distant the artist may appear, never lose sight of the fact that the artist is the boss. Even though they may have a manager or group of managers running the day to day details, including hiring and firing, the artist usually has the final say. After all, it is their name, image, and talent that provide employment for the rest of their organization. They are the president and CEO of their company (of course in many cases, they have to answer to an invisible money man somewhere or their boss at the record company).

Daryle Singletary at the Grand Ole Opry, 2005

Some Things To Consider When Working For An Artist

» Don't "crowd" the artist. Artists are regularly poked and prodded by everyone imaginable and, in most cases, don't want to deal with that from their employees.

» Work hard. If you always give 110% there isn't much they can complain about.

» Read body language. Some artists are shy and don't volunteer their thoughts. Learn to read between the lines.

» Avoid the star territory. The front line of the stage is for the artist. Some artists want their players more forward during performance and some don't. Know the acceptable boundaries and work within them.

» Always follow their lead. Listen to them and watch them closely during performances so you won't be caught off guard.

» Give the artist their space, both onstage and off. Artists may like attention, but sometimes they just want to chill. It's all about balance.

» Make them look good. That's why you are there in the first place.

Rhett Akins and band performing at Country Rendevous in Crapponne, France - 2007

Touring Musicians

"Being on tour is like being in limbo. It's like going from nowhere to nowhere." — Bob Dylan

Landing the all-so elusive road gig can be quite a task. As it is hard to make a living just from nightclub work and the session goal can be quite a long term endeavor, getting a gig with a national level touring act based out of Nashville can be more practical, lucrative, and immediately attainable. Assuming you can work your way into getting hired for a road gig, here is a little of what you can expect, and what might be expected of you:

Job Requirements Of A Touring Musician

» Be able to ride well with others. A lot of your time on the road will be spent hanging with the band in a small lounge on a bus and you need to learn how to take up as little space as possible (mental space as well as physical space).

» Leave your baggage at home. Not your luggage-baggage, your attitude-baggage. An empty bus might look spacious when you first walk on one, but it gets real small real fast, and one bad attitude can totally kill the hang.

» Have good, reliable gear. Your rig should sound great, be fool proof, be able to set up and torn down quickly, and be in professional road cases.

» Be able to sing harmony. This isn't always required, but being able to sing harmony can increase your value to the artist and help job security.

» Be able to learn an artists' repertoire note for note.

» Be able to perform that repertoire with conviction, under all conditions.

» Be able to look like you are enjoying yourself even if you're not.

» Dress appropriately onstage and off. If your boss doesn't care, wear what you want. If he does care, wear whatever you must to fit in with the group.

» Represent your organization in a positive manner. Whether you are on tour or out on the town on a night off, your peers know about your gig and people love gossip. Don't do anything that will reflect negatively on yourself or your tour and you will keep your job longer.

» Don't be a "gherm" (pronounced "ger" as in "girl" plus "m"). A gherm is someone that is overly infatuated or star struck with celebrities, and is often annoying to everyone around them. *(See the chapter on gherms on page 127.)*

Honky Tonk Tailgate Party 2005 - Left to right: Randy Smith, Darryl Preston, Eric Normand

How To Get A Job Playing For A National Act

If you are interested in getting hired to play on a national level tour based out of Nashville, it is important to first understand the nature of a touring band. A touring band is like a family or an extended family. Although the musical performance may be the priority and main focus of each day on a tour, the performance and the setup/sound check will only account for roughly 10% of the day. This leaves a lot of time to be spent hanging out with the band (unless you are a complete recluse), and this is why it is so important for a road band to be comprised of people who get along with each other and have a good "hang factor."

When a player leaves a touring band, the band leader will want to replace him or her with someone they already know and feel comfortable with. The band leader might go to the artist and say, *"I've got someone in mind to replace Jimmy. This guy is a great player and a great hang. I've known him for 5 years, and he's a solid, reliable, stand up guy. I think he'll fit right in."* In many cases the new player is hired on the basis of a brief conversation with the artist or manager, and it is the band leader vouching for this player that gets the new guy the gig.

Getting one of these gigs in Nashville is all about who you know. Although there are some "cattle call" style auditions, in most cases when a player leaves a band, the band leader will replace him or her with someone they already know. While some may refer to this as the good ole boy network, I prefer to call it the buddy system. They are simply hiring one of their buddies that they already feel comfortable with. I've heard of situations where a national act has already picked the new player but holds auditions anyway, and then still hires the player they already had in mind. Maybe they are just looking for options, or it might be a formality to appease the record label and/or management. Some feel that this buddy system is unfair, as it makes it difficult for newcomers or players that aren't in the loop to have much of a chance. For better or for worse, this is just the way it is. Knowing and accepting this is essential! If it is your goal to land a road gig, you must know and become friends with people that are in road bands.

» **Be Visible:** Whether you are new to town or have been here for several years, nobody is going to know you are a competent player if you don't play some gigs in town or do some sitting in. Try to land a regular weekly spot with someone performing in clubs on Broadway, Printers Alley, or other in-town music venues. Know the Country standards that everyone plays (see The Nashville 100 under chapter 5 - Nashville Specifics) and look for opportunities to sit in with bands playing around town.

» **Spread Out:** Over time, work your way into as many different in-town gigs as possible. Rather than being in one band that plays out 5 nights a week, you would have more irons in the fire if you played in 5 different bands that each played 1 night a week. This way you are playing with and building relationships with a larger number of players thus, increasing your possibilities that one of them will call you for something else. Little gigs can lead to bigger gigs.

» **Hang Where Road Guys Hang:** If you want to get to know some guys in road bands, hang out where they hang out. Over the years there have been different clubs on different nights that have had good hangs for road musicians. Although there is no specific hotspot at the time of this writing, there are certain musicians and bands that perform regularly around town that tend to attract more "players." A couple of weeks of nightly exploring might reveal some of these situations. Be on the lookout for standout players and bands and engage in conversation whenever possible, as they will be more likely to provide insight about the more happening groups or artists to check out. Also keep in mind that road guys are usually out of town Thursday through Sunday, so Monday through Wednesday are the nights they are most likely to be out on the town.

» **Let People Be Aware:** When you are hanging out at the clubs and meeting people, let them know what you are working towards. People come here to work in many different aspects of the music industry and won't necessarily assume that you are looking for a road gig.

» **The Nashville Handshake:** If you meet some new players and they like you and/or your playing, they may ask you for a business card. "Hey man, I really enjoyed playing with you, you got a card?"…"Sure, let me grab one of yours, too." This is what is known as the Nashville Handshake.

» **Phone Calls:** After you have made some friends with different musicians and industry people, call them every once in a while to touch base. People are busy in general and have a lot on their minds, so a little monthly chat will help keep you more to the front of their minds; just don't overdo it. If they're friends, call as often as you feel it's appropriate. If it is someone you only met once and barely know, you might want to call sparingly; it's a fine line. A little goes a long way, but the squeaky wheel does get the grease.

» **Be Patient and Don't Panic:** If it is taking a long time and you haven't gotten any bites, don't freak out. It can take years to land a road gig. There are somewhere in the vicinity of 500 touring bands based in Nashville, but there are thousands of players trying to get hired by them, very stiff competition. Five hundred touring acts means there are 500 drummers, 500 bass players etc, but it does not mean there are 500 job openings for each band position. Many artists have had the same players in their bands for years, and with times being tough, most players are sticking around longer. Therefore, at any given moment there are only a handful of job openings for those thousands of players looking for gigs. There are no guarantees in this town; you just have to be patient, wait your turn, and work it.

"Check your ego, don't offer "your opinion" unless someone asks you, roll with the less than ultimate touring situations WITH A SMILE and remember that you're getting paid to do something you love." — Randy Smith

Touring Musician Pay

Most touring country artists pay their musicians on a per show basis. $300 per show plus $25 a day per diem is a pretty standard wage. $250 per show is respectable, but anything below that is considered less than optimum if it is a real national act. Some tours can pay $350 to $500 per show and occasionally more, but $250 to $300 is the reality for most road musicians that aren't on the highest profile tours, 'ala Chesney, Paisley, Straitt etc. A daily per diem of $25 to $35 is usually paid for every 24 hour period of a given road trip. Although a set amount per show is most common, there are a few acts (very few) that actually pay a salary. Most national acts pay you as an employee and withhold taxes, but do not provide health care benefits.

Most country tours are weekend tours that are on the road for 3 to 5 days a week (Wednesday through Sunday for example) and leave and return to Nashville each week. This can be ideal for many players who wish to have a life outside of the tour.

Typically rock and pop tours pay more, often upwards of $1000 per show; however most of those tours are based out of LA or New York. These tours will usually go out for extended periods of time, often 6 weeks to 6 months or more of nonstop travel and shows, never staying in a given location for more than 2 or 3 days.

Bandleaders

In a national act, the band leader is almost always one of the players in the band, and may be responsible for hiring and firing players, distributing new material, organizing rehearsals, coordinating sound checks, printing and distributing set lists, providing visual onstage cues during performance, and acting as an intermediary between the band and artist. Usually, but not always, the band leader receives some extra pay for this additional level of responsibility. The unique position of a band leader on a tour makes him an important person to know if you are looking to get hired by a national act.

The Life Of A Touring Musician

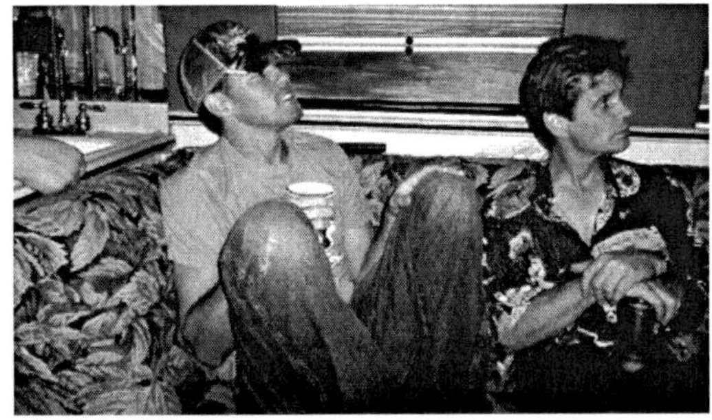

Top left: Honky Tonk Tailgate Party tour bus. Right: Waiting on the tarmac at London's Heathrow airport. Second row left: Chilin' on the HTTP bus. Right: Corey Smith concert in Chastain Park, Atlanta, GA, 2008. Third row left: "Wade and Cowboy" with Jamey Johnson, 2006. Right: After show "cheer" - Milledgeville,GA. Bottom left: Rhett Akins in Gstaad, Switzerland, 2006. Right: Backstage in Montgomery, AL, 2006.

Road Managers

"A guitarist, a drummer, and a road manager are walking on a beach when out of the sand pops a genie. The genie says, "I usually grant 3 wishes to the person who frees me, but as there are 3 of you, I will grant each of you one wish." The guitar player says, "I want to be on a deserted island surrounded by beautiful women, with plenty of food and booze." The genie grants his wish and poof he disappears. The drummer says, "I'll have the same" and poof, he's gone too. The genie then asks the road manager for his wish, and the road manger barks out, "I want both of those guys back here right now!" — Anonymous

Road Managers or Tour Managers are responsible for the day to day operations of a national level tour. Their duties will usually include making travel arrangements; booking hotel rooms; making food arrangements; budgeting and payroll; advancing the details of each show day with event coordinators, promoters, and production companies; taking care of settlement; communicating the daily itineraries to artist, band, and crew; and acting as a general liaison and peacekeeper between everyone on the tour. On a large tour, a tour manager might have an assistant and delegate some of this workload to others. On many small to midsized tours; they might be doing all of this by themselves and then some. It's not uncommon on a smaller tour for a band or crew member to perform the tour manager duties.

A good tour manager has excellent people skills and is also a problem solver. As any tour relies on the interaction and cooperation of a large group of people, it is the tour manager's job to make and allow everything to flow smoothly. Behind every successful show, is a small army of people, most of whom go unnoticed by the audience and fans that work tirelessly to make that show happen. The tour manager needs to see the big picture of each day and show of a tour, connecting and coordinating the members of the tour with the event staff, applicable media, production companies, and local laborers.

Many tour managers were once either band or crew members that worked their way into a tour managing job. I don't think very many tour managers ever thought as a small child or teenager "I think I want to be a tour manager when I grow up." If you are interested in this line of work, the best way to break into it is either by landing a job on a tour as a crew or band member, or getting a job at a local venue that hires national touring acts. Either scenario will give you experience, insight, and help you establish connections that could lead to this kind of work.

The pay for Road Managers varies. It can be per show, in which case it might be comparable or a little higher than that of the band members ($250 to $500 per show). It could also be salary or even a percentage.

Effective tour managing is a twofold operation. Half of the job is the advancing of each show, usually 1 to 4 weeks prior to each engagement. The other half of the job is the daily managing of each day and show of the tour as it occurs. For weekend tours, the advancing is probably done from the tour manager's home office. For acts that are touring for more extended periods of time, the tour manager will do much of his advancing on the road, using a lap top, cell phone, and working out of bus lounges, hotel rooms, and venue production offices.

One of my jobs since moving to Nashville has been working as tour manager and lead guitarist for country music artist Rhett Akins. This tour has been working about 40 to 50 dates per year with most of the shows occurring on weekends. A Thursday midnight leave time for shows on Friday and Saturday, returning to Nashville by mid-day on Sunday would be a typical weekend run. Most of the advancing for this tour has been done out of my home office.

A Day of Advancing

> *"Normally, we do not so much look at things as overlook them."*
> — Zen Quote by Alan Watts

My job tour managing a weekend of shows begins 2 to 4 weeks prior. I begin by examining the contract and then plugging some of that info into an itinerary. With some help from my wife, I have created an itinerary template spreadsheet using software called Excel in Microsoft Office. Venue address, show time, doors, and event coordinator contact info are included in most contracts and all this information will be entered into the itineraries for the weekend being advanced.

Using a program called Microsoft Streets and Trips, I will then determine the mileages and travel time between each leg of the trip. This allows me to determine times of departure and arrival for each day of the tour, and this info is then put in the itinerary. With all this information as a starting point, I now call the event coordinator to coordinate the details of the show day. During a 15 to 20 minute phone conversation we will work out a flow for the day that covers our arrival time, meal times, load in, sound check, meet and greet, opening acts show times, show time, set length, load out, autograph signing, and departure time. I will also discuss other details such as the location of our merch sales, the stage size, the location for bus parking, bus stock, number of stagehands needed, runner schedule, production company contact info, security, rain contingency (for outdoor events), and radio or other related interviews. All of this info gets entered into the itinerary.

For each show, I will usually book 3 to 4 hotel rooms at a hotel that is as close to the venue as possible. One room will be for the bus driver to sleep in, and the others will be used as cleanup rooms for the band and artist. The hotel info also makes it to the itinerary.

Some tours travel with their own sound and lighting, and some do not. In our case, we require each event buyer to provide adequate production for our shows, and these requirements are listed in our rider. I will usually make a call to the production company to advance the basics (load in, soundcheck, show times, and opening acts) and our FOH (front of house) engineer will usually make a follow-up call to discuss some technical aspects of the production.

As we travel by bus for most of our engagements, these trips must also be coordinated with a bus leasing company. An email or phone call to them a couple of weeks in advance is needed to insure that a bus is reserved for when we need it. On the week of each show, I will receive a proposal and contract by email which I sign and return.

Upon completion of all of these tasks, I post the finished itinerary on a hidden spot on the artist's website for the band members to view, and I send a copy of it to the event coordinator and production company. Go to page 52 to see an itinerary that reflects a typical show.

The people I deal with to make a show happen - event coordinators, production companies, bus companies, media personnel, band and crew members, even the artists - can have varying levels of competence and communication skills. When the person on the other end of the phone is organized and efficient, things come together quickly and easily. When they are not, advancing a show can be quite painful. I have found that redundancy helps. An extra phone call and email a couple of days prior to the show can go a long way to insure that things will go as planned.

Artist X

Daily Itinerary - 08/03/2011 - Hampton, NH

Eric Johnson
615-444-4444
info@comcast.net

Tuesday, August 02, 2011 — **Travel Day**

Travel: **Nashville TN to Hampton, NH**
Straight to Hotel
Time Zone: **Central**
Distance: **1140 miles, 18 hours**
Driver info: **Steve Jobs** 615-444-4444
Bus call: **4:00 PM**

Bus parks behind stage - load in up ramp

Wednesday, August 03, 2011 — *Time Zone:* **Eastern** — **Show Day**

Day Transportation:

Weather: **93°/70° mostly sunny**

Arrive: **11:00 AM**
Depart for venue: **noon**

HOTEL INFORMATION:
Ashworth By The Sea
295 Ocean Boulevard
Hampton, NH 03842
phone: **603-444-4444**
fax:
contact: **Jim**
distance to venue: **1/2 mile**

4 rooms under:
Eric Johnson
4 kings - non smoking
conf.# 81930950
189 e

AMENITIES: high speed wireless, pool

VENUE INFO:
Wallys Pub **603-444-4444**
144 Ashworth Ave
Hampton, NH 03842

Don Kirshner **617-444-4444**
info@yahoo.com

Loaders: **2-3**
Load in: **1:00 PM**
Load out: **11:00 PM**
Security: t-shirt
Runner: provided
Stage Dimension: 20 x 12
Smoking: causes respiratory illness
Bus Stock to bus at: **1:00 PM**

MERCH: adjacent to stage
event will provide table, 6 chairs, and electricity

Runner Schedule: Times are approx.
1:30 PM bus driver to hotel
TBD band to hotel (7 people)
TBD pick up band at hotel (7 people)
11:00 PM pick up bus driver at hotel

TODAY'S SCHEDULE:

Breakfast: **on your own**
Lunch: **bus stock**
Load in: **1:00 PM**
Soundcheck: **2:00 PM**
Dinner: **buyout** *$20 x 8*
Doors: **all day**
Meet & Greet: **7:00 PM** *15 backstage*
Show Time: **8:00 PM**
Set Length: **90 min**
Other Acts: **Shockwave - 7:00 PM**

Depart: sleep over
bus call Thurs 10 AM
Next Destination: **New Haven, CT**
180 miles, 3.5 hours

SOUND COMPANY INFO
We Rock Em' Hard Audio **603-444-4444**
info@aol.com
wireless: yes

Arrive: **2:00 PM approx.**
Next Date: **Thursday, August 4**
Location: **New Haven, CT**

A Day of Tour Managing

"Check your daysheet." — Anonymous

For a typical weekend run, my tour managing duties usually begin the night before the first show day at the place of departure. For a midnight leave, I will usually arrive at the bus around 11:30, load my gear and luggage, disperse the per diem to the band and crew, post itineraries, discuss the trip with the bus driver, and begin drinking like a fool (just kidding). The bus departs, and after a little hang with the guys, I retire to my bunk to sleep.

A show day for the tour manager is usually 15 to 18 hours of seemingly nonstop activity. Upon our typical mid morning arrival to a hotel, I will attempt to check in to our rooms (early check-ins aren't always easy to achieve as most hotels have a 3:00 PM check in time). After a short time at the hotel, I call my event contact, and we depart for the venue. Once we arrive on site, I will help determine the best spot for the bus to "live" for the day. I will then take a brief tour of the grounds with my contact to assess the layout and discuss some details. I then organize a pick up time for the driver, coordinate his transportation to and from the hotel with the runner, and get him back to the hotel so he can sleep.

Next, I will direct our designated stagehands to load our stage gear onto the stage, and our merch (merchandise) to the merch area. Assuming our bus stock is delivered on time, I will then stock the drink coolers and have some lunch.

On this tour I am also the lead guitarist and band leader (you really do have to wear a lot of hats in this town). The next 2 to 3 hours will be spent setting up our stage gear and sound checking. After sound check, it's usually a trip to the hotel for everybody to rest and shower for the gig. An hour or 2 at the hotel is typically the only quality downtime I will get for the day, so don't bother me if you don't have to.

It's then back to the venue for dinner, and then I will usually assist our merch person in setting up the merch selling area. An hour before the show, I will deliver the artist, sharpie in hand, to a meet and greet (which is also occasionally referred to as the "weigh in" or "grip and grin"). With his patented movie star smile and switched on charm, he will then meet, sign autographs, and be photographed with anywhere between 20 and 40 VIP's, fans and a few overly excited event staff.

About 15 to 20 minutes before show time, I will tune guitars, check monitors, put out set lists, and coordinate with the MC how to introduce Rhett. At downbeat we're off and running for anywhere between a 45 minute and 2 hour non-stop onslaught of rockin' fun. If the crowd warrants it, an encore is played, and then the show is over.

After the show ends, I quickly strike my gear and then go to the bus to accompany Rhett to the merch table for an autograph signing. I leave him in the hands of local security so I can return to the stage to direct the stagehands through load out, and then I'll return to the merch table to help wrap up the signing. Once the merch is torn down and loaded, I'll find the event coordinator for settlement. After settlement, I make sure the runner is on target to pick up our driver. The driver returns, we are off to our next destination, and I am done for the day. A shot of Cuervo, a cold beer, and I'm spent!

On the road, things don't always go as planned. Many unforeseen situations come up that need to be dealt with, and this is where problem solving skills and diplomacy come in handy. A bus might break down, it could rain on your outdoor gig, a member of your entourage could become sick, a buyer might try to skip out on settlement, the artist could disappear for several hours after the show, band members could have an altercation, a piece of gear could get left behind, the hotel might have bed bugs, anything you can think of will eventually happen and it's usually the tour manager's job to find a solution.

Finishing Up

After a weekend run, the tour manager has several end of tour duties that need to be performed over the next couple of days. The first task is to send an email to the accountant stating how much money was collected, what will be deposited, and what each member of the tour should be paid. I will also send her the bus company invoice to be paid. A road report which details every expense of the trip is then created and mailed with the receipts to the accountant, and finally, a trip to the bank to deposit the collections.

Sound Engineers

"If all of the World is a stage, where is FOH?" — Anonymous

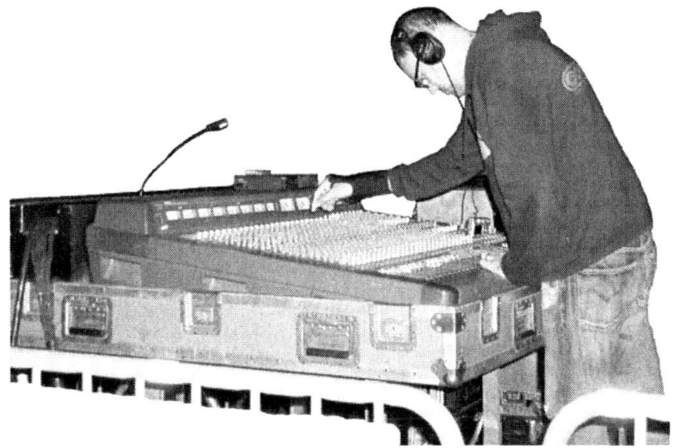

Eli Akins at the board.

Live sound reinforcement is considered by many to be an art form, and there is work in the Nashville music industry for qualified sound engineers. There are a few different ways engineers can earn income from their craft; working for a touring national act as a FOH or monitor engineer, mixing bands in local nightclubs and music venues, or working as a system tech for a Nashville based sound company. As is the case for most musicians in Nashville, nightclub work doesn't pay enough to make a real living, therfore, many engineers pursue touring work. Either FOH (Front of House) or monitors would be the two positions they are vying for with FOH engineers being most common (not all tours employ monitor engineers).

FOH sound engineers in Nashville, especially the really good ones, can be hard to come by. I use the term "engineer" loosely as it does imply a high level of competence and sophistication that is not always found with some people that consider themselves engineers. A bad engineer can ruin a great band's performance, and a great engineer can make a marginal band sound decent. Most national acts travel with their own FOH and monitor engineer, but on many of the smaller tours they may only take a FOH engineer.

Depending on the specifics of the touring situation, an engineer's duties and responsibilities can vary greatly. On large tours carrying their own production (PA, lighting, video, etc.), the engineer may or may not be required to oversee the assembling of the PA and perform systems diagnostics prior to the sound check and performance. On many high level tours, the FOH engineer simply walks in to the venue once the PA and monitors are fully operational and is only responsible for mixing the sound check and show.

On smaller or lower profile tours, engineers might wear several hats. In addition to mixing, their duties might include advancing production details with the venue, overseeing the load in and assembling of the PA, performing diagnostics, making repairs, mic'ing up the band, recording the shows digitally from a live board feed, and overseeing the tear down and load out. In some cases the FOH engineer might also be the backline and guitar tech, stage manager, road manager, monitor engineer, and or bus driver. In a few scenarios they also might be in charge of acquiring hookers and blow *(just kidding)*.

"What's the difference between a toilet seat and a monitor engineer? A toilet seat only has to deal with one ass at a time."

Monitor Engineers

Monitor engineers have one of the most challenging, yet thankless jobs on the planet. In most performance situations on a national tour, there is an area to the left or right of the stage referred to as monitor world. This is where the monitor engineer will run a mixing console that is solely dedicated to the monitor system. From this side stage vantage point, a qualified monitor engineer will have all eyes on the artist and band for the duration of the performance, making minor adjustments to wedge or in ear mixes that are conveyed to the engineer with subtle hand gestures.

It is also in monitor world where the engineer will periodically duck to avoid objects hurled at his head by unhappy artists. I personally witnessed an artist grab his monitor engineer by the throat midway through a show and proceed to scream at him in view of a crowd of 5,000. On another occasion, I saw an artist pick up and throw his JBL wedge at the engineer. No one was physically hurt in either case except the engineers' pride. This is what *can* happen when engineers take their eyes off the band and artist for the exact second they happen to look over for an adjustment.

The Pay for sound engineers on a national level tour based out of Nashville is usually comparable to the musicians in the band. $300 per show plus per diem is average pay for an engineer working for a mid-level act, and the pay can be more on higher profile tours. Occasionally, a salary is offered.

Obtaining work as an engineer on a tour based out of Nashville is almost solely obtained by word of mouth. All of the best engineers know other qualified engineers and commonly pass around work. Knowing road managers from different tours also helps engineers obtain work. Having a good attitude and a good hang factor will go a long way towards obtaining work and getting callbacks. If you are new to town and don't have any contacts, working in the clubs or rehearsal halls can be a good starting point. If you already have experience in this field, the websites www.roadie.net and www.roadiejobs.com can be also be useful in obtaining work.

In-town work for engineers consists mainly of mixing bands in the local nightclubs or working as a tech or engineer for production companies that rent or install PA systems. Nightclub work for engineers pays about as poorly as it does for musicians. In most cases they get a higher base pay but no tips. Depending on the venue, $50 to $75 per night is typical with a few that pay $100. Working for a production company might be more lucrative, as the work will be more consistent than most nightclub work. Working as a tech or repair person at one of the major rehearsal halls such as SIR or Soundcheck is also an option, and working a cartage gig (transporting, setting up, and tearing down music equipment for recording sessions, live performances, etc.) is yet still another option.

Recording engineers are in a different category than those who work as live engineers, even though some engineers work in both fields. Both situations require some highly developed skills, and just because you spent your career mixing bands live doesn't mean that knowledge will translate into instant studio chops or vice versa.

Merch

"The best of merchandise will go back to the shelf unless handled by a conscientious, tactful salesman." — James Cash Penney

A merch person is the person on a tour who is responsible for selling, ordering, and schlepping around the artists' merchandise. It can be hard work and is perhaps one of the most thankless jobs on a tour, rivaling perhaps the monitor engineer in that respect. The duties of a merch person can vary greatly depending on the level of the tour.

If a tour plays large venues such as sports arenas, summer sheds, and big outdoor festivals, the merch person will probably need to advance with the venue's merch person. In an initial phone call, they will discuss what the artist has to sell, how much they are bringing, what the selling price is per item, what the percentage split will be, where the merch will be sold, and what times to count in and count out. Tours on this level will usually have a truck or trailer that is solely for transporting their merch.

A Typical Day For A Merch Person On A Big Tour

The first duty for a merch person on a given show day is usually to supervise the loading of the merch on to golf carts or pallets, have it delivered to a pre-determined area, and oversee the venues' merch person in a count-in. The count-in can almost look like a goodwill store, with thousands of shirts strewn about the front lobby of a given arena. Every single piece of merch is individually counted, and spread sheets account for all of the merch present. The merch is then dispensed to the different selling stations throughout the venue. Most large scale arena style shows provide their own merch sellers and prefer the artist's merch person not to be involved in the direct sales. This means that the merch person has a long period of downtime in between count-in and doors. During this time, they might be doing some of their daily record keeping and accounting on a lap top, or placing orders for merch that is getting low in supply. They also might overeat at catering, take a long nap, and walk around trying to pick up chicks.

Once the doors are open, the merch person might spend the next several hours periodically checking on the different merch selling stations to insure that the merch is being correctly displayed and to keep an eye on overall sales. Once the show is over and the fans have dispersed, it's time for the count-out. The merch is gathered and returned to a central area for counting, and *this* is where it can get ugly.

Merch sales on this level can be in the tens or even hundreds of thousands of dollars nightly, and the venue gets a percentage of the total sales. This commission-based system breeds the same kind of dishonesty and sleaze factor of a car dealership. It should be rocket science: number of shirts counted in minus number of shirts counted out equals number of shirts sold. Number of shirts sold times the shirt sale price equals total shirt sales in cash. That cash total minus the venue's 25 to 40 % and everybody's happy.

NOT! I can't think of how many times I have seen the math come out wrong, almost always in favor of the venue. You would be amazed how in this era of high tech, with laptops and portable printers at our disposal, how many merch people are still doing math (poorly) with a pen and paper and then handing off a piece of paper with barely legible chicken scrawl that they try to pass off as a count sheet. Sometimes it all comes out right the first time, but when it doesn't, there can be some heated arguments, perhaps a couple of more attempts with the math, and even sometimes another counting of all the merch. Once this count-out is done and both sides agree on the numbers, the merch is loaded out and the merch person is done for the day.

On lower profile tours the merch person has a similar but different list of responsibilities. Many smaller venues such as nightclubs, fairs, and small town festivals don't require a count-in or count-out, nor do they provide sellers. On this level, the tour's merch person will set up the selling station and sell the merch himself. Some of these events will still take a percentage.

A merch person on this level is responsible for keeping an accurate count of the merch inventory, daily sales, re-ordering when supplies are low, and even sometimes helping to design the merch. Typically, he will get paid a percentage of total sales (10% to 15%) and will also get daily per diem for being on the road. On higher profile tours, a salary or daily show pay is more often the case, although a percentage deal does occasionally happen.

Most musicians aren't interested in merch jobs, as selling merch is not music performance related. Unlike some of the other crew members such as engineers and techs, the merch person is often isolated from the band during soundchecks and performance. He doesn't share as much common ground of those directly involved in the musical performance. This doesn't mean that musicians shouldn't consider this job. If you can't make ends meet working in town, and haven't yet landed a job on a tour but desire to, working a merch job might help bridge the gap. It will put you on a tour, provide you with some networking opportunities, and give you some life experience while paying you to see the country. It could also be a way for those interested in tour managing to see and learn how a touring operation works.

Got Merch?

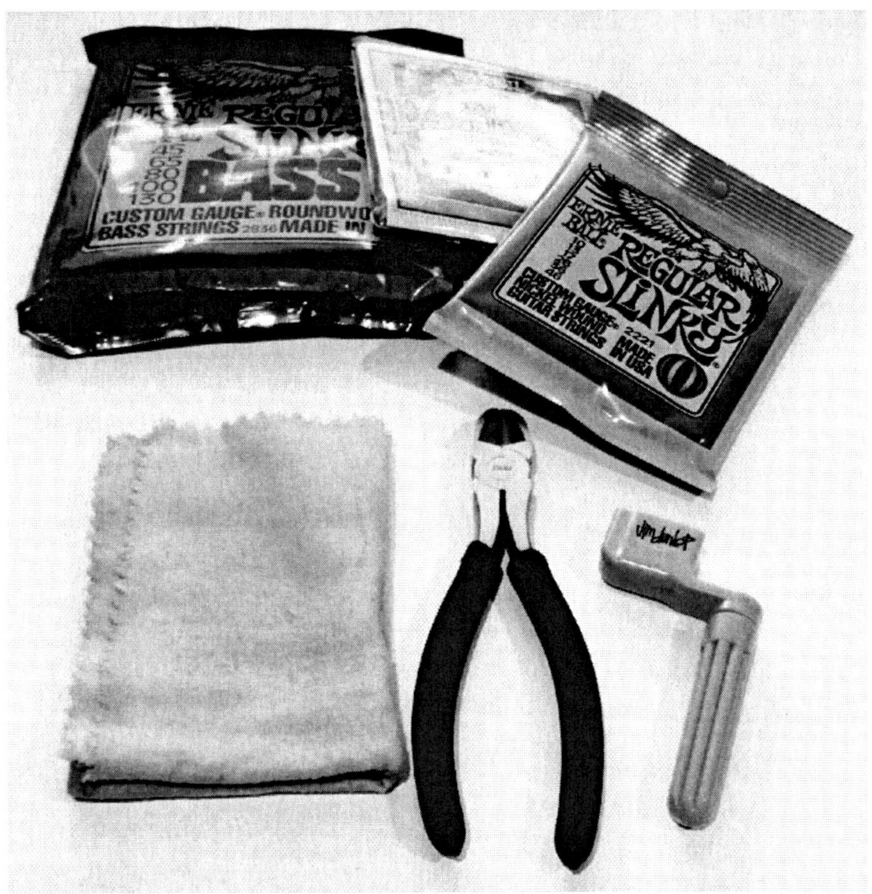

Guitar tech essentials: Ernie Ball strings, polishing cloth, wire cutters, and string winder

Techs

"These all go to 11." — Spinal Tap

Teching on a national level tour can be a good way for musicians or engineers to gain valuable experience, make industry connections, and make ends meet while they are working towards their long term goals. On most high profile tours, there are at least one or more techs that are responsible for the daily set up and care of the band's instruments and backline (amplifiers, speaker cabinets, etc.). Some of the biggest tours might have a different tech for each player in the band, while other tours might have one or two techs that take care of everything. On low to mid level tours, one of the other crew members, such as a sound engineer or merch person, might double as an instrument/backline tech or there might be no designated tech at all. In situations where there is no designated tech, the band members each set up their own gear, and the band leader or an engineer would most likely take care of the artist's instruments and gear.

Techs on major tours often have a challenging and thankless job, as do many of the crew members that work on these tours, and their duties can vary greatly. Most tours that have designated techs would typically have at least a guitar tech and a drum tech, making those the two most common tech jobs available.

Job requirements for a tech aren't as technical as the job title implies. Most techs are or once were players or engineers themselves, as this background provides basic knowledge about maintaining and caring for musical instruments and equipment. You will need to know how to change strings, change drum heads, tune instruments, clean and polish instruments, and troubleshoot and repair simple things like a loose guitar jack or some broken drum hardware. The best techs might also know how to intonate instruments, but this is not always required. Aside from having these kinds of skills, perhaps most importantly, a good tech is usually good at dealing with people and stress. It can be a high stress job, as the show coming off glitch-free night after night is largely in your hands. If you can gain the players' trust and make them comfortable, your job will be that much more secure.

The pay for a tech on a major tour is typically comparable to that of the musicians in the band. Depending on the tour and how long you've been working on it, you might make anywhere from $250 per show to upwards of $400 or more per show, with the rare and occasional salary position being offered.

Finding work as a tech is just like finding work in any other area of this business, it's all about who you know. The same kind of networking applies. Become friends with people that work for touring artists, hang where they hang, etc. If you already have experience in this field, the websites www.roadie.net and www.roadiejobs.com can also be useful in obtaining work.

One Downside for serious musicians who take on work as techs is getting pigeon-holed. If you are trying to make a name for yourself as a player, teching for a short while might help to pay the bills, give you some valuable experience and insight, and some otherwise unattainable connections while you are working toward your other goals on the side. But if you work as a tech for too long, everyone will know you as a tech, and even if you are a great player it might become difficult to ever become known as anything other than a tech. If you are a great player whos's teching just to make ends meet, you still might not get offered much work as a player because everyone assumes that you are out on tour teching and not available.

A Day In The Life Of A Guitar Tech

Nigel Tufnel: "The sustain, listen to it."
Marty DiBergi: "I don't hear anything."
Nigel Tufnel: "Well you would though, if it were playing." — Spinal Tap

It was the summer of 2003, and I was working as the guitar/backline tech on Toby Keith's Shock N' Y'all Tour. Toby's 12 piece group on that tour, known as "The Easy Money Band," consisted of drums, bass, guitar, steel, keys, utility, 3 horns, and 3 backup singers. On this tour, one of the truck drivers doubled as the drum tech, the horn section took care of their own instruments, and I was responsible for everything else. Everything else consisted of 20 electric and acoustic guitars, 2 basses, 1 fiddle, one steel guitar, 1 bass rig, 3 electric guitar amp rigs, and 1 keyboard rig consisting of a midi controller with a rack of electronics, one Hammond B-3 that broke down every other day, and a Leslie that broke down on the days the Hammond didn't.

This was a monster job for one tech and consumed roughly 10 to 12 hours per show. My work day would begin at load-in, usually sometime between 7:00 and 10:00 A.M. depending on our arrival. I would direct stagehands to load the gear from the back of the semi to the arena or shed floor, where the gear at this point would be stowed off to the side until the sound, lights, video, and set were in place. In between load-in and the time that the deck was ready for band gear was a period of several hours that I would use to restring guitars. I would find an out of the way area backstage and build myself a temporary guitar world consisting of a work table, work box, guitars, a tuner, a boom box, and some coffee. I would then begin restringing and tuning guitars.

The last thing a guitar tech wants to see happen during the show is breaking strings. So to avoid this, strings should never be played for more than 2 shows. Of the 22 guitars on this tour, 5 or 6 were backups that didn't need to be changed regularly, so the remaining 15 or so instruments were done on a rotating basis. I would usually change strings on 5 or 6 guitars each day, thoroughly stretching the strings, and then tuning each guitar with a strobe tuner. Over the next 2 show days, I would change the strings on the remaining instruments and then start the whole process over on the day after that.

After a couple of hours of changing strings, tuning guitars, and making occasional minor repairs, the deck was more than likely ready for the load-in and setup of the band gear. Depending on the situation, gear was either loaded onto the stage by ramps or forklifts by stagehands under my direction. The amps and racks were all placed behind a large set wall that was erected on stage about 2/3 back from upstage. The back side of this set wall was a maze of steel crossbars, cables, pyro and gadgets. It was also fairly dark in this area as this wall had a roof over it that served as risers for the horn section.

As you can imagine, this made for a less than optimum place to set up and wire a bunch of equipment. Once the amps and racks were in place, cables and snakes were run through small holes in the set wall out to each musicians dedicated stage area and connected to pedal boards, keyboards, steel guitar etc. Four stagehands were required to lift the 450 pound Hammond B-3 onto the 3 foot riser (I cringe just thinking about that daily nightmarish routine). Once the backline was all placed, wired, and mic'ed, it was on to guitar world.

Toby's lead guitarist, Rich and me before a show. *Photo courtesy Brittany Allyn*

Guitar World on this tour was set up either on stage directly behind the set wall, or off stage adjacent to or behind the stage depending on the space available. Some tours use giant coffin style road cases that each contains a series of padded slots inside for guitars, each case holding 6 or more guitars and allowing quick, safe, and easy storage and access to the guitars. Unfortunately, this was *not* the case, pun intended, for me on this tour. On this tour, all of the 22 guitars and basses were each in their own hardshell case and transported on a very large and very heavy set cart (picture 22 guitar cases, standing upright, strapped together in a long row, with wheels on the bottom).

All of these instruments were individually taken out of their cases and placed on stands and racks in guitar world. After straps with wireless transmitters were attached and capos clamped to headstocks, the tuning would begin. All of these instruments needed to be tuned twice on each show day, once before sound check and once before the show. This process would take me about an hour each time. Once all the guitars were out and tuned, I would then place some of them at each player's stage position on stands and get ready for line check.

For me, line check was one of the more enjoyable moments of the day, as I got to check and play the bands instruments though a 100,000 watt PA system in a gigantic arena. Although the arena was basically empty, this was still a thrill, as I had never before even stood on one of these concert stages, let alone strummed power chords to imaginary crowds of 20,000 while literally standing in the same spot where many of my idols had previously stood. One of my rituals was to play different classic rock and blues riffs on each instrument, changing the riffs daily. This was mostly for my enjoyment, although the sound engineer and crew seemed genuinely amused and would occasionally yell out some requests.

On most tours of this level, techs and monitor engineers are equipped with in-ear wireless systems for communication and to allow them to hear what the players are hearing. The FOH engineer's commands for line check would be done through a talk back at FOH to my in-ears. Assuming there weren't any problems during line check, or once we corrected the ones that arose, we were now ready for sound check. Soundchecks on this tour were typically short, with the band and Toby typically playing only 2 to 3 songs (the same 2 to 3 songs every time) and making some minor adjustments to monitor mixes. Once sound check was over, it was usually time for a dinner break and a brief pause before I would begin my pre-show duties.

Blake Shelton was the opener on this tour, and I would listen to his set every night as I prepped the instruments for Toby's show. His set was basically the same 12 songs in the same order nightly, and by the end of the tour, after hearing his set about 90 times, I could have probably played every guitar lick in his show, as I probably could have done for Toby's set as well. Beginning about an hour and a half before show time, I would start tuning, lightly polishing the guitars that needed to look pretty. Once the guitars were all tuned, I would replace batteries in all of the wireless transmitters and some foot pedals, and then quickly test each rig. Upon completion of Blake's set, I would begin placing instruments at different positions around the stage and put guitar picks on the pick clips.

By the time I was finishing these duties, the band members would usually start to file in, and I would assist some of them with their in-ears. One player in particular required a seemingly odd procedure. He would put his "axe" on, and then face away from me with his hands by his ears. I would hand him his in-ears, and once he had them in, I would meticulously tape the in-ear wire excess to his strap. It had to be just right or when he turned his head there would be not enough slack. If this procedure was done incorrectly, it would not be discovered until sometime during the set, and there would be hell to pay after the show. This guy was truly *wired* and not just for sound.

Another ritual that seemed a little more natural was to provide one of the players, upon his request, with a "bottle switch." There was a "no drinking before the show" rule on this tour, and minutes before downbeat, a bottle of spring water was placed at each player's stage position. At this point, I would take one of the bottles, run out to one of the busses (which were sometimes up to a quarter mile from the stage), and exchange the water for vodka. The tricky part was to switch the bottle on stage un-noticed just minutes before the show started. Everyone on the tour seemed to know this was going on, but I was nevertheless instructed to treat this procedure like a top secret spy mission.

As odd or uncomfortable as some of these tasks may have been, this was all part of the job, and taking care of the players' needs for a show is what it's all about for a tech. Give the artist and band some in tune instruments, make them comfortable, maybe a little bar tending duties here and there, and you've done your job.

Once the show started, it was my job to stand side stage for most of the set, listening to the show through my in-ears and watching the band members in case anyone needed something. Some of the 22 guitars and basses used by the band and Toby were instruments that were only played for one or two songs, so once an instrument was done for the night, I would retrieve it and return it to its case. For me, the 90 minute set was a methodical tearing down and packing up process of most of the equipment I had set up over the course of the day, and by the beginning of the last song, all but 6 or 7 instruments were cased. Throughout the course of the show I would also assist some of the players with some guitar changes, and if someone broke a string, I would hand them a back up instrument, take the other back to guitar world where I would change the string and re-tune the guitar, and then return the axe to them. Because of the regular, organized, string changing of these instruments, breaking strings rarely happened. I believe we only had 5 or 6 strings break out of 90 shows.

Toby and band on stage in Portland, ME, 2004. *Photo courtesy Brittany Allyn*

As soon as the last note of the last song was played, the most stressful and dangerous part of my job began. A small army of roughly 30 to 40 crew members, techs, and stagehands literally rushed the stage and began dismantling the set, audio, lighting, and video components of this mega-production. I was assigned 2 stagehands who assisted me in retrieving the remaining instruments and dismantling the backline amidst a sea of workers and equipment on the move. Time was not on my side, as every moment that passed more and more things were dismantled and becoming obstacles and potential WGDs (Weapons of Guitar Destruction). A flimsy old telecaster on a guitar stand stood no chance against a 10,000 pound video wall. It would usually take me about 30 minutes to completely pack up guitar world, tear down the backline, and have my gear loaded onto one of the 6 semis.

Then it was finally Miller time!

PREVOST

Bus Drivers

"Finding a good bus driver can be as important as finding a good musician."
— Reba McEntire

In many ways, bus drivers are the most important members of a tour, as the lives of everybody riding on the bus is in their hands. Good drivers don't just think of their jobs as safely driving around a group of people; they are safely driving around a group of people who are *sleeping*. If a driver understands this as a key component of their role, he or she will always be in demand.

Having good people skills is also an extremely important trait possessed by the best drivers. Just being a good driver is only part of the job. As they are also part of this extended family, they will be spending some time with the other tour members and need to make everyone comfortable. As they are a member of the tour, even if only temporarily, they are also representing the artist, sometimes calling a hotel for info or dealing with event coordinators when arriving at a venue.

A night of driving will typically begin sometime between midnight and 2:00 AM, and this allows the driver to drive through the night when the roads are the least travelled, and the band needs to sleep. Many tours have at least a few folks who may stay up every night until dawn, and this can be great, or not so great, for the driver depending on the personalities and habits of these night owls. Like everyone else out there, the driver must also learn to adapt. After the bus has arrived at its destination the driver will have some down time in a hotel room, and this ideally will be at least 12 hours away from the bus.

In order to provide the safest and smoothest ride possible, a good driver looks ahead and anticipates the road ahead, as well as the actions of other vehicles around them. Most of the better drivers don't drive too fast, as that will make a rougher and more dangerous ride. Rather than waiting to the last minute to apply breaks, a good driver might let off on the gas up to a mile away from an exit ramp allowing the gears to slow the bus more gradually. Good drivers will also allow enough space between the bus and the vehicle ahead of them, so they won't get caught having to brake hard. Many great drivers have spent some time sleeping in a bunk while another driver drives the bus, and this teaches them the perspective of a bus rider.

Sometimes artists may not want to leave a venue at the predetermined departure time, often because they are enjoying some after show hanging with friends, and occasionally because they are trying to get laid. This can cause a driver to have to wait to leave anywhere between an hour and sometimes up to 5 or 6 hours later than expected. While this isn't typical for most tours, it does happen sometimes, and when it does, the driver must learn to adapt. Courteous artists will tell the driver they are going to be a while and to go back to the hotel room, but not all artists are courteous.

Extra Duties

Checking the "genie"

In addition to driving, there are several other duties that the driver will be responsible for, and these can vary depending on the bus company or the tour. The bare minimum on many tours would be the daily rituals of filling the water tank, emptying the trash, and vacuuming or sweeping the floors. Washing the dead bugs off the front windshield can be optional.

On some tours the driver might be requested to do a little more extensive cleaning - throwing away unwanted food and drink containers, washing down the counters, adding chemicals to the toilet water, etc. Even a daily washing of the exterior and polishing of the rims is not all that uncommon.

If the satellite TV goes out or the wireless Internet stops working, the bus driver will be the first person asked to fix it. This would also apply to literally anything that goes wrong mechanically with the bus such as if the lock or latch on a door or bay malfunctions, if the AC stops working, if the "genie" (generator) breaks down, if the bus breaks down, etc. While not all bus drivers are mechanically suited to fix all of these problems, they will be the ones, along with the road managers, who will inevitably be called upon to fix them.

Other extra duties might include checking into hotel rooms, checking out of hotel rooms and obtaining the needed receipts, stocking the coolers with beverages and ice, and even on some tours carrying luggage or acting as a part-time bodyguard. Typically, anything beyond the most basic cleaning duties and essential maintenance would be discussed in advance.

Obtaining work as a bus driver is completely different than it is for musicians and crew members. Although some more established artists will have the same driver for years, with the driver being considered an employee of the artist, most bus drivers in Nashville obtain work initially through one of the several major bus companies based here. Word-of-mouth applies in this industry as well; however, bus companies are one of the rare exceptions within the music industry where a good old-fashioned job application possibly followed by a phone or face to face interview can land a job. Among the largest and busiest bus companies currently based out of Nashville are Roberts Brothers Coach, Diamond Coach, Hemphill Brothers, All Access Coach, as well as several others.

The pay that bus drivers receive helps compensate for the long hours of driving and some of the inconveniences they might experience. Quite often, the bus driver makes more money than most of the musicians and crew on a given tour. The following rates are an unofficial industry-standard followed by most bus companies and tours.

Day rate: $200

1st overdrive - 450 miles = $200

2nd overdrive - 650 miles = $200

3rd overdrive - 850 miles = $200

If you are traveling some long distances between shows, the driver will get overdrives at the intervals stated above. For example, if the total distance from one destination to the next is less than 450 miles, they will earn $200. But if it's over 450 miles (even if it's only over by a couple of miles) they will earn an overdrive of $200, for a total of $400 for that trip. If they drove more than 650 miles in a straight shot, they earned $600, and if more than 850 miles they earned $800. Of course, if they drove more than 850 miles in a straight shot, they should probably stop and sleep for a while.

If they are hauling a trailer behind the bus the day rate and overdrives are typically increased by $25, for a total of $225. If a driver is driving a designated "Star Coach" this also increases the day rate and overdrives by $25. A good entertainer coach driver who is in demand can easily earn $70,000 a year or more.

The World Through a Bus Wndow

Top left: French countryside. Right: St. Louis, Missouri
Middle left: Shelbina, Missouri. Right: Lake Mead, Nevada
Bottom left: Golden Gate Bridge, San Francsisco. Right: Eclectic, Alabama

Booking Agencies And Booking Agents

"I wish to be cremated. One 10th of my ashes shall be given to my agent, as written in our contract." — Groucho Marx

Although most musicians working in the Nashville music scene will rarely cross paths with booking agents, they are nevertheless an important part of the touring industry, and their function is worthy of understanding. The role of booking agents in Nashville is the same as the role of booking agents found in any music scene, on any level, in any city or region. They sit around waiting for the phone to ring while creating confusion and stress within your organization, all for a mere 10 to 15%. Just kidding, of course. On the contrary, booking agents have one of the most stressful jobs in the industry, as they, along with managers and labels, have a great deal of responsibility while being the only ones that aren't guaranteed a paycheck.

A good booking agent often acts as the "quasi-manager" for the artist, working diligently to map out the artists career and touring path. As an artist becomes more and more popular, the agent needs to know not to over saturate the artist in certain territories or markets. They also need to realize what the artist is – a future headliner, or one that is going to top out as a mid-level or "soft ticket" act. An agent has to understand rent deals, insurance, production, and every element that goes into an event so promoters don't take advantage.

For many national level touring acts, booking agencies not only book concert dates, they also provide a safety net for the artist by drawing up a contract which will be signed by all parties. In most cases, the contract prevents either party from backing out and helps to guarantee full payment to the artist. Most contracts also state that a deposit must be made within a certain time frame prior to the show with the remainder of the balance being due on the day of show. The fact that most booking agencies represent multiple artists adds another dimension to the safety net, as it will be less likely for an event to cancel an act as they will not want to diminish their credibility with the agent for future bookings.

The level of popularity of a given artist greatly impacts the role of the booking agent. It actually becomes more difficult as the artist becomes more popular as this creates the need to structure shows with percentages. This doesn't mean that smaller acts necessarily fall to the bottom of the priority list either. Ultimately, a lot of what an agent does depends on the passion and the team that is with the artist.

From the perspective of a working musician on a Nashville based tour, you will rarely cross paths with a booking agent, although you will at times hear road managers and artists complaining about them. Similarly to the job of a monitor engineer, a booking agent gets no credit for everything that goes right, but plenty of complaints for everything that goes wrong. And things do go wrong.

There are several major talent booking agencies with offices in Nashville, and they act as a go-between for national touring acts and event buyers from all over the country (and world). Some of these agencies are multi-faceted, also representing comedians, actors, models, speakers, etc. If you ever work as a road manager on a tour, as an artist manager, or become a successful artist, you will more than likely develop a relationship with a booking agent or group of booking agents.

Booking Agents and Working Bands/Startup Artists

There are some booking agencies in Nashville and beyond that will work with local bands, regional bands, and start-up artists. Some unsigned Nashville based bands and artists tour regionally playing nightclubs and casinos, and there are some booking agencies that will work with acts on this level. Just because you don't have a song on the radio doesn't mean you aren't a useful commodity to a booking agent. Don't be afraid to pick up the phone and start cold calling booking agencies to sell them on your band or artist. A gig is a gig and a commission is a commission. Some of them will work with you.

Employment

Becoming a booking agent is not something most musicians ever aspire to do (especially if they don't want their hair to fall out before the age of 30). However, working for a booking agency as an administrative assistant or secretary could be a potential job for some music professionals looking to build relationships within the music industry as it will put them in contact with many tour managers and some artists directly.

A Few Of The Bigger Nashville Booking Agencies:

» Agency Group

» APA Talent and Literary Agency

» Buddy Lee Attractions

» Harper Agency

» Integrity Events

» Junction Entertainment

» Paradigm Agency

» William Morris Agency

» Universal Attractions

Offices of Buddy Lee Attractions on Music Row

Photo courtesy Mike Holmes

Chapter I.3

Nashville Recording Industry

"It was just like a dream. I could have ended up with an album that's not all that different from anything else coming out of Nashville. Mutt made the difference. He took these songs, my attitude, my creativity, and colored them in a way that is unique." — Shania Twain

The Nashville recording industry and recording music in Nashville are two different things. There is a relatively small group of session musicians, studio owners, engineers, and producers that are individually and collectively involved with a large part of the paid recording work that happens in Nashville. Then there is everybody else, fighting for table scraps. While this elite group of professionals within the Nashville music industry has had a corner on the market for decades, this doesn't mean that some paid recording sessions can't happen for others.

Historically speaking, the Nashville recording industry has been a conglomerate that includes major record labels, major recording studios, A-team session players, producers, songwriters, publishing companies, and major recording and touring artists. Under this old business model, major album projects and demos alike were spit out with extreme efficiency, almost daily, for decades. That old model also included a group of smaller studios in which another group of lesser-known session players (referred to as the B-team) recorded many of the demos.

While this old model still exists, it downsized greatly during the early 2000s. Although there are still some big time recording studios here that regularly record major artists from Nashville and beyond, a whole new crop of home-based project studios have been part of a new wave of recording in Nashville. The affordability of home recording is perhaps one of the greatest gifts the post-digital revolution has given to the freelance musician.

While it is the world of home recording that perhaps offers the best opportunities for the up-and-coming session players of today and tomorrow, there will always be a need for high-end studios with their majestic sounding live rooms and superior consoles. And the level of musical and technical ability needed to record in that environment will never go out of style.

High rise on Music Row

Songwriters

"You have to wait until the wheel turns around to where you are creatively. Sometimes you have to sit on the bleachers and wait for it to catch up to what you're doing or you catch up to what it's doing. In writing there is a suffering that goes on. It's scary sometimes; you'll sit on the bench for a couple of years as the town does what it does." — Bill Luther

Songwriters are considered by many to be the lifeblood of the Nashville music industry, as it is their work that ultimately employs most everybody else working in this town. Many songwriters in Nashville who don't have a publishing deal are trying to land one as this will give them immediate income and industry connections and put them in a better position to get their songs out there. Songwriters without a pub deal will have to self-finance their songwriting career every step of the way, and it can become very expensive quickly.

Unlike performing musicians and singers who can play gigs regularly for pay, most songwriters don't make any immediate income from their craft. For songwriters to earn money from their work, they must either get their songs cut by an artist, land a pub deal, or figure out alternative ways to license and sell their songs. In most cases, a pub deal *will* give the songwriter a weekly draw, and for some writers this financial lifeline allows them to work at their craft without working a full-time job.

Publishing companies (at least the good ones) will help finance your songwriting career, team you up with other songwriters, critique your work, pitch your songs to artists, and help to track the success of your songs so you will get paid. For these services, they will own your ass, in the form of a percentage of future publishing and songwriting royalties. They will also, more than likely, own and control the songs you write under their direction even after you are no longer working for them. A standard pub deal might pay you a draw of $250 weekly which is recoupable to them if you ever make any money. You will be required to submit a minimum number of songs monthly, and depending on your deal, you may or may not have to cover the up-front recording costs. If the publishing company pays for the recording, it will be added to your running tab, which will come out of your end if you ever get a successful cut.

Songwriters are at the very beginning of the song production line, and the path that a song takes will cover a lot of ground. It goes something like this:

A song is written by a songwriter or co-written by a group of songwriters. They will usually make a rough work tape on the spot. (Everybody still calls them work tapes even though the recording is almost always made digitally and turned into an mp3 or burned to CD.) The song may then get professionally recorded or "demoed" either as an acoustic vocal or a full band production. If it is a full band demo, this process will employ several session musicians in addition to the recording engineer and the studio itself. If the writer or writers have a pub deal, the publishing company might have it's own studio or a studio that it regularly use for all of their writers. If the writer doesn't have a deal, it is up to them to find their own studio, or perhaps record it themselves if they are tech savvy enough.

The cost of recording a full band production of a song can vary greatly. However, many studios in Nashville can accomplish this for $300 to $500 per song, depending on the instrumentation and how many songs you record at a time. (Of course quality can vary greatly depending on the studio, players, and engineer.) An acoustic vocal demo can usually be accomplished for between $75 and $200 with the variance in cost largely dependent on whether or not the writer sings and plays on the demo, or hires studio musicians.

Once the writer has a finished recording of his new song or songs in hand, he might submit it to his publishing company if he has a deal, use it to try to land a deal if they don't already have one, or use alternative means to license or sell his work.

Writing appointments are an odd but common scenario within the Nashville songwriting community. One well-known successful Nashville writer described the concept to me as being "a really strange way to write music." He told me that on many occasions, his publishing company would schedule him for a writing appointment with another songwriter that he had never previously met. He would walk into a room, pull out his acoustic guitar, and then ask "What do you got?" The other writer would start playing a song, and then they might work to improve it, or move on completely if it's not working. There are, of course, many writers who write regularly with a writing partner with whom they have an ongoing working relationship. It is often the goal of new or unknown writers to obtain opportunities to write with established writers, as this increases their visibility, clout, and chances of getting a cut.

Networking for songwriters in Nashville is all about relationships and perseverance. If it is your goal to work your way up the songwriting ladder, you should try to find some nightspots that established writers frequent and insert yourself into that scene. Songwriter nights are held weekly at places like the Bluebird Café and the Commodore Lounge and can be good places to show your work and make some connections as well. Cold calling publishing companies is another avenue to explore. If you can afford it, hiring a professional songplugger is yet another option. Using the internet can also help to get your work out there. Post mp3's of your songs on your MySpace page or website and try to steer traffic there.

Session Players And Recording Musicians

"The only thing in your mind was to do that particular song, then go onto the next one. Then you'd walk out of the studio and not remember one song you did." — Gordon Stoker, original member of the Jordanaires

Ask any musician who is new to town what he or she is looking to do and many will say, "I'm interested in getting a road gig and/or session work." Not to be a buzz kill, but get in line; everybody wants those jobs. Session work is highly sought after and very appealing to players who want to make a good living with their craft without leaving the city. Although some gifted players with great contacts might get walked through the door shortly after arrival, most of us will have to sweat it out and slowly build and nurture relationships that might eventually lead to paid session work on a regular basis. It can happen; it just takes time.

There Are 3 Ways To Attain Recording Session Work In Nashville

1. Build relationships that will lead to session work.

2. Build your own studio and hire yourself.

3. Become good friends with an A-Team session player and ask him to leave you his spot in his will.

Of these three options, I have found the first two to be the most practical. Over time, slowly build relationships with as many singers, songwriters, musicians, engineers, and producers as you can. If you are a good to great player with a great attitude, you might eventually get hired to play on some projects through these contacts. This doesn't happen for everyone, but if it is one of your goals and you build the right relationships, over time, this can work. This approach can take a long time, and I would like to quote a great line from my mentor and friend D:

> *"The people you are meeting today and the relationships you build with them are what is going to give you work five years from now."*

So while you're working towards that goal, why not consider building your own studio and beginning to learn the recording process. Most players who have little to no recording experience aren't as ready for prime time studio work as they think. You can't get real studio chops and experience without playing on a bunch of sessions, but nobody wants to hire you for their session if you don't have much experience.

This was the case for me when I moved to Nashville. After three years of living here without any real session experience to speak of, I put together an inexpensive home recording rig and began to learn the recording process. Recording with and learning from friends, my studio chops and engineering abilities gradually improved, and I eventually started recording some demos and projects for hire. It takes time to learn how to set up and run a recording rig, but in the end, this might be one of the best ways to develop your studio chops and get paid for them without having to wait 5 or 10 years for the phone to start ringing.

"On The Card" Union Scale Session Pay As Of 2011

» Union Scale 3 hour demo session for side musician $156

» Union Scale 3 hour demo session for band leader $312

» Union Scale 3 hour master session for side musician $380

» Union Scale 3 hour master session for band leader $760

In most situations where musicians are working for a major label *and* a major established artist, they are getting paid double scale. But, if it's a major label with a brand-new, unproven artist, the budget will be smaller, and therefore only pay single scale, even for the A-team. This is also true for independent or smaller labels. In addition to scale, musicians will be paid "Health and Welfare" in the amount of $22.50 for the first session of the day, and $17 for each additional session on that day. Each musician that carries in more than one piece of gear can mark "cartage" on the union card and get an additional $12 for the first session of the day. So, for example, a sideman will take home $190.50 for doing one demo session. An amount equal to 11% of scale ($17.16) is paid by the employer into a pension fund for that musician at the Musician's Union. When musicians turn 55, they can start drawing a partial pension, or they can wait till they're 65 and draw the full pension

Most of the union scale paying session work in Nashville is done by what is commonly referred to as "the A-team." If you are not on the A-team you typically won't get called for these jobs. The only way to become a member of the A-team for most players is through luck or genetic engineering. Since genetic engineering is off of the table for most of us, that leaves luck as the only way in. There is a great quote by drummer Neil Peart that says "Luck is when preparation meets opportunity." You can't exactly schedule "opportunity" on your day planner, but you can work towards being prepared for the day it presents itself, and try to put yourself into situations that are more likely to lead to opportunities.

"Off the card" or non-union session rates can vary greatly. This kind of session work is more attainable although still a hard nut to crack. Here are a few common scenarios:

» 3 to 4 hour songwriter demo session - $100 to $150

» Songwriter demo per song - $40 to $75

» Recording session for a friend on a budget - whatever you think is fair.

Session Leaders/Bandleaders

On recording sessions, the band leader, or "session leader;" will usually be a player on the session as well. His duties might include hiring the other players, writing charts, creating arrangements, rehearsing the band, providing visual cues during the session, getting everybody paid, and even acting as a producer on many occasions. A good band leader will also help create a fun, laid-back atmosphere that will allow the session to flow smoothly. On all union sessions (and nearly all non-union sessions) the band leader gets double pay for these extra responsibilities. On union sessions, the leader is also responsible for getting all the musicians signatures on a union card and filing a contract with the union. If wages are late getting to the musicians, he will do what he can to make sure everybody gets paid. In general, a session band leader is an important person to know if you're looking for studio work.

Requirements Of A Freelance Studio Musician Working In Nashville

If you are ever hired as a freelance studio musician, here is a little of what might be expected from you:

» Be punctual. You should be prompt or early for your sessions. If you hold up a session because of tardiness, it is unlikely that you will ever be called back.

» Be competent. You should be a highly skilled player with great timing, great tone, great intonation, and a great feel.

» Be friendly and courteous. A good session is all about having a good vibe. Getting along with everybody else at the studio is a key element, so blend in and don't make waves.

» Be versatile. You should be familiar with all styles and genres of popular music new and old and be able to call up a given feel, tone, or style on a second's notice. Knowledge of other types of world music is useful as well.

» Know the radio. Some producers and artists might ask you to play in the style of a specific song or artist currently on the radio. Know the trends and you won't get caught with your pants down.

» Own the right gear. Session players need a wide variety of textures and tones readily available. If you're drummer, you should have a few different snares and some different sounding cymbals. Guitarists should have different guitars, amps, and effects. Keyboard players should be able to accurately reproduce piano, Rhodes, B-3, strings, etc. Make sure your gear is reliable and sets up as quickly as possible as well.

» Be efficient and effective. You should be able to play for the song and come up with tasteful, appropriate parts quickly. The player that holds up the process is unlikely to be called back.

» Be meticulous. If you made a mistake or two and hear it during playback, point it out and ask if you can punch it in. Things move quickly at many sessions, and the engineer or producer might not notice the mistake till later, after you are gone and unable to correct it.

» Know the numbers. You should be able to read and write Nashville number charts, as this is used on the majority of Nashville sessions. The ability to read traditional notation and other types of chord charts, i.e. Real Book, can also be helpful, although less common in Nashville recording sessions.

» Be able to play to a click track. Many Nashville recording sessions require players to record to a click track. Although this is not always the case, more often than not, a click is used. Learn how to sway your time around the click, i.e. playing slightly behind the beat on the verses, a little more on top on choruses and solos, etc.

» Have nerves of steel. If you are unable to deliver a part or overdub to the liking of the producer or artist, be prepared to do 10 or 20 takes with everyone watching you through a control room window. Of course, if this happens, it is unlikely that you will ever be called back.

» Be able to follow directions. Many producers and artists have very specific ideas and will convey these to you with varying degrees of efficiency. In these situations, do your best to deliver the part they request.

» Don't ever say to a producer, "I've got a better part in mind." If you have an idea for a part that you think might work better in a song, be very tactful in the way you present it. Perhaps say, "I have an idea, what if we do it like this?" and then demonstrate your idea. If your idea is well received, you'll be a hero. If it's not, just do it the way he originally wanted and you'll still be a hero.

» Look presentable. Casual is fine on many sessions, just don't forget that your appearance will be a part of how you will be remembered.

» Possess computer knowledge. You should be knowledgeable about MP3, WAV and all the other kinds of file attachments as employers might be sending you song files and charts via the Internet.

Station West, Nashville, TN *Photo courtesy Bart Busch*

MASTERFONICS
CURB
PRODUCTIONS
LOUD Recording

Recording Engineers

"It's quite ironic: We got rid of our analog equipment, replaced it with digital, then spent the next couple of decades trying to get the digital to sound like the analog we got rid of." — David Williams

Over the past 20 to 30 years, the job opportunities and landscape for recording engineers have gone through a complete metamorphosis. While the small handful of million dollar studios in Nashville and beyond still produce great recordings, there is a whole new wave of home based "project studios" that have completely changed the way in which music is recorded. In this new digital world, computers, software, and recording equipment have become very affordable allowing many bands and artists to record themselves. This new generation of self recording musicians has taken away some of the demand for the professional freelance studio engineer as many artists and bands now engineer and mix their own recordings.

Pro Tools is by far the most common recording software used currently in Nashville and has been for many years. Other mediums such as Nuendo, Cubase, Cakewalk, Logic Pro, and others are commonly used as well. In this new digital world of recording, great ears and a thorough knowledge of recording techniques are still essential, but a good understanding of computers is now required as well.

For big budget album projects recorded in high-end studios, an engineer who is in demand can earn between $1000 and $1500 per day, with his assistant earning in the neighborhood of $250. That kind of pay scale was typical in the record making industry for many years, but now, the kind of major projects that warrant an engineer on that level happen with much less frequency. Only a very small handful of great engineers with long lists of credentials ever earn that kind of pay anymore. Many mid-level operations pay engineers an hourly fee ranging somewhere between $25 and $50 per hour for a typical 4 hour session. Like the rest of the music related jobs in Nashville, there is a clique for this part of the industry, and most jobs are acquired by engineers with good reputations through word of mouth. These kinds of good paying regular studio gigs are hard to find as the level of competition for engineers is similar to that of the musicians.

One option for finding work as an engineer could be to start as a "grunt" assisting, setting up, cleaning the studio, etc. This could eventually lead to a regular position as an engineer. Another approach is to build your own studio and hire yourself, or partner with someone who owns a small to midsized studio. Carve out your own niche over time by slowly establishing a great reputation with your work. If you can build a cost effective project studio with a good vibe, charge competitive rates, while building as many relationships as you can with songwriters and aspiring artists, there can be some steady work in this town for you. Just don't expect it to happen overnight, Rome wasn't built in a day (or even a year for that matter).

For a more in-depth look at the evolution and ever-changing role of the recording engineer read the extensive interview with recording industry veteran Bob Bullock on page 207.

Bart Busch and his assistant recording Hank Williams Jr. at Station West, 2005. Photo courtesy Bart Busch

Producers

"I know the material better than the artist who may have written it before we hit the record button. After careful thought I'll discuss my ideas and gather other ideas that may have developed from the artist. I know what I want it to sound like in my head and know how to achieve that sonically and through the music/arrangement end. I like to write a lot of notation and make a lot of notes – even if it's just for me. That's producing in a nutshell as far as I'm concerned." — Jack Hale

When it comes to making professional recordings, it is the producer's job to hear the big picture of a song, a singer, and/or band and steer the recording session towards that end result. A modern day record producer has many roles, among them managing the recording sessions, coaching and guiding the artist/musicians, organizing and scheduling the production budget and resources, and supervising the recording, mixing and mastering processes. Typically this is not a job that one applies for through an ad in the classifieds; it is a career of evolution. Many great producers also have extensive recording engineering experience and may have worked as a studio engineer for many years before they became producers. Many are also proficient musicians as well.

If an artist has obtained a record deal with a major label, more often than not, the label will choose and hire a producer to oversee and control the recording process. A producer working on a major project might also assist in choosing the material that the artist will record and the session players that will be used. On this level, the producer will probably receive a large upfront payment upwards of $25,000 and some kind of points on the record if it gets released and becomes successful. It is not uncommon for self-promoted independent artists to hire a producer for their recordings as well, although most of them will hire one that works for a substantially smaller fee.

In some cases, a studio band produces itself. The producer, engineer, or artist will appoint a band leader who will chart out the chord changes and arrange the song. The best studio musicians are good enough to invent interesting parts, have a sense of what an arrangement calls for, and know how to "build a song" without an actual producer being present, and it is these qualities that a producer is ultimately looking for when choosing session players. Many Nashville recordings are recorded by great players with no producer present and still achieve a polished and "produced" sound.

If you are chosen by a producer or band leader for a recording session, chances are that you are already going to have a clue of what is expected from you or you wouldn't have been called. In many cases, the producer will discuss the direction of the session in a process called pre-production (which will be explained in more detail at the end of this chapter). However, that's not always the case. I have heard stories of a new player being tried on a session, not able to deliver what the producer is looking for, and then being "ejected" from the session never to be called again. If you are hired for a session and the producer doesn't schedule a preproduction session, don't hesitate to give him/her a call to discuss the material. Ask for worktapes, the tone, vibe, etc of the record. If you show an interest in being fully prepared for the session, you will be more comfortable when it comes time to record and increase your opportunity to be called back in the future.

As a player, you may wind up in a situation someday where you are working with a producer. If you ever get the call, don't be too nervous or you'll undermine your performance. And if you screw up, don't worry; it's just your career on the line.

Musicians Networking With Producers

There are a number of ways that musicians can network with producers, and this can be approached just as networking would be in any other profession - joining organizations, attending industry events, treating them to lunch, building relationships, referring projects to them, etc. Rather than handing them a business card and hoping they will call you some day, keep in touch and add value to what you have to offer. If a player can offer something of value to a producer and, in turn, begin to establish a relationship, he's more likely to get called (or called back) than if he touches base every once and while to "see if you have any work for me."

Another way is by networking with a producer's inner circle. Just as in the corporate world, where you have a much better chance of connecting with a CEO if you make nice with his/her assistant rather than a company sales rep, players can extend their network to include those individuals with whom the producer works closely with. Chances are there will come a day when the producer asks one of these individuals if they have a certain type of player in mind for a project. If you have developed a good relationship with him/her, your chances of being brought up in conversation are much better.

Becoming A Producer

If you are interested in a career as a producer or you are a musician who is interested in recording, learning about recording techniques is essential, and working in a home studio environment is a great place to start. Learn how to make a good recording from start to finish using whatever tools you have at your disposal. If you only have a PC with basic recording software like Ableton or Garage Band, start there and build on that foundation as you can afford to. Read online articles about recording techniques, experiment with drum loops, explore the use of different instrument sounds and mixing concepts, learn how to use space to give depth to a recording, learn how to write good parts that naturally sit well in the mix. By learning how to "produce" a good, professional sounding recording, you will slowly evolve into being a competent session musician, a skilled recording engineer, and an effective producer.

RCA's historic "Studio B," located on the corner of 17th Avenue and Roy Acuff Place, was a nerve center for major recordings made in Nashville between 1957 and 1977. Chet Atkins, one of the pioneers of the "Nashville Sound," was instrumental in conceptualizing this first studio built specifically to record on Music Row. Throughout the 60's and early 70's, Atkins produced hits for most of RCA's Nashville acts and brought many of country music's greats to the label, including Waylon Jennings, Willie Nelson, Connie Smith, Dolly Parton, and Jerry Reed, among countless others.

Preproduction: The Neglected Vital Stage Of Record Production

By Ronan Chris Murphy

The following excerpts are from the article "Preproduction: The neglected vital stage of record production" written by internationally acclaimed recording producer and mixer Ronan Chris Murphy, and are printed with his permission. Ronan works internationally as a recording producer and mixer with credits that include: King Crimson, Steve Morse, Nels Cline, Terry Bozzio, Steve Stevens, and countless others. For more info on Ronan check out www.venetowest.com.

Many people make the mistake of confusing production with drum sounds or something you "add" to a recording, when in truth production is inclusive process of making a record. As important as the sound of a record can be, what is far more important is that the song itself and the performance of that song be musically and emotionally engaging. One of the most overlooked and often neglected aspects of production is actually the most vital to this: Preproduction.

Preproduction is the work a producer and the artists do before the actual recording of a record begins. While many high budget albums and some poorly planned low budget albums will work on preproduction in the studio, this does not have to be the case. Preproduction is the single most cost effective, "bang for your buck" stage of producing a record, and critically important to making the best use of time, energy and budget in the studio. I would prefer a short amount of time in the studio to record an album, plus sufficient time for preproduction, than twice that recording time and no preproduction. Quite often people will compliment my production by commenting on the sound of particular instruments, voice or elements of a mix. While I am always flattered that people enjoy elements of my work, I usually consider my most important contributions to a record to be those that I made before we walked into the studio. Even the "sound" of the drums or a singer, usually has more to do with performance and arrangement strategies developed with the artist than a particular recording or mixing approach I may have used.

For most records, the only things necessary for successful preproduction are musical instruments and a room where people can play music together and exchange ideas. Certain modern styles of music, which are dependent on electronics, may require computers and samplers, but these things are really only modern musical instruments. Additional technology or complications serve only to pull the focus of the producer and the musicians away from making music and exchanging ideas. Preproduction should be a simple low cost stage of record production that helps save (or at least better spends) money and make better records.

The goal of reproduction is to address three fundamental areas: 1) Songwriting and song crafting. 2) Defining the vision of the record. 3) Making sure that the performances serve the vision of the record. These areas will continually be addressed and developed throughout the recording process, but the more work that can be done on these issues before entering the studio, the more effective your time in the studio will be. The studio should be a place to explore nuances, charge emotional energy and capture the magic of a performance and the moment.

By the end of preproduction I want to have established a vision for the record. What is the feel or mood we are going for? What is the sound we are going for? What is the process we will use to record? Who are we making this record for? How long should an album be? What songs will be on the album? How do we integrate the desires of the artist and the record company? All of these questions should be answered before the artist and the producer step into the studio. Will you leave the studio with the same answers to those questions? Probably not, but it is important that there be a vision that these questions define, so there is a common goal for the entire team to work towards. If a team of people enter a studio with a clear goal and all work towards that goal, even if you miss that goal you will probably end up somewhere interesting and of value. If there is no clear vision for a record this will be reflected in the final product.

Once a vision for a record has been established, it is important that the performances of the musicians work to support that vision. The performance of the musicians is the single most important element in determining the "sound" of a record and how a song will be translated to a listener. If someone compliments me on the drum sound of a record I have produced, I usually express my gratitude for the compliment and confirm that "yes, the drummer did play great." I more accurately say to myself "yes, the drummer really played to serve the song and the vision of the record we were trying to make". The foundation of great sounding instruments and recordings is great sounding performances. If a drummer wants a big rock sound, playing like a jazz musician will not serve that goal and visa versa. If a guitarist wants the vocals to sound great then the guitarist must play parts that support the vocal and don't compete with it. Every performance affects not only the sound of that musician's instrument, but of all the other instruments and the entire mix.

The preproduction needs for every project will be different. In some cases it can be a matter of a short period of time to define the vision of a record with artists whose songs and performances are already in great shape. In other cases it might involve several months of songwriting and performance coaching with the artists. Without proper preproduction it is impossible to truly establish the needs of a record and make the best use of your time in the studio. Preproduction is a 2-way education for the producer and the artists. It is a time to share ideas, to grow as musicians and develop the trust and skills that will be necessary when it is time to bring your best into the studio.

Photo courtesy Jim Handley

Cartage

"Cartage: conveyance of merchandise by cart or truck."
— Babylon Dictionary

Working a cartage job is another option for musicians trying to make a living in Nashville. When a studio musician shows up for a recording session, his equipment is already there, set up and ready to go. This is because the cartage person picked up his equipment from a storage facility, delivered it to the studio, and set it up before the session player arrived.

Most of the session players that work the "on the card" sessions pay a cartage company like Soundcheck or Nashville Cartage to store, haul, and set up their gear for their sessions. These cartage companies also do airport pickups and drop offs for touring and studio musicians. The people that are working for the cartage company must have at least enough knowledge about music gear to set it up properly for the recording sessions. They must also know how to drive a van or box truck and have a strong back.

Cartage can be a physically demanding job as most of this gear is kept in anvil style road cases. Most cases are on wheels, but you would still need to be able to do some lifting as there can be some stairs to deal with here and there. Working a cartage job in Nashville is going to put you on a first name basis with people that work for some of the higher end studios as well as some A-team studio musicians, and over time these relationships could be valuable.

To obtain work from a cartage company, just perform a Google search and start cold calling or stopping by the cartage companies in town. Put in an application to as many places as you can and do periodic follow ups. The starting pay is usually $8 to $10 dollars per hour over the table, with $12 to $15 per hour attainable for workers that are able to stick around for a while. The biggest downside (aside from a potential hernia) is getting pigeon-holed. You don't want to move Nashville and then have ten years go by with the music community only knowing you as a cartage guy. However, for musicians in town who can't make ends meet performing, cartage can be a good short to midterm way to bridge the financial gap.

Major Cartage Companies In Nashville:

» Sessions Services Unlimited

» Soundcheck Nashville

» Xpress

» Central Studio Service

» Drum Paradise

Finished drum setup at Oceanway Studios. *Photo courtesy Jim Handley*

Music Business Support Industries

"There exist limitless opportunities in every industry. Where there is an open mind, there will always be a frontier." — Charles F. Kettering

Depending on your background and abilities, there are several music related support industries in Nashville that offer employment opportunities. These jobs include music retail, instrument and electronics repair, rehearsal studio staff and technicians, production company technicians, music teachers, local union event workers, and administrative work. The following outline provides a basic overview of these industries and lists the names of several major businesses within each industry. For a more complete listing of these businesses including contact and website info, refer to the Nashville Musician's Survival Guide Website (www.survivenashville.com).

Music Retail

Nashville is home to dozens of music stores ranging from small, mom and pop type operations, to specialty stores, to giant corporate behemoths like Guitar Center and Sam Ash. If you are considering applying for work in music retail, here are a few of the stores that have been around for a while and might be worth checking out.

» Rock Block Guitars

» Gruhn Guitars

» Nashville Used Music

» Corner Music

» Forks Drum Closet

» World Music

» Sam Ash

» Guitar Center

These are just a few of the bigger stores; an Internet search will produce many more in the Nashville metropolitan area.

Instrument and Electronics Repair

If you have a background in instrument, amplifier, or electronics repair, you could apply for work at any of the previously mentioned and other music stores. Many of the more popular music stores have had the same techs employed for years, but sometimes they have overflow work and sub out jobs periodically.

Rehearsal Studio Staff and Technicians

Nashville is home to some world-class rehearsal studios, with Soundcheck and SIR being the largest and most popular. These two rehearsal studios in particular feature multiple practice rooms of various sizes, most of which contain large stages, complete PA systems, and separate monitor systems. Both facilities also offer extensive backline rentals and have in-house techs that service the equipment. The facilities also employ administrative personnel and techs to assist bands and artists with PA and monitor setups. There are a few other smaller rehearsal studios around town that also employ techs and administrative personnel.

Production Companies

Nashville has a few large production companies and several small ones that provide PA, lighting, video, and staging for concerts and events. These companies employ sound and monitor engineers, system techs, lighting designers, video technicians, repair technicians, and administrative personnel. Here are a few of the Nashville based production companies you could check out if you're looking for work in this field.

» Claire Brothers Audio Inc Nashville

» The Spencer Daniels Agency

» Meeting Tomorrow Audio Visual

» Gateway Productions

» Hurricane Mountain Sound

» Northern Lights Productions

» Gault & Associates, Inc.

» Sam's Video Productions

» Thompson Music Rental

SIR Rehearsal Studios on Cherry Ave.

Music Teachers

If you have a background as a private instructor, many of the previously mentioned music stores offer private lessons and might be good places to submit an application. This field is extremely competitive as many of the teachers working in these stores have had these jobs for years. It wouldn't hurt to submit applications anyway as they will often be put on file. Another option could be starting your own teaching business out of your home and advertising on the Internet.

Local Union Event Workers

Nashville has concerts and corporate events on a regular basis, and many of these events hire production companies that employ local union stagehands, riggers, and carpenters, etc. The production staff at the Grand Ole' Opry is also comprised of union workers. If you have experience in these areas you should speak to somebody at the Local Musicians Union 257 to find out more about how to proceed.

Administrative Personnel

If you have experience as an administrative assistant, there is potential employment in literally every aspect of the Nashville music industry. Included would be jobs working for recording studios, publishing companies, BMI, ASCAP, booking agencies, management companies, as well as most of the previously mentioned industries in this chapter.

The San Francisco - Oakland Bay Bridge

Chapter 2

Touring Life

"With my guys and with the way that we live out there, we work out a lot and try to eat right, but we try to basically keep it our own rhythm and our own world." — Brad Paisley

Over the past several years I have spent much time on the road, touring the country. I have been very fortunate to have had the opportunity to work with many great artists, meet many interesting people, and experience all sorts of scenarios both good and bad along the way. I have traveled on everything from million dollar tour buses to beat up old vans, 747's to mail carriers. I have performed on small stages in honky tonk dives and concert stages in arenas, plywood stages in the middle of fields in Georgia and Texas and the Grand Ole Opry at the Ryman Auditorium, in front of crowds ranging from 7 to 70,000 and everything in between. All of these experiences have enriched my life, and I am grateful for the opportunities I have had.

Touring is hard work. There are many great moments, but there are also many long bus rides and a lot of down time. Many people, myself included, have spent the majority of their life growing up in a small town or region, never experiencing or seeing the rest of the world. If you have never seen the rest of the country, touring with a national act is a great way to do it; much can be seen out the window of a bus. Traveling can help broaden your perspective and view of the world, and it can also help improve your self-confidence.

This next section of the book gives some insight and perspective to the daily life on a tour. The daily activities for touring musicians, artists, and crew members can vary greatly depending on the level and characteristics of a given tour, but the basic principles are the same. Long hours of travel, late nights, living out of a suitcase, being constantly around people, and living on a bus for days or weeks on end are all part of the job. The lifestyle can be hard on your body, and this makes it typically a younger person's game. (You don't see too many 60 year olds on a tour.) This lifestyle can also be hard on family relationships as touring requires one to be gone for extended periods of time. Of course in some situations this might actually help save the relationship.

To live day to day on a tour and not have it take too great of a toll, an almost scientific approach can be taken. The better you understand the finer points of the different components and variables of touring, the better prepared you will be to survive touring for a long period of time. A common theme you will find throughout this part of the book will be "learning to adapt." Touring is not for everyone, but for some it can be a great way to see the world, meet people from many different walks of life, and gain some otherwise unattainable life experiences, while earning a living from your craft.

Roberts Brothers Prevost XLII

Bus Leasing

"In the early days we didn't have the bus, we had a station wagon."
— Mel Tillis

Most artists and bands touring on a national level lease tour busses for a majority of their travel. There is a common misconception among fans and others that most artists or bands own the bus they are traveling in. While some may buy a bus outright, most touring acts cannot afford to do this as a brand new Prevost XLII (the bus of choice) costs somewhere between $400,000 and $700,000. In addition to being very expensive to purchase, the useful lifespan of these busses is relatively short, as a busy tour may cover more than 100,000 miles in a year. One more reason not to own one of these is the maintenance. If you own it, you pay to fix it. If you lease it, the bus company is responsible for repairs.

So, for most tours, leasing is where it's at. There are several major bus leasing companies based out of Nashville as well as the other major music cities in the U.S.; among them, Roberts Brothers, based out of Springfield, TN with a fleet of 150 busses, is currently the biggest. For most weekend tours, a bus is leased only for the days needed and then returned to the leasing company. The per-day lease for weekend tours is usually between $400 and $500 for a band or crew bus and a little more for a star coach. On tours that are going out for extended periods of time, artists and bands will usually have the same bus for the duration. A long term lease can help reduce the per day leasing rate.

There are several other fees in addition to the daily leasing fee that need to be covered by the artist. Bus driver, driver hotel rooms, fuel, end of tour cleaning, satellite and internet fees, and engine, transmission, and generator maintenance fees based on mileage. These busses by the way, average about 5 to 6 mpg (ouch). With leasing, driver pay, fuel, and all other fees, it costs about $1000 to $1200 per day to lease and travel on a tour bus. You can find some bus companies that will lease busses for less ($300 per day); however these will typically be older model busses and more likely to have problems and breakdowns. You get what you pay for.

Knowing the basic cost and expenses of leasing or owning a tour bus will help you gain an appreciation and respect for the bus that will ultimately be your second home.

Honky Tonk Tailgate Party Tour enroute to California - 2005 *Photo courtesy Brian Beihl*

Bus Life

*Family: **1:** a group of individuals living under one roof and usually under one head. **2:** a group of people united by certain convictions or a common affiliation.* — Webster Dictionary

Living on a tour bus with a band or crew is an interesting experience, to say the least. The members of a tour living on a bus are very much like an extended family, and for many, they *become* their family, at least by definition. As most families are dysfunctional, a band is no exception, and this can vary greatly. The biggest challenge for many is learning to adapt to this new life.

Most people in our society grew up in a family of at least 3 to 4, in a house or apartment that was probably 1200 to 2000 square feet. You probably had your own bedroom and shared a kitchen, living room, and at least 1 bathroom (if not 2) with the other family members. You had your own space and shared the rest of the house with the family. Well, living on a bus is based on the same principal except the family is bigger (probably between 8 and 12), and the house is smaller - MUCH smaller. The interior of a bus is roughly 40 feet by 7 feet, or 280 square feet. Your only personal space is your bunk, which is about the size of a coffin; the rest of the bus is shared space.

A Typical Band Or Crew Tour Bus Layout Is As Follows:

The front door to the bus is opposite the driver's seat, and there is usually a "co-pilot" seat right behind the stairs by that door. The front lounge comes next with a couch that seats 3 to 4 running down both sides of the bus and a small kitchen table with another seat for two behind it. There is typically a TV, DVD/CD player, and stereo in this area as well. Just past the couches is a kitchenette in this same room, consisting of refrigerator, microwave, sink, and cabinets and drawers for storage. The bathroom is probably somewhere in this same area and about the size of a bathroom on an airplane.

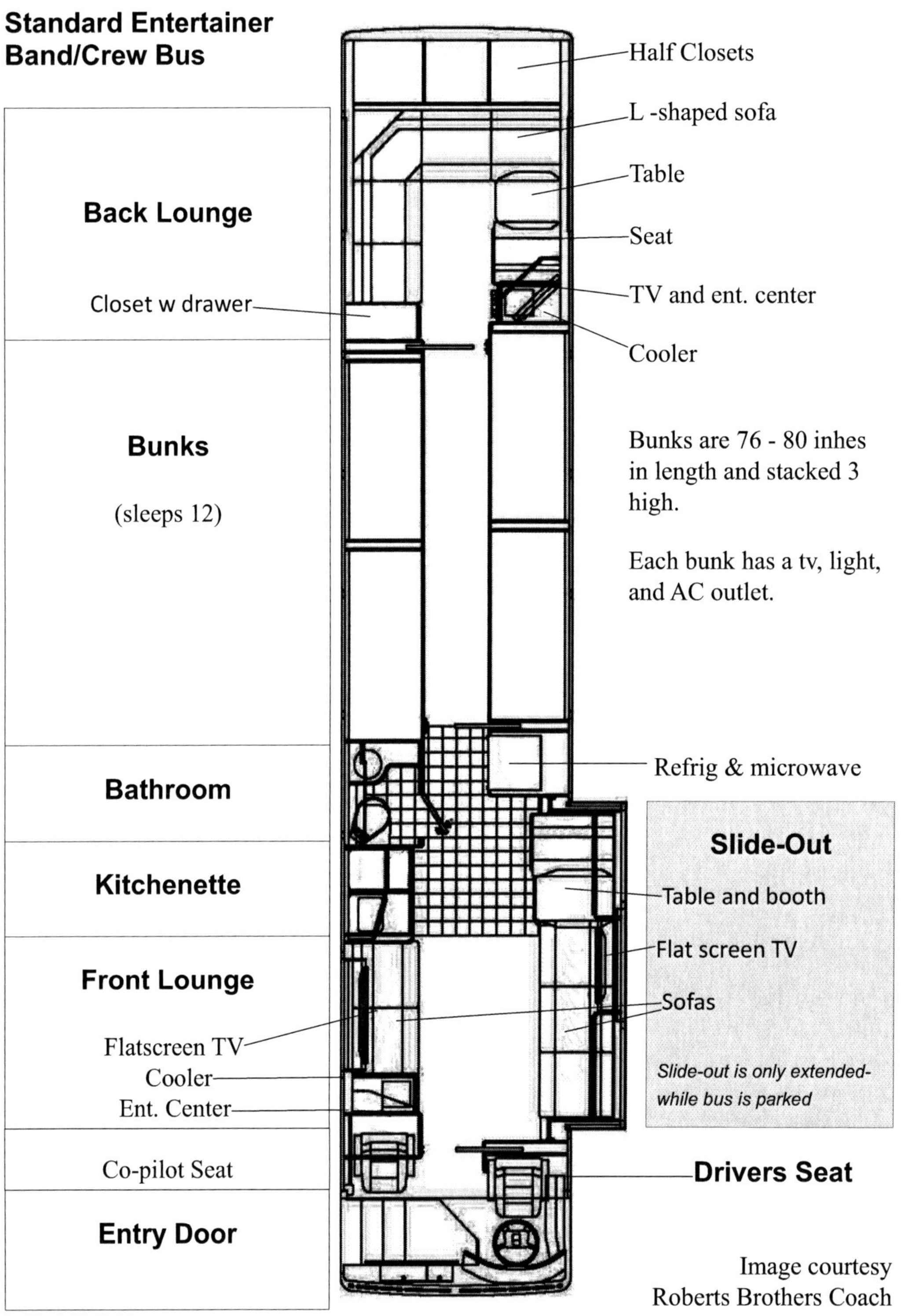

Image courtesy
Roberts Brothers Coach

The bunk aisle will be next which consists of a hallway down the center of the bus with a row of bunks on both sides. The bunks are typically three high, with a total of 12 bunks (6 on each side) in the aisle. The middle bunks are usually the most desired as they are a good tradeoff between the noise and rumble of the bottom bunks and the sway of the top bunks. The top bunks can be a little difficult to get in and out of for some. Each bunk has its own curtain and interior light and can be pitch black when the curtain is shut, if desired, and many busses have a small TV and DVD player in each bunk as well. The bunk aisle is usually separated from the rest of the bus by a sliding door at each end.

Just past the bunk aisle is the back lounge, which is usually a much smaller version of the front lounge consisting of an entertainment center and seating for about four comfortably. There are some closets and drawers throughout the bus for storage, and if the bus isn't full you may have some "junk bunks" for storage also. There are many different variations of this layout, but the basic amenities are going to be the same on most crew busses.

As far as hanging out, the front lounge is usually where most congregate. The bunks are used for sleeping or lying down, and the back lounge is the noisiest (right above the engine) and roughest riding part of the bus. So your nice, cushy 280 square foot rock and roll palace on wheels has just shrunk to an area roughly the size of a waiting room at the doctors' office. This still beats the hell out of a van or an airplane. The bus is really a house on wheels and should be viewed as your home away from home.

Most bus drives are made during the night with anywhere between midnight and 2:00 AM being a typical leave time. The driver will have an opposite schedule from the band or crew and do their driving between midnight and noon. Most of the tour members will sleep during this time and wake up at the next destination, ready to begin their work day (with the occasional night owl being an exception). During the daytime hours the driver will have his down time and will usually be put up at a hotel to sleep. I have been trying to explain this concept to my family and friends back home for years, and they just can't picture it. They will still ask, "Doesn't the driver get tired driving all night?" and I will respond, "No, he drives thru the night so we can sleep, and then he sleeps during the day when we work." They still don't get it.

Living on a bus with your band or crew requires a different mindset than living in a house with your parents and siblings, or an apartment with roommates. Because of the limited space, you have to learn to adapt, both physically and mentally. As members of a tour don't always share the same life views, most tours practice the old "don't talk about politics or religion at work" concept. Going with the flow is where it's at. Sometimes the only thing to do in the front lounge is watch TV, and you won't always like what someone else chooses. Learn to adapt. On some tours, the artist may ride with the band and sit in silence for most of the trip (while controlling the TV). This can create an unspoken tension that permeates the entire bus. Learn to adapt.

I have been on tours that have a walking-on-eggshells vibe, others that have a great close knit family quality, and some that lie somewhere in between. The individual personalities of the tour members form a collective overall vibe, and this provides the social setting in which you will live on that tour. One person's mindset and attitude can completely change this chemistry. If just one person is in a bad mood he can bring down a whole bus full of tour members, and this is why getting along and being respectful of your fellow tour mates is of utmost importance. Learn to adapt. (*Thanks Rhett!)*

Sleeping At 75 MPH

"He who sleeps in continual noise is wakened by silence."
— William Dean Howells

Sleeping on a tour bus comes easier for some than others. No matter how nice the bus, how good the driver, or how respectful your band mates are, you are still traveling at 75 MPH down an interstate. Depending on what part of the country you're traveling through, the quality of the roads can vary greatly. A bumpy road can make for a rough night of sleep. One bus rider once described the experience of sleeping on a bus as being similar to that of sleeping on the back seat of her parents' car while being driven to her grandmothers' house as a child.

Aside from getting used to sleeping while in motion, there are other elements that may affect your ability to sleep on a bus. From inside of your bunk you may be able to hear conversations coming from the lounges, the sounds of the TV or stereo being played, the bunk aisle door opening and closing, people getting into their bunks, and possibly the rumble strip on a regular basis if your driver isn't that great. If you sleep in a bottom bunk the engine noise and vibration will drown out a lot of this noise, but you will hear and feel the road and diesel drone intensely. If you have a top bunk, the engine noise will be much quieter and you will feel the road the least, but sounds from inside the bus will be louder and you will experience the most amount of side to side sway. Many bus riders consider the middle bunks to be the most desirable for sleeping as they are a good happy medium and the easiest bunks to get in and out of.

Of course, as these are the most coveted bunks they are usually already spoken for by the senior members of the tour. On many tour buses there is a pecking order regarding bunk status, with the artist always having first choice. Behind the artist, the bunk preference order is usually established by seniority within the rest of the group. When someone leaves a given tour, the most senior member of the tour gets first dibs on the newly vacant bunk, and so on.

Hopefully you will get used to sleeping while in motion, the sound of a loud diesel engine, the sounds of distant conversations and maybe some random TV blaring. Another

Bunk aisle (Be very, very quiet!)

variable will be your band or crew mates' ability to be considerate. If your co-riders are respectful of the bunk aisle, you won't hear much else than the steady sounds of a diesel engine moaning through the night. If you are traveling with some inexperienced bus riders or maybe some road veterans who just don't care, there is a long list of things that might ruin your sleep. People talking loudly while walking through the bunk aisle, talking on cell phones in bunks, doors slamming, excessive noise or light from the lounges because someone left the door open, unattended cell phones ringing in a bunk, and excessively loud TV or stereo noise from the lounges are a few. The use of foam ear plugs while sleeping can greatly reduce the noise coming from outside of your bunk, but the best case scenario is to have a bus full of considerate riders.

There is one other HUGE variable to be considered for good sleep on a bus, and that is the bus driver. For me, knowing and trusting the driver is crucial when trying to sleep on a moving bus. A great driver will be able to provide a fairly smooth ride even on bad roads, as they will know the limits of the bus and consider the fact that people are trying to sleep. A bad driver *can* and *will* scare the hell out of you. If your driver sucks, you will feel a variety of unpleasant sensations while traveling and *trying* to sleep ranging from hard braking, over accelerating, weaving side to side, and riding on the rumble strip at regular intervals. If you are stuck with one of these morons, complaining about their driving will usually make it worse. The only thing you can do in these situations is to complain to the road manager or artist and hope they don't like it either. If all else fails, learn to adapt.

Assuming you have a good driver and some considerate co-riders, sleeping on a bus is *much* better than sleeping in a van or on a plane.

Sleeping Tips

It is commonly accepted that the only safe way to sleep in a bunk is with your feet pointing forward, toward the front of the bus. This is done in precaution to the possibility of an accident (a broken ankle would be better than a broken neck). Most bus bunks come with a comforter and pillow; however some riders bring their own pillow and/or comforter if it helps them to sleep better. If you're a light sleeper and easily awoken by sounds, ear plugs are essential. They can also help reduce fatigue.

If you have a hard time falling asleep here are a couple of tips you can try.

The Alphabet Game

Pick a subject you enjoy like movies, bands, world history, etc. For this example I will use movies. Start with the letter A, and name three movies that begin with the letter A, (for example, *Avatar*, *A Few Good Men*, and *Austin Powers)*. Now move on to the letter B; *Back to the Future*, *Behind Enemy Lines*, and *Born Free*. Keep going through the alphabet naming three movies per letter until you fall asleep. This has worked for me many times, and in general I can't even get halfway through the alphabet before I'm asleep. Some of my favorite topics to use with this particular game are movies, bands, song titles, and towns and cities in my home state. Pick something fun that you enjoy, and you'll be sleeping like a baby before you know it. If you start to get bored with the routines, start with the letter Z and work your way backwards.

Number Games

Most people are familiar with the old trick of counting backwards from 100 or 1000 to fall sleep. The problem with this is it's too boring after you've used it a couple of times. Step it up a little. Try counting backwards from 1000 at intervals of three, 1000, 997, 994, etc. This is much more challenging and will keep you engaged longer.

Take a Walk or Ride a Bike

Go back in time to an earlier part of your life, maybe as a teenager in your hometown. Picture yourself walking or riding a bike away from your home. Pick a destination a few miles away. Try to visualize the scenery as you travel down the street. Picture the houses, landmarks, fences and overall scenery. You are traveling the entire time viewing each house or business as you pass it. If you do this correctly you will be asleep before you have even gone a mile.

Sleep on a Flying Carpet

This only works on a moving bus. Get into your bunk, get comfortable, and close your eyes. Try to picture yourself lying on a magic carpet and flying through the sky. Tour buses tend to have a cushy boat like motion inherent to the way they ride, so just transfer that sensation. Use the subtle bounces and sense of motion to visualize yourself lying on a magic carpet, flying through the sky, through the clouds, to some far-off destination. Maybe picture some scenery of the countryside below, the sky above, etc. This has worked well for me many times; however, you might not want to try this if you are afraid of heights.

The concept behind these methods is that by concentrating hard on one concept or thought, you are clearing your conscious mind of all other thoughts. This allows your overall thought patterns to slow down and helps to stop your mind from racing so you can fall asleep.

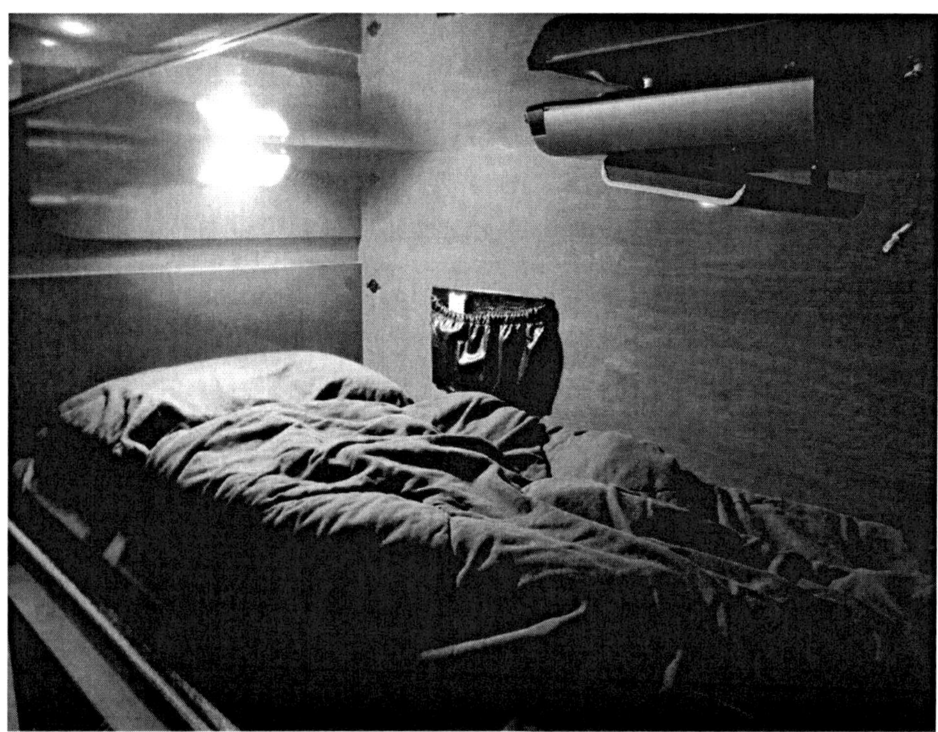

No Number Two

"Always go to the bathroom when you have a chance." – King George V

One downside to life on a tour bus is the bathroom rule "pee only." Most modern tour busses do not have a system adequate for anything other than *pee only,* which means the bus needs to stop at a rest area or truck stop if someone needs to do anything more. If you have ever been on a bus where this rule was broken, you know why this rule is so important.

The people who break this rule most commonly are friends, fans, or gherms that are hanging out on the bus after the show. Tell some 22 year old floozy, "The bathroom is pee only, no poop or paper," and she will probably forget before she even closes the bathroom door. Starting sometime the following day, and lasting for the rest of the trip, will be an unpleasant and constant reminder why the pee only rule exists.

Bagging One

If you are traveling on a long stretch of road where there is no place to stop for hundreds of miles, such as through a desert or Kansas, sometimes "bagging one" is the only option. This practice is not encouraged, but sometimes may be the only option.

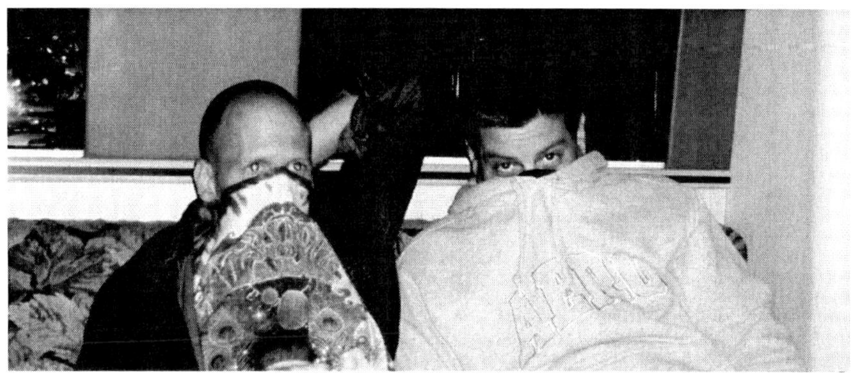

Photo courtesy Brian Beihl

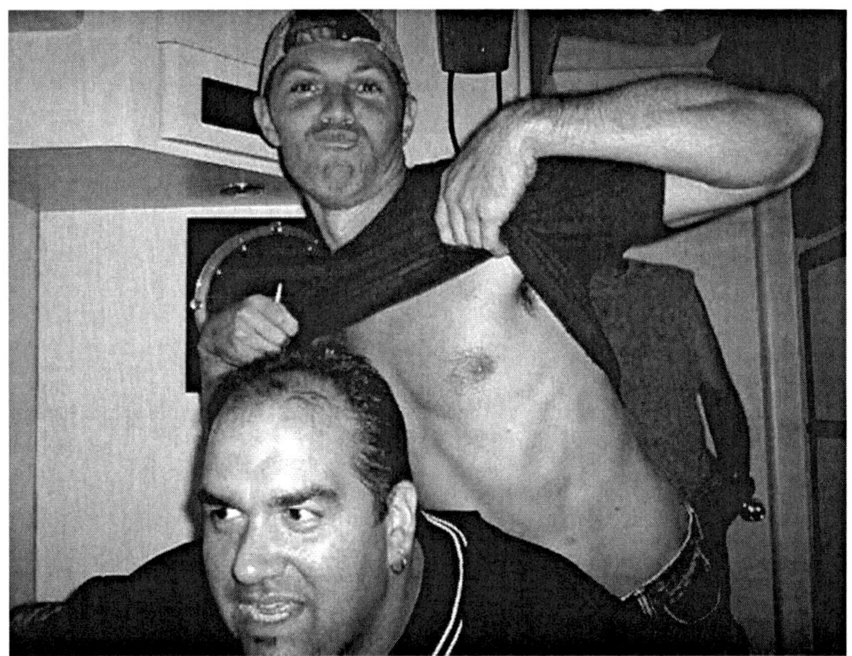

Randy Smith & David Kersh clowning around on the HTTP bus. *Photo by Brian Beihl*

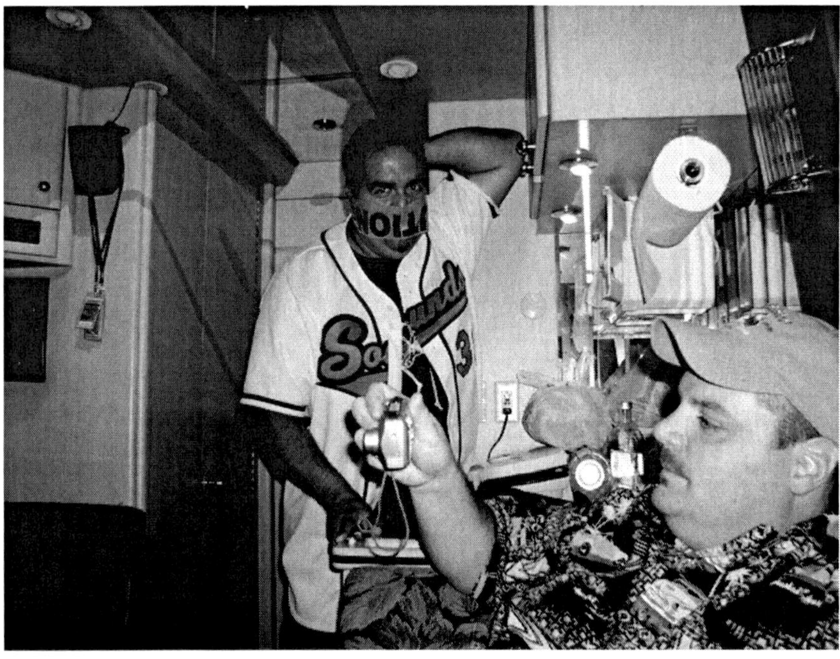

Does something smell kinda foul on here?

Bus Etiquette

"Etiquette requires us to admire the human race." — Mark Twain

From being on many different tours with many different groups of bus riders, I have come up with a set of "bus etiquette suggestions" that is designed to improve the overall bus experience for all.

While working on the Toby Keith tour in 2003, I rode on a bus with the video crew and backup singers. When I first began riding on that bus, the video crew chief held a brief meeting with all of the riders. He rattled off a short list of guidelines that were designed to give all of the bus riders the most amount of space and the best night of sleep possible. The most important thing he emphasized other than the "pee only" rule, was to always treat the bunk aisle as if someone were sleeping, even if you knew nobody was sleeping. His reasoning was that this approach would guarantee good habits by all in the bunk aisle. I believe his words were, *"It's a bedroom, think of it that way. A bedroom is for sleeping."* He said this once at the beginning of the tour and everyone magically followed his lead. I slept better on that bus than any bus before or since. Of course there was no artist on that bus.

That experience inspired me to create a list of what I call "Bus Etiquette Suggestions." Many of the suggestions on my list came from his list, and I have added a few more of my own in the years since. These are simply suggestions based on my perspective on this matter; however I believe if you follow them, at the absolute least, you will never piss anybody off on a tour bus.

"Bus Foul"

Bus Etiquette Suggestions

1. No poop or paper in the toilet, pee only. This is a mandatory rule!
2. Always treat the bunk aisle as if someone is asleep.
3. No smoking, except out the front window while the bus is moving.
4. Don't slam doors; you might wake somebody (or piss off the boss).
5. Always lock the bus when it is unoccupied.
6. Don't crank the stereo or TV too loud when people are sleeping.
7. Don't sleep in the lounge as that is what your bunk is for (this is called "bus foul").
8. Keep the lounge clean by throwing away your empty food and drink containers.
9. Use the junk bunks and closets to store luggage.
10. Be courteous and considerate to your driver.
11. Be aware of your driver's condition; is he tired, or hungry, or in need of a coffee?
12. Don't talk on your cell phone in your bunk or in the bunk aisle.
13. When you go to sleep, switch your cell phone to vibrate.
14. Don't be a "flipper" with the TV remote.
15. Ask permission (from the artist or road manager) before inviting guests onto the bus.
16. Don't leave the TV on the porn channel when you are done watching it.
17. Turn your bunk light off when you are not using it.

18. Keep the bunk aisle doors closed at all times.

19. Don't talk in the bunk aisle.

20. Don't take up too much SPACE.

21. Don't sprawl out and hog the whole couch.

22. The front lounge is for hanging; the back lounge is for banging.

23. Don't ever give the bus door code to anyone who is not a member of the tour.

24. If the driver stops for fuel during the night and you leave the bus, leave something on the driver's seat (or else you might get left in Fargo).

25. Don't give the bus stock to the "gherms"; it's for the band.

26. Don't be surprised when the artist doesn't follow any of these suggestions.

Every touring entity is comprised of a unique group of individuals. Not everyone will see eye to eye regarding basic common courtesy. Do your best, and forget the rest. When all else fails, learn to adapt.

Rhett Akins band and crew 2009: left to right - Clint Jacobs, Penn Robertson, Eric Normand, Rhett Akins, Kelly Normand, Cliff Thompson, Scott Tweten

This Is Our Home, Damn It!

"Home is where the heart is." - Gaius Plinius Secundas

The bus you are traveling in might be a home away from home for everybody on the tour, but to the rest of the world it is a party waiting to be crashed. Most fans, and even many event staff personnel have never seen the inside of a tour bus, and this fact can create a sense of curiosity and mystique. For shows at most major festivals, amphitheaters, and sports arenas, busses are usually parked in a secure and inaccessible location to the masses, and this helps to put the bus and its tour members out of reach for most. However, when a tour is playing a small town fair or a nightclub, the bus may be parked in a spot that will allow easy access for the curious fan, gherm, or stalker.

When a concert at a nightclub ends, many people in the crowd will figure out that the bus is parked right out back and will quickly find it. To them, the bus is simply an extension of the nightclub party. Some tours have a stiff policy about allowing "guests" on their bus, while others can be more lenient and open. If your tour is on the more lenient and open end of this spectrum, you will find that many people will walk right up to a tour bus, open the door without knocking, and walk right in. Quite often they might leave the door wide open, and this usually creates a steady stream of bus invaders. Once on the bus, if they are not ejected by a grumpy tour manager, they will usually proceed to eat and drink you out of house and home while taking up all of the available seating space meant for the band members. They might annoy the artist, insult a band member, spill drinks, put paper in the toilet, vomit, or commit just about any other offensive act you can imagine, and this can be very frustrating for some tour members.

Some tour members are not fazed at all by a bus full of partiers, and may enjoy a good K-tel dance party in the front lounge after the show. However, some prefer a quiet and tranquil after show hang and might prefer the bus to be free of riff-raff. If the artist doesn't want any guests on the bus, there won't be any guests on the bus. But if he or she doesn't mind, or you're on a band or crew bus with no artist, it is up to the tour manager to attempt to control the leakage. If the tour manager is off doing other duties, it is up to the crew or band members to watch the door. Locking the bus door as you come and go can also help to control unwanted traffic.

Most fans, gherms, and even some friends and family members will fail to see the bus as your home. They're just there for the party, and they don't care who bought the beer. If you're on a tour that frequently allows the bus to be overrun, do your best to ignore the riff-raff and keep your bunk curtain closed. Perhaps use the back lounge for your hang out and keep the door closed, or find a spot somewhere outside the bus to hang until the party subsides. If you enjoy watching your house get trashed, none of this will bother you. If you don't enjoy it, learn to adapt, as this is often out of your control. You *will* eventually leave the parking lot fiasco.

Watch Each Others Back

"Move calmly and move cautiously; you'll never regret it." — Joel Weinstock

While on tour, you and your group will be spending many hours and days traveling by bus, van, and airplane. Your tour and your travels will put you in some strange and sometimes dangerous places; like airports in the middle of nowhere, hotels in the wrong part of town, truck stops, and dark seedy nightclubs. Some of the people you come in contact with in your travels might be less than sincere, and this will not always be obvious. These reasons are why it is a good idea to watch each other's back.

» If you are traveling by air, try to keep an eye out for your other bandmates while going through airports. In the post-9/11 world of airport chaos, it's easy to get hung up at security, lose luggage, or miss your connecting flight. Try to stay with your group and help make sure no one gets left behind.

» If you are traveling by bus and stop at a truck stop, make sure everyone is back on the bus when it leaves. It is not uncommon for someone to get left behind and for the bus to need go back for them.

» If your bus is full of guests after the show, try to keep your bunk curtain shut and the bunk aisle door closed. Most people won't go into your bunk, but it only takes one unbeknownst thief for someone to lose a wallet or an iPod.

» Watch your gear during load-in and load-out. Depending on the level of the tour, you may or may not get quality stagehands. A bad stagehand can equate into your gear being dropped or broken.

» Beware of jealous spouses. I've seen women (and men) throw themselves at an artist with their significant other in sight. This can cause a dangerous situation if the signifigant other becomes angry and retaliates. You might not see this coming.

Most of this is common sense, but it can take a few harrowing experiences for some tour members to see the big picture. Be ahead of the curve.

Gherms

"I call it fan fatigue. I went to see Bob Dylan last year, who I think is absolutely incredible, but he suffers from his audience." — Roger Daltrey

Gherm, pronounced "gir" as in girl, followed by "m," is a term used by music industry professionals to describe overly obsessive and often out-of-control fans. A gherm can be anybody including fans, event staff, band and crew members, friends and family, even some artists. No one is immune. Before I moved to Nashville I had never heard this term before. But very quickly into my touring years I understood the term, its meaning, and made the realization that at different points of my musical career I had already been ghermed and had even done some gherming myself. There are no physical attributes specific to the gherm; it is their behavior that will ultimately set them apart.

How To Identify Or Spot A Gherm

» If a fan manages to make it through the autograph line two or three times, they are probably a gherm.

» If the runner tells the artist that they have been a huge fan since the age of five, have all their albums, and have been waiting their whole life to meet them, they are probably a gherm.

» If an event promoter is overly ecstatic upon meeting the artist and needs to hang with the artist at length although uninvited, they are probably a gherm. In this case they are actually a gherm/promoter combo, known as a "ghermoter".

» If a band or crew member inserts their head up the artists' ass on a regular basis, they are probably a gherm.

» If a fan or group of fans has figured out what hotel you're staying at, has booked their rooms there as well, and are waiting there in their vehicle in the rain before your arrival, they are definitely gherms.

How To Tell If You Are A Gherm Or Have Gherm-like Tendencies

» If you are constantly trying to be the center of attention while in the presence of the artist, you might be a gherm.

» If you are always looking to the artist for approval, you might be a gherm.

» If you are constantly going out of your way to pamper the artist, you might be a gherm.

» If you have to verbally agree with every word that comes out of the artists' mouth, you might be a gherm.

» If you ask to have your picture taken with the artist more than once, you're probably a gherm.

» If you act like you have a deep spiritual connection with the artist even though you just met them, you're probably a gherm.

A touring national act can and will attract people from all walks of life. Everybody wants to meet and hang out with the artist and band. Sometimes this curiosity and interest is accompanied by a sense of entitlement. Because they bought your album, or saw the artist's music video, they feel like they know you on a personal level. This false perception of friendship will cause some people to do some strange things. Many people will stretch the truth or lie to get to meet and hang out with the artist. Complete strangers will claim to be old friends, distant relatives, or high school buddies. Fans will lurk in the shadows and approach band and crew members with amazing stories of their deep connection and alleged relationship with the artist. They will act like they are interested in you and even show a great deal of sincerity if they think this will give them a chance to meet the artist. While most gherms are ultimately harmless and never consciously harbor any bad intentions, their inherent nature can be somewhat self-serving and manipulative. If you are working on a tour, try your best not to be a gherm.

Fly Dates

"Flying is hours and hours of boredom sprinkled with a few seconds of sheer terror." — Pappy Boyington

Sometimes the distance to be traveled for a show is too great or impractical for a bus or van, leaving air travel as the only viable option. While some entertainers seem unaffected by flying to shows, most that I know detest air travel. If air travel was ever perceived as being fun, that all changed after 9-11. For those of you that fly on any regular basis you know what I'm talking about.

If you are a musician flying to a show, there will most likely be backline provided. Backline usually encompasses a complete drum kit, bass amp, guitar amps, and keyboards. This means you will be flying your guitars. While some musicians don't mind checking their guitars in a hard-shell case, many are uncomfortable with the thought of putting their expensive delicate instruments in the hands of baggage handlers, who are notoriously rough on luggage. I use a padded gig bag with shoulder straps which allows me to walk through airports hands free and carry it on to the plane. With this approach, the guitar never leaves my sight, and I don't have to worry about it getting damaged or lost.

Here is an overview of a typical one-off fly date I recently went on.

4:00 am: Wake up, eat breakfast, and prepare to leave

4:30 am: Leave for Nashville airport

5:00 am: Arrive at airport, check bags, receive boarding pass, proceed through security

5:30 am: Board plane

6:00 am: Depart for Chicago

7:15 am: Arrive in Chicago; change planes

8:30 am: Depart for Omaha

10:00 am: Arrive in Omaha, proceed to baggage carousel

10:30 am: Locate our day transportation; ride an hour and a half in a van to hotel

12:00 pm: Check in to hotel rooms; eat a quick lunch (mini-mart gack)

1:00 pm: Ride to the concert site (20 min)

1:30 pm: Set up and sound check (1:30 to 3:00)

3:00 pm: Ride to hotel for showers and get ready for the show

4:00 pm: Ride back to the concert site

5:00 pm: 45 minute performance (on this date we are playing first, opening for Terri Clark and Randy Travis). We play our set on an outdoor stage to a receptive crowd.

6:00 pm: The performance part of our work day finished, we hang out for a couple of hours watching the other acts, and then ride back to the hotel to get some sleep.

11:00 pm: Sleep

Day Two

5:00 am: Wake up call, shower, and breakfast

6:00 am: Depart for airport

7:30 am: Arrive at the airport

8:30 am: Depart for Chicago

10:00 am: Arrive in Chicago; change planes

11:00 am: Depart for Nashville

1:00 pm: Arrive in Nashville

1:30 pm: Retrieve luggage; drive home

Thirty-three hours of planes, vans, hotels, and airports were needed to play a 45 minute show. In reality, you are playing music for the love of it and getting paid to travel and be away from home.

The long hours and activities of a fly date are exhausting, and there are some things you can do that will make the experience easier and less taxing.

Here are a few tips:

» Hydrate. The number one cause of jet lag is dehydration. Drink plenty of water on the days prior to and following a fly date. Avoid soda, coffee, or too much alcohol consumption on the days you are flying as they will dehydrate you.

» Use "Earplanes." These are specially designed earplugs made for air travel. Changes in cabin pressure can cause sinus problems and headaches for some passengers and these ear plugs can help alleviate these problems. They also reduce noise while in flight, which is the second biggest contributor to air travel fatigue.

» Chewing gum during flights can help your ears avoid "popping."

» Brings some snacks. Most flights no longer provide food, and airport food is expensive and typically unhealthy. Take a homemade sandwich, or maybe some nuts, raisins, and other foods that are calorie dense and able to last unrefrigerated for several hours. This will not only save you money, but will also allow you to arrive at your destination without being completely drained.

» Take a nasal decongestant before and after your flight to help your sinuses combat the dry and stuffy air on the plane. This can also help some of the ear and sinus congestion that causes your ears to pop.

» Bring something to read. Flights can be boring. Some people are able to sleep during flights but some can't, and if you can't, reading is a great way to pass the time. I can't think of how many times I have read a good magazine cover to cover on a long flight.

» Move around and stretch. If your flight is anything longer than an hour, you may start to get stiff and uncomfortable. Take a walk to the bathroom, even if you don't have to go. There is usually a little space near the bathroom where you can stand and stretch out for a minute. This will help your circulation as well as prevent blood from pooling in your legs.

» Wear loose clothing. Planes can be cramped, hot, and stuffy, so loose-fitting clothes can allow for a more comfortable flight.

» Pick an exit row seat. Not always, but quite often, an exit row seat has more leg room than any other seat on a plane.

» Check in on-line. Most airlines allow on-line check-ins 24 hours in advance. This can minimize time spent standing in lines and possibly give you a better choice of seating. With some airlines, you can also print out your boarding pass and pay any luggage fees in advance, saving you more time on the day of your flight.

» Stay together. It's easy to get lost in big airports. Do your best to stay with your group, and you'll be less likely to get lost or miss your flight.

» Use the buddy system and watch each other's backs. Airports are a great place to get robbed or lose personal belongings. Keep an eye on your band mates and have them do the same for you.

» Travel light; the less you bring, the less you have to worry about losing.

Road Gack

"You can find your way across this country using burger joints the way a navigator uses stars." — Charles Kuralt

The way in which sustenance can be obtained on the road can vary greatly, and a lot of this depends on the level of the tour and the specific requirements of the tours rider. High-profile tours can have a long list of hospitality items and very specific meal requirements that are usually catered. Some high-end tours even have their own catering company that travels with the tour and supplies daily meals for the duration of the tour. Other tours on the middle to lower end of the spectrum will have a more limited list of hospitality items and a greater variance in the quality of its daily catering.

There will also be many instances in which you'll either need to eat in restaurants, purchase takeout from fast food chains, or eat real food that you brought from home or purchased at a supermarket on the road, such as travel days, layover days, or at events that don't provide bus stock or catering (the latter of which is somewhat common on mid to low level tours).

Pulling in to a truck stop, a very common sight for the road warrior

It is common practice for a national act to require the event buyer to provide the tour with a list of food and beverages that will be delivered to the busses and/or dressing rooms early in the day. This list of food and beverage items is commonly referred to as bus stock or dressing rooms supplies. Here is an example of a bus stock list that was on the rider of one of the tours I worked on. This list was for one bus that had 7 people on it.

» 3 – 10 lb. bags of ice

» 2 case spring water

» 1 case diet Coke

» 1 12-pack Coke

» 2 cases Bud Light

» 1 case Bud Light Lime

» 1 bottle Crown Royal

» 1 Bag Levi Garrett Chewing Tobacco

» 1 lb. sliced Turkey (Boar's Head or Prima Della)

» ½ lb. sliced low-fat Cheese (any kind except American)

» 1 loaf 100% Whole Wheat Bread

» 1 jar mayonnaise (fat free or light)

» 1 Vegetable Tray

» Fruit assortment – Bananas, Strawberries, Red Seedless Grapes

» Hoody's Peanuts

» 1 jar Smucker's All-Natural Peanut Butter

» 1 bag Corn Chips

» 1 jar Salsa

» 2 9V Batteries

» 1 roll Paper Towels

This list of items would usually be delivered to our bus upon our arrival and would serve as our lunch and snacks for the day (the alcoholic beverages were typically for after the show). This list was a compilation of the individual requests of the band and crew for that tour. Some venues would provide this list verbatim, while others might cut some corners or even blow it off completely on occasion.

This bus stock or dressing room hospitality list is usually separate from dinner, which is usually a hot catered meal (specified in the artist's rider) served somewhere at the venue. Sometimes the dinner might be a meal at a local or on-site restaurant, paid for by the event buyer. In some situations where it is not practical for the buyer to provide a meal, a buyout is offered instead, usually somewhere between $15 and $25 per tour member. In a buyout situation you are on your own and can go to a restaurant of your choice.

If you don't like the food options on your tour, you can bring some of your own food. Most busses have a kitchenette consisting of a refrigerator, microwave, toaster, and coffee maker. There is also cabinet space for dry storage and typically plenty of paper plates and cutlery.

I personally do not care for most of the food available to me on the road and therefore bring most of my meals from home. If I am going on a 3 to 4 day run, as is typical on a country tour, I will cook some meals that yield a lot of leftovers on the days preceding the run. I will also bring some bread, sliced turkey, cheese, cereal, granola bars, etc. and this will allow me to eat what I want, when I want, *and* keep my buyout money when it is offered. Many tour members will do a combination of bringing some of their own food and utilizing some of the food provided by the tour.

Some folks might think you're anti-social if you don't eat at catering or restaurants with the entourage. I personally don't care what anyone thinks of my eating habits. I know how I prepared my food, and I feel good when I eat it. This is not always the case when experimenting with a home-cooked mystery casserole or some "BBQ" served at a county fair in the middle of nowhere.

The diet of many members of the modern day touring community consists of a nonstop barrage of fast food sludge and truck stop gack, as this has become somewhat typical of the modern American diet. It's no secret that this food is unhealthy, but all too often this is the only kind of food available on the road. Unless you are on one of the higher profile tours, your choices will be limited if you don't bring some of your own food.

Touring is hard on your body, so eat well and hydrate often if you want to feel good and survive the rigors of the road.

Kenny Chesney fiddler, Nick Hoffman and his band opening for Rhett Akins in Bowling Green, KY , 2010

Local Bands And Opening Acts

"We were a band who made it very, very big. That's all." — John Lennon

Opening Acts

If you're working on a high-profile tour playing arenas and festivals, more than likely, the opener will be another national act. They will probably have their own bus, their own dressing rooms, and share the headliner's catering. Their work day is short, as they are the last to sound check and the first to play. Their set, (typically 30 to 45 minutes in length) often takes place during a part of the night when the audience is still coming in and the venue is only half full. This short performance played to a half-full house is still great exposure for the opener, as this situation puts them in front of a much larger audience than they would otherwise attain.

On many major tours it is common for the opener to be on the bill for the duration of the tour, or at least a solid portion of it. In these situations, a coworker mentality usually exists between the two or more different touring entities (some major tours have two or more openers). It is kind of like a traveling circus or rodeo, with everyone working together to put on a successful show night after night. It is also common for members of one group to become friends with, and establish long-lasting relationships with the members of the other group. Not always, but in most situations there is an overall sense of camaraderie, not competition.

Local Bands

If you're working on a middle to lower level tour, there is a good chance that you will play some shows where the opener is a local band. The purpose of a local opener at one of these concerts is to warm up the audience for the headliner, help re-enforce the shows attendance, and in some cases, to increase the overall length of the event to allow for more liquor sales.

Some local bands are quite good, and some are not. While some can add a good boost to attendance, many only bring their girlfriends. Many local bands, regardless of their talent or draw, feel and act as if they were the headliner, expecting and demanding the same kind of provisions and complaining when they don't get them. This is not always the case as some local openers are respectful and appreciative. It is noteworthy to mention that most musicians that play for national acts were once in a local band themselves.

Local bands don't always get fair treatment from the headliner or event staff. Some tour managers and sound engineers see the opener as a pain in the ass, potentially screwing up FOH and monitor mixes, playing too loud or too long, and being overly ghermish to the headliner. There are two sides to every coin, and when these problems occur, it is not always their fault. A good stage manager or house sound engineer should be able to protect the headliner's mixes and control the length and volume of the opener's set. A good tour manager should be able to control the backstage leakage, etc.

Many musicians in local bands aspire to be on the level of the national act they are opening for. Most of them won't ever make it to that level, but some will, and the rest will die trying. If you are in a local band and have the chance to open for national act, be sure to give them the space they need and the respect they deserve. If you are on a tour and have a local band opening for you, don't forget where you once came from.

Opener soundchecking in front of the cloaked Toby Keith set at the Germain Arena, Estero, FL - 2006

Older Touring Musicians

"Men do not quit playing because they grow old; they grow old because they quit playing." — Oliver Wendell Holmes

Touring is typically a young person's game, and there are many reasons for this. Historically, record companies signed artists and bands that were in their late teens, 20s, and sometimes early 30s, as a youthful look was desired to help market the band's image to the young people who bought most of the records. If a musician begins his touring career in his 20s, there is a good chance that if he's still touring 20 or 30 years later, that he's had his fill. Life on the road can be hard on the body and mind. Sleeping while in motion, living out of a suitcase, eating on the go, and missing out on your family life at home are just a few of the things that can get old.

There are some musicians who spend most of their adult life on the road and never get tired of it. Just ask Willie Nelson and his band, who have spent most of their time on the road since the early seventies. While this is an option for some, more often than not, by the time a musician is into his 50s, he is either losing his desire to be on the road, or he has become less in demand by the industry as he no longer has a youthful image. The lack of a youthful image problem can begin for some musicians as early as their 30s or 40s. This is an unfortunate shortcoming of the music industry and society, and while it is unfair, it is a reality.

This reality often leaves many musicians unprepared for the day their touring career ends. Many people start touring in their 20s and spend their next 20 or 30 years working and living on the road. By the time they are tired of the road, or the road is tired of them, they are well into the middle of their life. It can be very hard to start or find a new career at this point for a musician if they have not been developing one along the way.

If you are a young musician on a tour, show some respect for the older members of the tour. Many of the veteran players have a lot of great qualities that they acquired over their lifetime and career. They've been at their craft for a long time and often have good advice and insight to offer younger players. And don't forget, all young players eventually become older players.

From my experiences, most of the great musicians in the world are at least into their 30s if not older. In his best selling book "This Is Your Brain on Music", author and neuroscientist, Daniel Levitin explains how many scientific studies have shown that it takes approximately 10,000 hours of practice to reach an expert level on any given instrument.That's about an hour a day for 30 years. It's just hard to cram that much practice in by the time you're 25. A player who is well into the middle of his life is often more mature, more stable, and can have a deeper sense of time and harmony because of all the years of practice and performance that he has put in.

If you are an older touring musician and wish to tour as long as possible, do your best to maintain the most desirable youthful qualities you possess. Two things that you can have some control over would be your attitude and your appearance. Nobody likes being around an ornery old grump, so try to have a positive outlook and avoid being overly cynical. Work at staying physically fit, the better shape you are in the younger you will look and feel. In my book, age is an attitude not a number anyway.

Wall paintings - downtown Nashville

Impact On Relationships

"I met my wife by breaking two of my rules: never date a girl seriously that you meet at a nightclub and never date a fan." — Corey Feldman

The lifestyles of touring musicians are unique and complex. They are often living two completely different lives - their life on the road, and their life at home. While on tour, they are probably spending most of their time living on a bus with their band mates, and this environment is very much like an extended family. On a tour you are constantly in motion, always around people, keeping late hours and probably having limited communication with your family and friends at home.

No matter how hard you try to explain to your family and friends that touring isn't all fun and games, they will usually perceive your life as the life of a rock star. After all, you are getting to perform in front of thousands of people, see the country and the world, meet people from all walks of life (including some celebrities), and be somewhat the center of attention on a regular basis. While this is all true, there are just as many downsides to the road, such as lack of privacy, lack of sleep, and the toll that touring takes on your body and relationships, to name a few. Of course if you try to explain this to somebody that's never been on a tour, none of this will register.

If you have a close relationship with your wife, husband, children, and friends, you'll miss them while you're gone. They will miss you. A couple of cell phone calls a day can help, but there is no replacement for lost time and you *will* be gone for long periods of time. If you are on a busy tour, you will be absent from a big part of their lives and vice versa. You might miss watching your kids grow up, your 10 year wedding anniversary, your child's first words, and holidays with your family. They might miss their dad at little league practice, your absence from family outings, and have an overall sense that you are missing from much of their lives, as you will be.

If you have a good relationship with your significant other, the touring lifestyle will test that relationship. The stronger that relationship is, the easier it will be to endure the long periods away from home. It will still be difficult. If your relationship is shaky to begin with, the strain of long-term touring can and will cause turmoil within it. While you are gone seeing the world, and doing interesting things, your family is living a routine life at home. Your counterpart is spending a long lonely night in bed alone. This situation can breed jealousy, animosity, and a sense of detachment.

Of course there are some odd relationships that only work when two people are apart. A good friend of mine, who has been a touring musician for most of his career, needs to be on the road for his relationship to work. When he is home in between tours, he and his wife are at each other's throats. The minute he hops on the bus everything is fine. As long as he remains a touring musician his relationship works. I'm not sure what will happen if he ever decides to stop touring.

If you are considering becoming a touring musician as a career, consider these factors. If you are on a busy tour that does 100 dates a year, you will be gone for roughly 150 days a year taking travel days into consideration. That's about half the time, or 3 to 4 days a week. Can the relationships in your life handle that kind of absence? Can your significant other deal with sleeping alone? Can your kids deal with having a part-time parent? If you are a young person with minimal family ties, most of this won't be a factor. If you are an important part of a close knit family, you might want to carefully consider these factors if you are thinking about becoming a touring musician.

Chapter 2.I

Tour Diaries

"The touring part is really mixed. You love to play and you can't wait to go, but you don't want to leave." — Nuno Bettncourt

If you ever have the experience of working as a touring musician, you probably won't get a big severance package when you're done. What you will get will be some great stories. Funny stories, sad stories, and unbelievable tales of debauchery on the high seas will be part of the fruits of your labor. It's perhaps one of the best parts of touring, as many real-life scenarios can be more outlandish and entertaining than most reality shows.

Over my years of touring, I have had the good fortune to work with several great artists and bands. My touring and travels put me in many strange places and situations that I would otherwise never have experienced. The following stories came from some of those firsthand experiences, and I have done my best to tell them in a way that is respectful to all those involved.

BB Watson, The Southern Rock All-Stars, And Barbeque Sandwiches

"The best thing about this gig is the barbeque; it's the best in the state."
— Anonymous

It was early fall in 2003 and I received a phone call to do a weekend of shows with country music artist BB Watson. I met the band leader downtown and received a CD of material to learn for the show. Our bus left Nashville on a Thursday morning for a weekend tour of three cities in the Deep South; Baton Rouge, Louisiana, would be our first stop. We had a full bus, as it was being shared by two bands, BBs group and the Southern Rock All-Stars. The Southern Rock All-Stars were a tribute to the great southern rock bands of the 70s, and featured members formerly of Lynyrd Skynyrd, 38 Special, and Rick Derringer's band, as well as a couple of guys who thought they were in those bands.

The bus was a 79 eagle with a manual transmission, and a real gem. Anyone that has had the experience of traveling on one of these realizes that this is by no means a luxury liner. The bus driver was in his late 60s, although he looked like he was in his early 90s, and probably weighed all of 73 pounds. He was a sweet old guy, but unfortunately lacked the strength required to fully depress the clutch pedal. This meant that we would be hearing *and feeling* every shift, or grind rather, for the entire weekend. Needless to say the ride was a little rough. To make things even more interesting, we quickly discovered that the air conditioning did not work at all on this bus, and by the time we reached Louisiana, we were all soaked with sweat.

Somewhere close to our destination, we pulled up to a busy intersection at which point the bus died. The driver tried to start the bus several times with no results. Finally, he utilized a method of engaging the bus generator to begin slowly powering the bus through the intersection. With no power steering, the turning of the steering wheel was near impossible, and three of us gathered around the driver, pushing and pulling on the wheel to make a nine point turn to get through the intersection. This nine point turn completely blocked the intersection in every direction for about 15 minutes. During this slow-motion turn, those not involved in the wheel turning ceremony crouched down low or sat on the floor of the bus to avoid being seen out the window by random motorists shouting insults and making various gestures.

After we finally made it through the intersection, we found a local garage and waited while the bus was repaired. Tired, hungry, and caked with dried-on perspiration from a long hot drive, we arrived at our gig an hour before downbeat and hurried to set up for the show. This first night of our poorly promoted three night weekend brought the biggest numbers with a crowd of about 75 turning out for our southern rock extravaganza in an old, rundown casino showroom right out of yesteryear. The place even had upholstered walls, circa 1950.

Two days, five fast food meals, and a couple of hundred-degree sleepless nights on the bus later, and we found ourselves in Lubbock, Texas, for our third and final fiasco. This venue, by far the most interesting we would encounter out of the three we experienced that weekend, was an old rodeo barn with a dirt floor smelling of dried cow dung in which, the promoter bragged, 18,000 people could fit, as they previously had done for Garth Brooks 10 years earlier. We set up on a small stage at one end of the arena facing an empty cavern that could have housed the Hindenburg.

After our sound checks we retreated into a small back room for our "barbecue dinner." The promoter had bragged earlier in the day that a local restaurant would be providing some world famous BBQ, something seldom experienced on a southern tour. Upon entering the "dining room" some confusion set in as we all viewed a small box containing 10 McDonald's hamburger sized barbecue sandwiches wrapped in wax paper. *"One sandwich each, boys"* the promoter gleefully exclaimed as he chowed down his puny sandwich. *"Sorry, but they forgot to send the fries."*

What was probably the most bizarre visual of the weekend came later that night when our bands each performed their roaring 90 minute sets to a crowd of about 20, all of whom were gathered around the sound board about 200 feet from the stage in a room bigger than most airplane hangars. Although I could not see them, I'm sure if I could have, the looks on the audience members faces would have been nothing but sheer amazement. If they could have seen our faces, I'm sure they would have seen looks of pure agony, as the sound was horrendous and the air was thick, smelly, and stifling. Finally, after the two band performances that seemed to last an eternity, we were done, and could hear an argument in the back room between the promoter and the event buyer as we were loading out our equipment.

The words *"Sorry everybody, but the venue lost their ass, and were going to have to wait to get paid"* reverberated and hung in the thick Texas air for what seemed like the longest load-out of all time. Needless to say, this is not something that any of us wanted to hear as we clamored back onto our smelly, hot bus for the long ride home. Morally defeated, we pulled back into Nashville late Sunday afternoon, each weighing about 10 pounds lighter from sweating bullets while riding around in a 100° sardine can all weekend.

In the end, we never did get paid, but we did get the barbecue as promised.

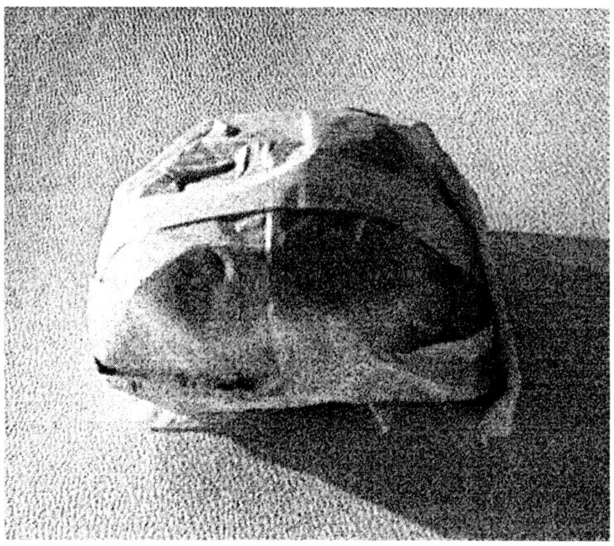

Toby Keith in Concert, 2003 *Photo courtesy Brittany Allyn*

Sammy Hagar In San Diego

"I've been drinking tequila for a long time now, and it's never been about drinking to get drunk. I don't do that. I never drink tequila during the day, and I don't drive at night." — Sammy Hagar

It was a hot summer night in August of 2003 at the Coors Amphitheater in San Diego, California and show-time was just a couple of hours away for Toby Keith and his band. It was just after dinner when Sean, the production manager, called me on my two-way radio and requested my presence at the production office. He informed me, as I was the guitar tech on this tour that it would be my responsibility on this night to set up an additional guitar rig for a surprise guest. Unbeknownst to the 20,000 or so anxiously awaiting fans, this surprise guest would be none other than the Red Rocker himself, Sammy Hagar.

Of course this was exciting news to me, as I had grown up listening to all of the guitar rock from the era of which Sammy was born. Years before I had thoroughly worn out a cassette tape of Van Halen's 5150, one of Hagar's shining moments with the group, along with some other recordings of his earlier work, and now I would be guitar teching for him. It was almost like I was working for Van Halen! With a sense of real purpose, I was off to guitar world where I set up a Gibson Les Paul and dialed it in for Sammy to use during his sit-in.

The concert began a couple of hours later, and the crew and I were busy with our regular tasks. I was watching the band from side stage by monitor world when Mr. Hagar suddenly appeared, seemingly from out of nowhere. A couple of minutes later our production manager formally introduced us and explained to Sammy that I would be setting him up with a guitar to play. We walked a few feet over to guitar world, and I showed him the Les Paul I had chosen for him to use. He tried it out for a minute and exclaimed *"This is a beauty! It'll work just fine."*

We returned to monitor world and watched Toby and band stomping through some more of their set. Sammy was all eyes and ears, watching the show intently. At one point he turned to me and commented, *"Country music is great. The lyrics are so direct. I love the stories."* Although I was trying my best not to gherm him, I couldn't resist this apparent invitation for conversation. I told him that I had listened to a lot of his music over the years, and even owned some vinyl records of one of his earliest bands, Montrose. His eyes seemed to light up with that comment. *"That was a great band!" he commented. "Out of everything I've ever done in music, my time with Montrose was my favorite musical experience."* I agreed that it was a magical band, and we both started naming our favorite songs from their early albums. I was very impressed and pleased to see that such a megastar could be so personable and down to earth.

A short while later it was just about time for Sammy to sit-in, and I handed him the Les Paul. Toby called him out onto the stage, and the surprised audience roared with approval. After a few brief words, the band launched into a spirited version of Led Zeppelin's "Rock 'n Roll". This was followed by a loose, but fun improvised slow blues in which Sammy took a couple of big guitar solos for which he received a more than warm reception. When the second song was over, Toby thanked Sammy, and the excited fans showed their appreciation while Sammy walked off. He handed me the Les Paul and thanked me for the help.

The moment subsided, and I got back to work. It was an exciting night, and I could hardly wait for it to end so I could call my wife and share with her what turned out to be one of the most memorable nights of the tour.

Toby Keith's Shock 'N Y'All Super Bowl Party Rehearsal

"I'm really just a country boy." — Steven Tyler

The week of January 20th, 2004, would be an interesting couple of days for all that worked on the Toby Keith Tour. We were in Houston, Texas, for a performance at Super Bowl XXXVIII as well as the filming of a CMT Crossroads Concert Special featuring Toby, Steven Tyler, Joe Perry, Willie Nelson, Sammy Hagar, Darryl McDaniels (Run DMC), and Chad Smith (Red Hot Chili Peppers). This live-to-tape performance would consist of Toby's band backing Toby for a couple of songs, backing the other guest artists for a couple of songs each, followed by a big jam at the end. What would prove to be the most interesting day of the week was the rehearsal that took place in a small studio the day before the taping.

We loaded the band gear into a small hall just outside of Houston, and set up for the rehearsal. The main rehearsal room was only about 20' x 20', which seemed rather small for the bigger than life superstars that we would be working with that day. The small size of the facility actually provided an intimate setting in which to meet and rehearse with these artists who were such huge influences on so many of us.

It was just after lunch, the gear was all up and we're getting close to downbeat, when in walked Steven Tyler, Joe Perry, and their entourage. Steven was very outgoing and full of life, much as he is on stage and during interviews. He greeted most of us with a handshake and a boisterous *"How ya doin!"* Joe Perry was a bit more reserved but was also very personable. While waiting for the rehearsal to begin, a couple of us guitar geeks were able to chat a little with Joe. Compared to Steven, Joe seemed almost soft spoken and shy, but gladly engaged us in some guitar talk. We picked his brain a little about some of his favorite guitars, and I'm sure we seemed a little giddy, like kids in a candy store. It was almost surreal, standing there talking to one of the greats of modern rock guitar as just another guy in a band. It was only two years ago that I was covering his guitar parts in my band back home, and now there I was talking to him face to face, and being treated like an equal.

The Toby /Aerosmith part of the rehearsal then began. Toby's band was backing Steve and Joe on two new Aerosmith tunes, and Steve led this portion of the rehearsal, stopping the band to fix mistakes and drill parts. It was an interesting glimpse into the mind of one of Rock and Rolls greatest frontmen/bandleaders, and his ability to hear the big picture of a band's performance was evident. At one point, he requested some steel guitar fills on one of the verses, and once that was achieved he looked at Josh the steel player and loudly proclaimed "*Schwing!*" We all broke out into laughter, and he further commented, *"That's one of the things I love about Nashville musicians. Ask them to play, and they will deliver."*

After a couple of hours, Steve and Joe left, and we broke for dinner at which point Sammy Hagar arrived. I had previously met Sammy a couple of months back in San Diego, California, when he came to one of our shows, and he seemed glad to see us. The overall mood of this day was high in spirits, and we continued rehearsing until fairly late into the night.

Photo courtesy Brittany Allyn

Toby Keith's Shock' N' Y'All Super Bowl Party

"Don't compromise even if it hurts to be yourself." — Toby Keith

Saturday, January 31, 2004, was a mild winter day in Houston, Texas, but a special day for Toby Keith, his band, and crew. On this eve of Super Bowl XXXVIII, a live telecast bearing the title "Toby Keith's Shock ' N' Y'all Super Bowl Party" would unite Toby and band with special guests Willie Nelson, Steven Tyler, Joe Perry, Sammy Hagar, Daryle Daniels of Run DMC, Chad Smith of The Red Hot Chili Peppers, and jazz bassist Wayman Tisdale for an action-packed historic performance. The show was part of a CMT Crossroads special and would require a long day of sound checks and dress rehearsals to prepare for the nerve-racking experience of performing on live TV.

"The Super Bowl always marks a time when friends can get together, enjoy the best game of football, talk about which television commercial they think is the funniest and be entertained by some of the best artists music has to offer," exclaimed Toby just 24 hours before the Carolina Panthers and the New England Patriots would take the field. *"It's an honor to be asked to be a part of the event this year and I can't wait to get on stage with my friends from country, rock and pop music for all our fans."*

This exciting day began with an early-morning load-in to a TV studio in downtown Houston. As Toby's band would be the core group of musicians to back the majority of the event's performers, my role as Toby's guitar tech put me in immediate proximity to most of the day's pertinent activities. The studio wasn't particularly large, probably 50 wide by 60 long, but did have a big stage at one end facing a multilevel floor plan in front, and a balcony above, almost creating the feel of a nightclub. The area designated for guitar world was adjacent to stage left, and right next to the stairs on which the performers would enter and exit the stage. There was a catering room side stage, and a suite of dressing rooms on the second floor, but it was in this main room where most of the action would take place.

At some point midmorning, after guitar world was up and all of Toby's backline placed, the guitar techs for Sammy Hagar and Joe Perry arrived with gear in tow. *"Hi, I'm Dugie. Pleased to meet you,"* stated a friendly and boisterous man by the name of Kevin Dugan.

Dugie was currently working as Sammy's guitar tech, a job which he was enjoying during the Van Halen hiatus of the early 2000's. He later explained to me that he had been Michael Anthony's bass tech since the band's origin, and that since Van Halen had stopped touring, he had stayed on with Sammy.

I was then introduced to Jim Survis, Joe Perry's tech, who had a couple of Marshall amps, and some of Joe's vintage guitars in tow. I had spent most of my career up until this point relating to musicians, but working as a guitar tech for the past six months gave me an instant connection with my fellow guitar tech comrades. After talking to Jim for a little bit, I realized my responsibility of 22 guitars and basses for the Toby operation wasn't so bad after all, as Jim was responsible for having 30 of Joe's guitars performance ready on a nightly basis. Jim was a total gentleman and allowed me to play a few licks on one of Joe's early 70s Gibson's through a couple of Marshall's at full blast. I guess that was the closest I had ever come to playing guitar for Aerosmith.

The day slowly progressed, and by mid-afternoon the sound check-dress rehearsals were in full swing. After Toby and his band ran through a few tunes, Steven Tyler and Joe Perry arrived to rehearse their portion of the show. Everything was going smoothly on this tightly scheduled day when suddenly in walks an unexpected Ted Nugent. With the words *"I hear you guys are having a big jam here tonight,"* it became quickly obvious that the list of special guest performers would have to be modified. After all, who's going to deny Ted Nugent? Following some discussions between Toby's managers and the slightly panicked TV producers, it was decided that Ted would sit in using Sammy's guitar rig near the end of the show.

After a dinner break and some brief downtime, the doors were open, and the audience began to gradually fill the room. As the show's producers and event staff were affiliated with MTV, it seemed that every other person in the room was either an employee of MTV or one of their guests, and the buffet and seemingly open bar quickly ignited a near out of control party atmosphere in this room now full of would-be superstars. The Super Bowl has always been as much, if not more, about the party than it is about the game itself, but these folks quickly took the concept of "party' to a whole new level in the hours preceding the show. The almost rabid-like over-consumption of alcohol by a few of our MTV "friends" led to a seemingly endless succession of puke fests around the room shortly before downbeat.

With the chaos and excitement factor in overdrive, the shows MC began the preshow broadcast while I was helping the band get situated with their instruments. During the last cut to commercial before show time, the band and Toby took their places as I watched from side stage in guitar world. The show began with a brief introduction by the host, and as he read down the list of special guest performers, Willie Nelson walks out onto the stage, apparently ready to play a little bit ahead of schedule. Although his designated appearance spot wasn't until about three songs in, he was apparently itching to do some jamming and proceeded to play along with Toby and band on the first few songs.

After Toby and Willie's duet of "Beer for My Horses", Tyler and Perry joined forces with Toby's "Easy Money Band" to rock the house for a couple of songs which would prove to be one of the evening's high points. Every commercial break was followed by a different array of special guest performances, and the crowd reaction and participation remained over the top in this beer soaked rock n' country adventure. The show roared on for the 1000 plus in attendance and 7.5 million television viewers with Toby and Sammy's duet "I Love This Bar". The hour-long program flew by with lightning speed, and as quickly as it started it seemed the final song was upon us.

"A Little Less Talk, and A Lot More Action" was set to be the final tune of this extravaganza in which all of the guest performers would take turns singing verses over the brilliant lead guitar playing of Ted Nugent. With some bussed in cheerleaders and dancing girls now also added to the mix, the stage was an ocean of activity, with Toby in the center of this building wave of frenzy. The producer's original plan was that the band would do a little extended jamming at the end of this tune while they ran the final credits. Strangely, the show was running ahead of schedule, which required a need to extend the extended jamming, allowing guests to bask in the sunlight of some unplanned and long-winded soloing. For me, the funniest part of the night was watching the look on Toby's face, which seemed to reek of "Get me out of here!", as he rocked out with his acoustic while towering over this ocean of musicians, entertainers, and dancing girls during this no-end in sight televised blues jam. — Final Score: New England 32, Carolina 29

Photo courtesy Brittany Alyn

Rhett Akins' Bus Fire

"THE BUS IS ON FIRE......THE BUS IS ON FIRE!" — Eric Normand

The night air of August 5th, 2006, was warm and muggy when Rhett Akins and band headed out on a leased late model Prevost tour bus bound for an outdoor show in Statesboro, Georgia. Sometime in the early morning hours, while we were all sleep, the power steering stopped working making it difficult for our driver, David, to turn the steering wheel at slow speeds. Despite this difficulty, he continued on, and we arrived in Statesboro mid-morning at which point he made several calls to find a garage. Being Saturday, most garages were closed, and it took a while to find one that was open and willing to work on a bus. Around 11:00 AM we got lucky, or so we thought, and found a garage that was willing to take it on.

The mechanic, an older fellow weighing in at about 85 pounds, worked on the bus while we all waited in the front lounge; now an oven because the engine and generator were no longer running. We watched in amazement as this tiny little fellow walked back and forth touting wrenches and tools that were almost as big as he was. He didn't seem to be making any headway and when a beer was spotted in his hand a little while later our concern began to grow. By 1:30 it was becoming obvious that he wasn't going to be finished in time for us to make our soundcheck, so I called the promoter who sent a truck and trailer for us, our equipment, and most of our luggage. After riding for a while on a seemingly endless maze of back roads we pulled into the Silver Creek Saloon, set up our gear on a plywood stage facing a field behind the club, and began soundchecking in the hot Georgia sun, the temperature now well over 100°F.

Around 5:00 I received a call from David saying he was on his way to the venue and would be there shortly. The mechanic had not been able to repair the power steering and had "capped off a line" that had been leaking. We continued on with our sweaty soundcheck until a few minutes later when I noticed I had missed two calls from him. I immediately called him back, and he excitedly answered with, *"Eric, the bus is on fire!"* "What?" I said dumbfounded. He answered again with, *"The bus is on fire! I must be close to you guys because I heard loud music a minute ago!"*

With that, I turned to everyone on stage and said, "Hey, I've got our driver on the phone and he said the bus is on fire and that he's close by!" Everyone just seemed to stare at me for a long moment as if I had three heads. "THE BUS IS ON FIRE…THE BUS IS ON FIRE! It's somewhere close by!" I shouted, my voice now reaching a heightened state of frenzy. Someone then pointed across the field and said, *"Look there's smoke!"* We all looked and saw thick, black smoke billowing up through the trees about a quarter mile away causing us all to run out to the street in front of the club.

At first glance you could barely even see the bus as there was so much smoke, but then our eyes adjusted and the eerie scene came into focus. Our bus sat about 500 feet down the

road in the middle of a wall of black smoke with flames coming out of the back, leaping 20 feet in the air. I asked a woman standing nearby to call 911. The fire intensified as we stood mouths agape in the hot sun, culminating with a loud explosion that only added to our horror. After what seemed to be an eternity, the fire department arrived and began extinguishing the fire.

After the fire had been out for about 20 minutes, our drummer, Cliff Thompson, and I were allowed to walk down to the bus, now a smoldering charred mess that smelled badly of toxic smoke and burned plastic. I found David making out a report with a police officer and spoke with him briefly. He was shaken, upset, and said that he had never been so scared in his whole life but that he was okay.

"I was driving down the road and looked in the rear view mirror and saw smoke and flames coming out of the back of the bus," he said. *"A few seconds later I heard an explosion in the back and knew that if I stopped where I was that the fire would ignite some mobile homes that were near the road."* He took a gamble and kept driving for a few hundred feet until he was past the mobile homes at which point he tried to shut the engine. Apparently, the engine wouldn't respond to the ignition switch and, no longer able to see the road because of the smoke, he had to jump from the bus while it was still moving, the bus rolling to a stop a few seconds later.

After hearing this heroic tale, Cliff and I were escorted onto the bus by a fireman and observed the ruins for a brief moment. We stood in the decimated front lounge in which we had all sat just a few hours before and stared in disbelief while the fireman walked down the bunk aisle to look for any salvageable belongings. The only thing he found was a small vinyl bag soaked and smelling of burnt plastic in one of the bunks. Fortunately, we had already taken most of our luggage and belongings off the bus when we had left the garage.

We gradually got back to our day, or living nightmare rather, which was now quite difficult as we were all upset, distracted, and bus-less. Obviously our ride home to Nashville was now an issue and had to be dealt with. A call to the bus company prompted them to send

another bus from Nashville, but it wouldn't be able to arrive until 6:00 AM the next morning.

We went to the hotel, ate, showered, and returned to the venue to perform, rocking the 1,000 plus crowd for an hour and a half. After the performance we tore down, loaded our gear into two pickup trucks, and went to a hotel in town where we made trip after trip through the lobby - carrying guitars, drums, and luggage, and wheeling road cases past a confused looking receptionist. We stashed the gear in a room and began to wait for our ride home. Physically and mentally drained, we sat around and talked about all that had happened that day and how lucky we all were to be alive. If a few things had been slightly different, the outcome could have been much more disastrous.

From where the bus caught fire to where it would have been parked for the rest of the day at the club was less than a half mile. If the fire had started just five minutes later, the bus would have been parked directly next to a plywood stage with PA and lighting equipment, our stage gear, and all of us in close proximity. This stage, which was about 20 feet from the club, was sitting in a field of dry, almost hay-like grass on this day where the temperature reached 108°F. Scattered across the field were several campers, vehicles, tents and people milling around. If the fire had started with the bus parked there, I am sure it would have quickly spread to the stage and club (also filled with people) and more than likely across the field. It takes but only a little imagination to envision how this horrific scenario might have played out.

Another possibility that came to mind was one in which the bus had made it to the venue without catching fire, had a chance to sit and cool, and not caught on fire until we were driving down the interstate on the way home. With all of us likely asleep in our bunks by that point it would have been unlikely that any of us would have survived. Boy did we get lucky!

Around 6 AM our replacement bus arrived, and we slowly trudged all the gear back through the lobby. A few minutes later, while rolling down the highway, we learned that this new bus had no AC. If you've ever been on a bus in the summertime with no AC you know the significance of this. With every window on the bus open, we all collapsed in our bunks attempting to get some sleep on this slow cooker. Sweating bullets the whole way home, we reached Nashville stripped down to our underwear feeling like a pack of wet rats. Needless to say, this would be the last time we would use this unnamed $300 a-day bus company!

Epilogue: This story should serve as a great teaching moment regarding tour bus leasing and bus safety.

Many people have died in bus fires over the years. And while most buses leased by reputable companies have smoke detectors and fire extinguishers, some do not. Smoke detectors and fire extinguishers could make the difference between life and death, so make sure your bus has these essential items and make it a point to know where they are (your driver should know their location).

You get what you pay for. During the summer in which this bus fire happened we had several other bad experiences with "$300 a day" bus companies. Typically, if the day rate seems low on a leased tour bus, it's for a reason.

Lastly, the bus drivers are arguably the most important members of a tour, as is the pilot of an airplane. The safety of all the passengers is dependent on the driver's ability, awareness, and judgment. Treat your drivers with consideration; talk to them while they're driving late at night. Ask them how they're doing and if they need anything before you go to sleep. If you get up in the middle of the night to go to the bathroom, don't be afraid to briefly check in, a friendly voice after hours of solitude can go a long way. Once you arrive to your destination make sure your driver gets a clean and quiet hotel room as soon as possible. Make sure your drivers' get whatever they need to do the job at hand, and always give bus drivers the respect they deserve.

Jamey Johnson, 2006

Rhett Akins & Jamey Johnson - Second Night Out

"When you go to write a song, you owe it to your listener to give them complete honesty, to tell them the full story in a way they can hear it, understand it and apply it to their life. If you can't do that, it's like peeing in your pants: You might get a warm feeling, but nobody else really cares to know." — Jamey Johnson

Friday, March 24, 2006, was a clear and brisk spring day in Cincinnati, Ohio, when the Rhett Akins and Jamey Johnson tour bus pulled into a strip mall parking lot that would be our home for the day. We parked on the backside of the mall and began loading in, rolling our road cases up a long concrete walkway that led into a large cavern of an empty honky-tonk style nightclub. The show we would be playing this night marked the second on what would be a two-month tour, hitting 30 major US cities by crisscrossing the country in "dartboard" style touring fashion, typical for many country tours.

The set up and sound check were uneventful other than the near impossible challenge of fitting our oversized backline of drums, SVT bass rig, and four guitar rigs onto a 16 x 12 stage. This two artist package tour combined Rhett and Jamey's bands, Jamey would be bringing his full five-piece band, while Rhett would bring Cliff Thompson on drums and me on guitar to be joined by three of Jamey's musicians for our nightly concerts. After a long afternoon of sound checks, we broke for dinner and showers.

By the time the show began around 9 PM, the place was hopping with probably 1000+ in attendance. As the tour served to promote both Rhett's and Jamey's recent releases on BNA Nashville, expectations were high, and members of both artists' management and record label reps were on hand. Jamey and his band would be the first to take the stage on this particular night, and they romped through their hour-long set of southern-fried, honky-tonk rockin' country. The terrible acoustics of this industrial building made it difficult to get the vocals above the groups' wall of Marshall half stacks, and their three guitar sound was more reminiscent of southern rock than country, rendering this cold northern audience lukewarm by the last song.

Even with the familiarity of Rhett's radio hits over the years, our set wasn't received with much more enthusiasm as neither the sound nor the crowd seemed to be on our side this night. We steamrolled through our 12 song set, fighting tooth and nail for whatever response we could get, and upon the set's conclusion were joined by Jamey for the "noncore." I call it a noncore, because I'm not sure the audience really wanted to hear us anymore by this point.

The band began what would be the most eventful part of the concert with a Hank Jr. cover in which Jamey stampeded onto the stage clenching a shot of Jaegermeister in each fist. After swilling down the shots of black gold back to back he proceeded to smash both glasses on the stage floor. He then grabbed the mic with one hand and, with the other hand, proceeded to tightly wrap the mic cable around his arm several times as if he were rolling up an extension cable. This essentially bonded him to the microphone in some sort of pseudo power stance from which he shared his sentiments with the crowd in the form of a deafening "*Yeeee-haaaah!*" At this point, time literally stood still. Apparently, the non-reaction from the crowd was not what he anticipated, and this prompted what would eventually become the most memorable one-liner from the tour - "*Did ya'all come here to rock, or are ya'all just a bunch of cross-stitchin' motherfuckers?*" If the look on the faces of the crowd could be described as confusion and subdued fear, then the look on the faces of the management in attendance was none other than sheer terror. After performing three or four more songs in this newly heightened state of awareness, the show concluded, and we began tearing down and loading out, anxiously looking forward to seeing this fiasco of a night draw to a close.

A couple of hours later, after the load-out was finished, Cliff and I retreated to the back lounge of the bus to enjoy some after show cheer and escape the mayhem of the party that was now roaring in the front lounge. After a half hour or so of chill time, we heard some yelling from the front lounge which was followed by the appearance of a now ornery Jamey Johnson lurking in the back lounge door way.

"You work for an asshole." He shouted from behind a cold stare that could have cut glass.

"What do you mean? What's the matter?" asked Cliff.

"What's the matter? Your boss is an asshole. He's causing trouble with my band!" Jamey shouted in a voice that was clearly agitated.

"We've been working for him for a long time and have never known him to cause any trouble. I'm sure it must be some kind of a misunderstanding," Cliff further defended.

"Look, I was a Marine for seven years, and that's all you need to know about me!" barked Jamey with a tone of voice that would have frightened the Terminator, and with that, he turned and stalked off.

Dumbfounded, Cliff and I stared at each other in amazement for a moment before collecting our wits to go upfront and see what was going on. We arrived to a near empty front lounge only to hear the yelling now coming from the parking lot just outside the bus. Apparently Rhett had got into an argument with the tour's merch person, Reg', also known as "rear-entry Gentry", when Reg' went on a tirade after being apparently caught off guard by a sarcastic joke directed at him. As this package tour consisted of Rhett, Cliff, and I joining eight members of Jamey's organization, on a bus leased by Jamey, we were technically on their turf. And with this being only our second day together, the two different groups were still relative strangers, so diplomacy was of utmost importance, as there were still 28 shows to go.

With Rhett ready to wail on Reg' and Jamey ready to pounce on Rhett, Cliff bravely got in the middle and helped to defuse an otherwise ticking time bomb that was ready to go off and derail our tour. It took a while, but things finally did cool down, and everybody got back on the bus. After a few brief apologies and a couple of friendly slaps on the back, our entourage seemed to return to a steady idle, although it was still a high idle. For a brief moment, it seemed like that second night of the tour was destined to be the last, but somehow the moment passed. A little more Jack Daniels and Bud Light and we were on our way, laughing down the highway. Edinboro, Pennsylvania, here we come!

Epilogue: Despite this rocky start, an overall sense of kinship developed between our two camps in the following weeks. Other than this one over-the-top incident, Jamey treated Rhett, Cliff, and myself with nothing but respect from that point forward.

The Eight Foot Naked Cowboy

"Life is tough, but it's tougher when you're stupid." — John Wayne

It was a hot July day in Briggs, Texas, with the temperature soaring to a record breaking 102°. The Rhett Akins tour bus pulled down a gravel dirt road adjacent to a large, deserted junkyard before landing next to a stage facing a large field. This would be home for the day. After our load-in and soundcheck, we were shuttled by limo to the hotel for showers and dinner. As we arrived back to the concert site around 7:00 PM, we were greeted at the bus by some locals who seemed to know Rhett. He invited them on to the bus to hang out for a bit before our show.

The three Texans, consisting of one heavyset girl and two lanky cowpokes, drank a fair amount of beer over the next couple of hours, and engaged Rhett in their stories of life on the range. One of the guys was well over seven feet tall, and his head lightly skimmed the bus ceiling when he stood. They were wearing the standard modern day cowboy uniforms - skin-tight Wrangler jeans up to the armpits, red and white plaid wrangler shirts (think Urban Cowboy), cowboy boots, and ten gallon hats. They were also loud and boisterous, getting louder with each beer they consumed.

We played our ninety minute set to a crowd of local concert goers with our three newly found cowboy friends cheering and yelling from their spot front and center. After the show, they were practically on the bus before we were, picking up where they had left off. At some point, Rhett mentioned that he wanted to take a shower before the long trip back to Nashville, and the cowboy crew offered the use of their shower at their ranch, just a couple of miles down the road. Before too long they added a drunken late night bush hog hunt to the offer, apparently a local ritual, and it was a done deal. Rhett, a skilled hunter himself, accepted their intriguing offer, and they promptly drove off into the night.

About an hour and a half later, Rhett appeared back on the bus. With his hair still wet he excitedly proclaimed, *"We went skinny dipping in a cow trough!"* - apparently another local ritual that occasionally replaced conventional bathing. A minute later the girl ran on to the bus wearing only her camouflage pants. Bare-breasted, she ran up and down the bus aisle with boobs and cellulite a'floppin'!

It was at this point that the eight foot naked cowboy burst through the doorway of the front lounge wearing cowboy boots, tighty-whities, and his ten gallon hat. With his BVD's covering his mid section, he wasn't completely naked, but the sight was comical enough, and we started to cut up. There was one scary moment when his half naked girl bent over in front of him in which we thought we were going to see something ugly, but the moment quickly passed as they barely gained control of themselves.

After a few more moments, things wound down, and it was time to go. The cowboy crew said goodbye, and we thought we had seen the last of them. Five minutes later, round two began as we approached the front gate. We came to a stop as the local police had stopped the vehicle in front of us. It was, of course, the drunken, eight foot cowboy who was now performing an embarrassing DUI test wearing only his boots and briefs. The moment was almost surreal, like some bizarre episode of "Real Stories of the Highway Patrol." We all crowded around the front windows of the bus to watch an angry sheriff putting this local hero through the paces. The eight foot lone streaker didn't fare well with the drunk test and we thought for sure that ole' Bart was a goner. The police wouldn't let them leave, as they were drunk, so we volunteered to drive them and their truck home.

A few minutes later, we delivered them and their truck to the entrance of their ranch, said farewell, and rode off into the night. This was the last we ever saw of the eight foot naked cowboy and his gang.

Rockin' On The Mountain

"Thousands of tired, nerve-shaken, over-civilized people are beginning to find out that going to the mountain is going home; that wildness is necessity; that mountain parks and reservations are useful not only as fountains of timber and irrigating rivers, but as fountains of life." — John Muir

It was just after 1 PM on Saturday, May 29, 2010, as we pulled into the Fast Lane minimart in Huntsville, Tennessee. The parking lot of this fine establishment would be our home base for the day as this was the closest our tour bus could safely get to the mountaintop concert site. The event we were playing on this hot and humid Memorial Day weekend was "The White Knuckle Event" at Brimstone Recreation, an annual ATV convention on which thousands converged from all over the country, some even traveling from as far as Canada.

Shortly after our arrival, the event coordinator arrived with a fleet of four-wheel drive pickup trucks, our gear hauling and runner service for the day. Some local fellows helped load the gear into the back of the trucks, and we hopped in to make the five mile, thirty minute ride to the top of the mountain. The first couple of miles of this trek were quite scenic, winding through a maze of fields and rolling hills spotted with picturesque homes and cabins. After about ten minutes of driving, the pavement ended, and we proceeded up some steeper inclines as the road turned to dirt and gravel. We were now going up the mountain, and the old logging road on which we were traveling was a flurry of activity, a steady stream of four wheelers and other off-road vehicles coming and going in every direction. The air was thick with dirt and dust kicked up from all the ATV's as we passed a couple of campsites along the way.

A little while later (it seemed like an hour) we reached the summit, and a spectacular panoramic view of the mountain range came into focus. We backed up the pickups to the stage and commenced our load-in and sound check. The stunning view off the back of the stage was that of several other peaks, jettisoning up across the horizon under some billowing clouds that seemed to stretch on for as far as the eye could see. The contrasting view off the front of the stage was that of a sea of four wheelers dotting the hilltop amidst several vendor tents, all viewed through a thick haze of freshly kicked up mountain dust.

By four o'clock we finished sound check and strapped in for the bouncy ride back to the bus. Chilling on the bus for a little bit, we dug into the event provided meal of country ham, green beans, steamed corn, and hot rolls. As this was the only store around for miles, the parking lot was a flurry of activity, providing varying degrees of amusement which could be viewed candidly through our tinted bus windows. At one point a truck pulled up towing a trailer upon which a four wheeler containing several young family members sat. A little while later, one bright fellow took off on a dirt bike with his toddler sitting on the handlebars. It was a regular ATV Woodstock, and after dinner and some showers we hopped back into the pickups for another bouncy ride up to the peak as it was getting near show time.

Now nearing dusk, we were in amazement upon reaching the concert site when the view of 10,000 concertgoers sitting on thousands of ATVs came into sight. We hit the stage running, and the powerful PA system filled the night air with the sounds of Rhett Akins music. We began the show with our appropriate onslaught of "Down South" and "I Brake for Brunettes" and the crowd was instantly on our side. After a few more tunes Rhett introduced me as the bands only Yankee and encouraged me to play some "southern-style" slide guitar. This led to our rendition of "Curtis Lowe" which was followed a little while later by some hunting songs from his new CD like "My Baby Looks Good in Camouflage," "Duck Blind," and "Hung Up."

We finished the show to a massive ovation which brought us back for a brief encore. Just before we began our short second round I was informed that one of the patrons wanted to propose to his fiancée on stage. A minute later, an excited young fellow stood on stage in front of the masses and told his girl he loved her and wanted to marry her. Teary-eyed, the girl made her way to the stage to meet her love, at which point he gave her a ring. Everybody got all mushy at this point as we played Rhett's hit "She Said Yes". Our mountain top adventure now complete, we tore down and loaded up our gear, road back down the mountain, and hit the road.

Chapter 3

Interviews

During the process of writing this book I was fortunate to have several Nashville music industry veterans agree to be interviewed. The music industry is a massively complex group of separate, but overlapping industries, and as I do not consider myself an expert in all these different arenas, I sought the help of others to provide a broader perspective. While I did my best to ask questions that reveal what it's like to work in each person's specific field of experience and knowledge, I also allowed the interviews to be somewhat autobiographical. After all, everybody has their own story to tell, and what better way to learn than from the journeys of people that have been there and back.

Conducting interviews is something I had never done prior to this project, and the experience was another great learning process, both challenging and rewarding. I am grateful to have had the help and support of these gifted and knowledgeable industry veterans; I think you'll find their stories are unique and full of depth and insight. While much of this book stems from my own experiences, these stories go directly to the heart of what it's like to work as a professional in the modern-day music industry. This next section contains some of my proudest moments of this project. I hope you enjoy our conversations.

Photo courtesy Clint Jacobs

Scott Tweten

Originally from Hesper/Decorah Iowa, Scott Tweten moved to Nashville in 2000 and has been earning his living as a freelance guitarist in Music City ever since. Growing up and working on a family farm gave Scott the work ethic he would need to succeed in the competitive scene of Nashville. To make a living as a guitar player, he supplements his touring work as guitarist for Rhett Akins with year round in-town nightclub work and some regional touring with club and casino bands.

{Eric Normand} You grew up in a small community in Iowa. What sort of musical situations, professional or otherwise, were you involved in there as a young adult?

{Scott Tweten} We didn't really have a lot of things. It was a small town and concerts were a rarity. I do remember going to see a Dave and Sugar concert, and Emmylou Harris. Her band went to a Perkins restaurant and Ricky Skaggs was her fiddle player at the time. My brother and I both got his autograph on napkins and then lost them. I just remember music as a part of the family since I could remember and an occasional jam session somewhere.

{EN} What made you decide to move to Nashville?

{ST} My uncle suggested it after a gig somewhere once. I laughed at the idea. As time went on and I became better, I started getting bored at concerts thinking or knowing that I could do (for the most part) what the guitar player on the stage was doing, then suddenly Nashville started becoming a reality.

{EN} When you first arrived in Nashville, how did you approach inserting yourself into the music scene?

{ST} I would go downtown and frequent the clubs and just listen, to mentally take in what was being played so that if I were to get a gig down there I would know what to expect.

{EN} How did your first paying gig come about?

{ST} That was actually kind of a network through one of the guys that played down town. He hooked me up with a guy that was looking for a guitar player. I went out to a jam session, got up and played a couple of songs, and he thought, he knows what he's doing even though he was nervous. He referred me to the guy that was looking for a guitar player, we hit things off, and that was it.

{EN} How did you financially survive your first several months in Nashville before you started gigging? Did you work another job? Use savings?

{ST} I had some money saved up when I first got to town, then borrowed some from my mother and grandmother and also took some from savings. Since then, a good prayer has blessed me with plenty of work and not having to borrow or take from savings for the last 3 years just showing that God does provide!

Gettin' down with Rhett Akins and band in France, 2007

{EN} How did your first road gig with a national act come about?

{ST} Guitar player buddy of mine was leaving a group and asked me if I was interested in the gig. I said yes, hence - The buddy system!

{EN} Who was the gig with?

{ST} Cowboy Crush.

{EN} Over your 10 years so far in Nashville, you've earned a living from a combination of touring and in-town nightclub work, with a lot of that nightclub work being in clubs on Broadway. How important is the Broadway scene in terms of your ability to make a year-round income from music?

{ST} A lot of players on and off the road frequent Broadway. It really helps for networking with both work for downtown and the road (per say an artist gig) simply because the musicians on Broadway are both workers of downtown and the road.

{EN} Have you seen many players land road gig from working on Broadway?

{ST} Certainly - hence the buddy system and also word of mouth. It's a great place to network if you don't get caught up in the party scene of it, well, to a degree anyways.... *laughs*

{EN} Can you tell me about any specific situations?

{ST} Sean Bailey is a fiddle player who sings harmony. Good singer, Awesome fiddle player. He came into town from I believe, Arlington Texas, and he was in town for six months. Gigging on Broadway led to a gig with Mark Chestnut, and the Mark Chestnut gig led to a gig with Big and Rich.

{EN} Didn't a steel player from downtown wind up with the Kid Rock gig?

{ST} That was Rusty Rhodes, but he had been down there forever, and of course he lost the gig not very long afterward... *(laughs)*. That was one of those attitude type of things that you don't want to end up with because it will get you canned as quick as it will get you hired.

{EN} Describe a typical busy night at one of the Broadway clubs. What kind of material is being played? What is a typical audience like? How long are the sets/breaks? What is typical pay?

{ST} Hmm, well, you'll hear everything from Merle Haggard to Lynryd Skynryd, Poison to Faron Young and Ozzy Osbourne. If you want to hear a certain song, you probably can and will. Breaks are almost non-existent anymore; sets are 3 1/2 to 4 hrs. Usually, you can get a bathroom break, and some can keep the music going, just depends on the crowd and what's going on. Weekends during the evenings, it is usually wall to wall people, so be ready for a music marathon, any and everything you know, minimal bathroom breaks. Clubs usually pay a small base pay of $30 to $50 dollars per person, depending on which shift you are playing, the rest is tips in a tip jar split equally by all members of the band.

{EN} What is it like to play a double (two shifts back to back), and how do your pace yourself to avoid injury?

{ST} Not bad depending on whether it's a split double (2:00 to 6:00 and 10:00 to close, versus back to back doubles). If you can, you should sit for some of these gigs. It may seem easy to play music for a living, but our bodies are human too. Don't overdo it standing up for too long if you don't have to.

{EN} Tell me about the most rewarding musical experiences you have had since being in Nashville.

{ST} Hmmm, I have lots of stories to tell. I guess the best so far is that I've played the Opry, been to Greenland, Switzerland and France, and met some of my musical favorites, sports stars and movie stars as well. You never know who or what is going to happen next!

{EN} As you know, there are rarely any benefits or long-term pension/ retirement plans provided for career musicians. Do you picture yourself still earning a living from music in 20 years or do you have other careers in mind as a fallback plan?

{ST} Myself, I try to save up as much as I can for a slow time, as a lot of what we do is seasonal, which means money is decent during the summer months and less during the winter months. Fortunately, I have been blessed with some retirement plans already. It's up to me now to keep trying to put more money away when I can.

{EN} For players new to town that are trying to break into the scene, what kind of advice would you have to offer?

{ST} Don't come to Nashville thinking it will be a piece of cake, or as a cocky person with an attitude, or looking at it as a competition, you won't last long. Mix, mingle, and try to feel out what is your thing. Don't try to force or fit in where you don't. Be yourself and let it happen, if it's meant to be, it will!

Danny Milliner

By the time Danny Milliner moved to Nashville TN in 1986 he had already been working as a professional bass player and vocalist for the better part of two decades. Growing up in a large, musically active family in rural Louisiana gave him the background and support he would need to pursue a career in music. By the age of 15, as a sophomore in high school, he was already playing for a living, working 2 to 3 nights a week throughout the South in various R&B bands on what was known as "The Crawfish Circuit".

Photo courtesy Danny Milliner

Danny continued to play professionally from the mid-60s through the 70s, performing and recording with a variety of bands and musicians that included Bobby Kimball of Toto fame, slide guitar legend Sonny Landreth, Dony Wynn from Robert Palmer's band, and Jon Smith and other musicians from Johnny and Edgar Winters' bands, among others. In 1981 he became a staff musician on a weekly radio program called "The Louisiana Hayride" where he worked for three years before moving to Nashville.

Danny's work ethic combined with his networking skills would eventually land him a permanent job as a bandleader and bass player for Brooks & Dunn, for whom he was employed with for almost the entirety of the duets career. Recently retired from touring, he is still musically active and continues to perform regularly around Nashville.

{Eric Normand} Tell me a little bit about your upbringing and background.

{Danny Milliner} I grew up in a large family in rural Louisiana. Both my parents were musical; my mom was a piano player and played gospel in church. My dad was an excellent fiddle player, a good singer, and was born and raised in Litchfield Kentucky, where Bill Monroe and all those bluegrass guys were from. He had a band with his brothers who all played. One played banjo, one played mandolin, and one played guitar. When he got drafted he was sent to Louisiana where he met my mom. Of course we all sang in church choirs at a very early age. In the third grade I was singled out by my music teacher. I guess I was just loud, we lived in the woods; I mean everything is loud, and when I sang out, I mean I sang out. She said *"Well you know we're going to have the real music teacher from the parish schools come around, and I want you to sing America the Beautiful."* What? *"Yeah, just stand up by your desk and do it."* I ate about three pencils...*{laughs}*... anyway, I sang it acappella and thought that would be the end of it. She came back the next day and wanted to take me around to the other classes, and that was the first time I got the adrenaline rush of the performance thing. That's kind of where I came from and where I got started.

{EN} What was your involvement in music as a young adult before you came to Nashville?

{DM} I started playing for a living when I was 15, and I ended up getting with a bunch of older guys, a horn band called the Capris. They had a record on Dick Clark's American Bandstand, *'Pass It on By'*. I'd been working for United Van lines during the summer, and then stocking grocery store shelves and cutting grass. So from cutting grass and doing that to making a couple of hundred bucks a week in three or four nights playing was huge. I ended up going through high school like that and ended up going to LSU and playing music the whole time.

{EN} How did you first become involved with the Nashville music scene?

{DM} I was singing with a horn band during the week nights when I was just about getting toward the end of my stay at the Hayride and ended up meeting Kix and his wife Barbara, and we just kind of hit it off. He said, *"If you ever decide to get out of Shreveport and come on up to Nashville, make sure you look me up."* And that was in 85. Ended up, he was true to his word. Got there, and he was very helpful, showed me around a lot. So that's how I ended up, just showed up cold.

{EN} So Kix was basically an unknown artist at that point?

{DM} No, actually, he had already had a couple of number one hits as a songwriter. I didn't know this at the time, but he had had hits with John Connolly and the Nitty Gritty dirt band. So he was unknown as an artist, but becoming known, and had a good situation with Tree. At the time, Tree was the largest independently owned publishing company in the world, and they had a bunch of great writers over there. Curly Putnam, Bobby Braddock, Kix, Deborah Allen, Ray Van Hoy, Hank Locklin. That's where he was, and we just started playing. We got some more guys from Louisiana, and he was writing a whole lot more. Then one day Jim Fogelson from Capitol said *"Why don't you do an album?"* So we ended up working on that in 86, 87, and just playing around town. Played Antonio's out in Bellevue, Douglas Corner, you know, the usual proceeds. We'd end up splitting three or four dollars a night, if we were lucky.

Then in 88 we had done the record and all three of the singles that were released were Billboard pick hits. We did a radio tour up to Maine and back and they all treated us like we were the Beatles. They said *"Man we keep wanting to add your record and your record company doesn't want us to do it because they want us to keep playing T. Graham Brown's record."* So Kix realized he was in the old record company shuffle. He went to a song meeting with the record company, and the head of A&R guy said *"I'll tell you what we should release Kix, I'm on to you."* And Kix said *"Well that would be great except that was the first single that we released a year ago"... {laughs}.*

{EN} They weren't paying attention.

{DM} We found out in person what the deal was there. That was in April or March of 89. He told me he was going to get off the label and get back to writing. Then I hung the phone up and I swear to you 10 minutes later the phone rings and it's Nanci Griffith's manager wanting to know if I wanted to gig. I didn't know there was a gig, but yeah I want it. She had kind of a pop record coming out and was doing a whole lot of dates in Europe at the time. Of course Kix and I had been buddies a long time, and I got a call out of the blue one day. *"Man I got this partner Ronnie Dunn and we're going to make a record. I don't know where it's going to go or what's going to happen, but I want you to be involved in it."* So, I spent most of 90 working with them *and* her, and then I finally came to a little crossroads.

{EN} So that was basically the formation of Brooks & Dunn, it kind of just happened?

{DM} Pretty much, it kind of evolved into that. Ronnie was new in town and couldn't get arrested, which was odd because he brought Neon Moon, Boot Scoot Boogie, Used to Be Mine, four or five songs that were later major hits. They ended up, as everyone knows, getting thrown together by Tim Dubois and Scott Hendricks, and writing Brand New Man, and of course it was a huge hit. That's kind of how it evolved.

{EN} Were you involved in the recordings at that point?

{DM} You know, I was supposed to be. I was also going to do Nanci's record, that was the thing. We had done demos, I had sang on it and the whole bit, and this was like in 89 into 90. But then Kix said *"You know I want you to do these demos."* And I said I can't because I'm going to be in Europe. *"Okay, so what about next year?"* I don't really know what's going to happen there, we're doing her record, supposedly in the middle of March. So as luck would have it *"Well that's when we're doing our record."* You're freaking kidding me? This can't be? Of all the months and weeks to be able to do both of these, they're cutting at the same time? So I called Nanci and said, look, am I going to end up doing this record? She said *"Absolutely"*. I mean, nobody knew that Brooks & Dunn was going to last five minutes; we had just gotten off of a sinking ship. Nanci was at least working, and her pay was good. So I called Kix back and they made other arrangements. Then they got Mike Chapman, or whoever played. I came to Nashville and went by Nanci's management office, and they said "*Oh by the way, we're not doing their record because*". I went what? *"She's changing producers, Larry Mullins, the drummer with U2 is going to produce the record."*

{EN} So then you didn't get to do either of them?

{DM} Exactly. She ended up getting Rod Argent, and he wanted to use guys and his band from England, so I didn't do either one of them, which was devastating at the time. I could have done both of them, and didn't do either, after I had done the demos and sang and everything on Nanci's record. When I heard the record, everything I played and sang, they did it just like the demos. Really, really, aggravating.

{EN} How did it evolve that you became band leader for Brooks & Dunn and did you choose the musicians for the touring band?

{DM} Kix called me in the later part of 89 and said *"I want you to be involved, and next time you're in town I want you to come meet me and we'll go have lunch with Ronnie."* They said *"We definitely want you to play, and we know you can sing."* I said I'm not going to road manage, I'm not going to drive the bus, I'm only going to do so much. So they said would you be the bandleader? I said yeah. So we ended up talking about people to play. Ronnie wanted to get a guitar player he knew from Tulsa, Kix wanted to get a couple of guys from around here, a drummer that he knew, and we got a keyboard player and just started small with a four piece group. And as things moved forward and people started getting slung off of the pile for various reasons - alcohol, whatever, you name it, all the issues that come along with people, I did have a little bit more say in who was going to be used and handled all that for them. It was always, here is the deal, here y'all are, I'm telling you what your options are. You've got these guys, we can hear them all play.

{EN} Present them options and let them choose.

{DM} Exactly, based upon who they were, how I knew them, and how they knew me. After the first couple of years, they were a whole lot more reliant on me to help make sure all that was steered along.

{EN} What are some of the other responsibilities you had as bandleader?

Photo courtesy Danny Milliner

{DM} I had control over pretty much all of the traffic. Telling them when we we're leaving, when we're going to be there, where we're going to be. That was also the tour managers deal. My job, more than anything else, was to make sure that you were prepared musically. If it was to learn some new songs, get a song rearranged, do a segway, or whatever. And I took care of the soundchecks. Pretty much the overseer of the whole deal. Like I said, if there was something I needed to talk to them about, I would wait until the appropriate time and sit them down, or get them both on one of their busses and tell them this guy's doing this. I know you don't see it, you just see him on stage, but there is this going on, this going on. How do you want me to handle it? That kind of thing.

{EN} Brooks & Dunn were on a separate bus?

{DM} In the beginning we were all on one bus, which was excruciating. But after it took off, after the first year, they ended up having their own bus.

{EN} Was there a disconnect between the artists and players? Did you see them much?

{DM} Yes, I saw them all the time. But, one of the things that happens, and this is nothing against managers or anything like that, but I've seen this happen several times. If there's a closeness between the band and the artist then the manager wants to get in there so he can deal with the artists, and use these guys as a utility. It's not derogatory to them, it's just how it plays out. Pretty much separated. The decision-making, we had a couple of guys in that band early on that kept thinking this was a band, and they kept saying that. *"I never did get treated like that in the last band I was in."* I said you're not in a band, maybe you need to start rethinking this. You work for these two guys. Now, perception wise, you're on stage with a band, but that's the only place it's a band. You're an independent contractor working for these guys, Brooks and Dunn Inc. So, as far as you having an input as to what we're going to do for the video, or getting to write with them just because you happen to walk by and they were writing a song while you were in the room, you're absolutely on the wrong end of the spectrum. This is not a band, it's a job.

{EN} A lot of people don't understand this.

{DM} A lot of people can't. Two or three of those guys just could not get that. And I was like, what do you not get about it? Did you sign the record deal? No. Your name isn't on the bus lease.

{EN} Being the bandleader on a tour puts you in a unique position in which you're working for the artist in a managerial context while performing as a player in the band and trying to fit into both worlds. How do those two roles conflict, and how do you find a balance?

{DM} I didn't let them conflict because I'm the messenger. These are not my decisions. I'm here to tell you how we're going to do it according to them. The fact that I'm bandleader doesn't give me any more priority than anyone else, other than when they want to tell the band something they call me and we talk about it. I get them two together and make sure they both sign off on it before I go talkin' a bunch of stuff. I make sure that what I'm going to tell the band is right, and exactly what they want. It's not with any authority for me, it's just what we're going to do. So pretty much I kept it separated like that, and I ended up dealing with the soundchecks and that kind of thing

{EN} How did you handle the soundchecks?

{DM} For us, early on, there was a few guys that would get up there and, I called it the random playing demon. If they had taken the time to really learn scales, arpeggios, or whatever, they'd have been really good. Instead they were just doodling, but loud! We ended up finally getting ear monitors, which was huge, and probably saved their musical careers, as well as a lot of other peoples.

When it was first presented to me that we were going to get ears, I said, you mean I don't have to have fiddle or steel in my mix if I don't want to? And the monitor guy said *"Yeah, you don't have to have anything, you've got a stereo mix, and you've got it panned, so you can put it how you want it."* And I swear to you some of these guys said *"I can't hear a thing"*. And I said, what are you listening to? The concept is less is more. You're not going to get everything turned up to 12 and then ask to go to 14. Why don't you try backing everything down. For me, I got kick drum, bass, electric guitar, and keys, panned out and spread out around my head. Well, obviously the loudest thing in my mix is going to be kick drum, bass, and click track.

{EN} So you played to a click live?

{DM} Yeah, we ended up having to go to that because I got sick of hearing people say *"I think that was rushing a little bit". "Really, I thought it was right on."*

{EN} Its tough playing in those sports arenas, they're just not made for good sound.

{DM} We played the first Houston rodeo without ears. Somebody said the time delay is something like 17 seconds. It was so bad that if you started thinking about something else and you heard something you played 10 or 15 seconds ago, you became disoriented. So the ears were a Godsend. But I still had to go through all those personal trials and tribulations of, okay, let's go early and try to get your mix straight and build a mix that you can live with instead of coming off stage every night going *"I can't hear nothing".*

{EN} What was it like on the first few years of the tour, when it was first starting to really take off?

{DM} Well it was one of those deals to where again, I never gave it 15 minutes. 15 years was way on the other side of what I thought might happen. We ended up getting in a bus and learning these songs, and I think our first gig was like the middle of April in 91. We played clubs from here to LA and back. And then all of a sudden they ended up snaring the tour with Reba in 93. We were the opening act of three acts, and first thing I noticed that I hadn't noticed before was that the place was full when we were ready to play. Usually for the first opener it's half-full and they're coming in, even the middle slot they're still coming in. But I noticed the place was almost full every time we came out there with Reba. We did five or six songs. Hey, boom, boom, boom, boom, boom, bye, that was it.

{EN} Well received obviously.

{DM} Yeah, really well received, it was kind of frightening. They ended up winning the ACM award that first year. I think it was 93. We were playing in Omaha Nebraska, somewhere the next day after the award show and I remember Ronnie telling Kix in the dressing room *"Look, don't brag about us getting that award or anything last night because these country people, they'll turn on you if they think you're cocky or anything like that."* And Kix said *"Okay, I won't mention it."* Of course the first thing he does is to walk out and say *"Anybody see us on television last night?"...(laughs).* And of course the place just went bonkers. Of course Ronnie looked at me, and that was the give and take of their little deal. Ronnie thought one way and Kix another. Kix did his own thing and Ronnie said *"Would you quit running around on stage?"* And Kix said *"Quit standing in one place."...(laughs)..."It's a show, its entertainment. You're not in a bar in Tulsa at 3:30 in the freaking morning singing a Merle Haggard song. It's called the entertainment business. And I've done this all my life, I'm not going to stand still like you, stiff as a board, and sing. I'm going to go have some fun."*

Photo courtesy Danny Milliner

So anyway, it was like that, and it kind of exploded pretty quick. We went from doing club gigs to all of a sudden on tour with Reba. Then we opened up for a bunch of other folks. By the time the third record, I think it was Brand New Man, Next Broken Heart, and maybe Neon Moon, and Neon Moon was a bona fide blockbuster. When you get there and you see everybody singing the words, it was like, you know this thing might work if it don't explode from within, which was another tall order. Anyway, it happened pretty quick the first two or three years, things evolved, and things got a little bit better for the band as well.

{EN} You were treated pretty well on the tour after it got established?

{DM} One of the things they did ask me was, what's the main thing about being on the road that you would covet the most? The biggest lubricant other than being on stage is time alone. I'm a grown man with two kids. I don't need to be talking to my wife, my kids, my mother, or anybody else and see some guy walking by in front of me scratching his…, I don't need that. I'm old. I don't mind riding 20 hours on the bus if I know when I get there, bye, go get a hot shower, and go to my room and enjoy my space, I don't mind then. And at the end of that first year, we got all single rooms, which was big. That was a little bit of a respect thing there that I thought was good, because it gives people a little bit of time away from each other. You know you're happy to see each other as opposed to, oh my God, I've been rooming with this guy, he's on the bus, now he's, you know.

{EN} How many dates a year did you play?

{DM} It might have been just under 180 in the first year. But then all of a sudden it came down, because obviously the record sales were going up. It came down to 90 dates, and down to 85, and then down to 75 and it ended up staying at 70 for a long time.

{EN} That's palatabe.

{DM} Yeah, gettin' paid pretty decent, and you still had some time, and you weren't gone all the time. It was pretty quick, things change fast and so do people. I call it false entitlement. When people think they're owed something that no one really owes them, and there's a lot of that. I think it's not a very attractive trait in humans, but it happens all the time.

{EN} What have been some of the more memorable musical experiences you have had since being in Nashville?

{DM} The first session I did was with Curly Putnam and Bobby Braddock, who wrote He Stopped Loving Her Today and other major country hits. I got to work with a lot of those people, Russell Smith, just tons of folks. It was great working with Kix, great hanging with him, because he knew a bunch of people and that was great for me. Getting the job with Nanci was really good because I had never been to Europe and spent most of 89 in Europe, Ireland, Scotland. That was memorable. My mom and dad saying *"Oh you're going to be on the Grand Ole Opry"*. To them that was huge. Even getting to do, as silly as it sounds, Hee-Haw, remember that show? It was in the very last incarnation, the last year or two, and it wasn't anything prestigious. I just thought it was funny that I was on Hee-Haw all of a sudden...*(laughs)*. Being able to meet and work with Brent Rowan who was in Kix's band for 2 1/2 years and certainly didn't need to be there. He would do sessions all day and then show up at SIR at eight or nine o'clock at night and rehearse for two or three hours and go back and do a full day of sessions. Just meeting different people and being able to get involved was huge. I bet everything I had to come up here, stuck my neck out pretty good to move everything I owned up here with no job. A lot of little things added up, let's put it that way, and it allowed me to be free and see my kids and do what I needed to do. It was pretty amazing that it worked out at all.

{EN} Being a touring musician can take its toll. It can be hard on your body, hard on relationships. What advice would you give to players that wish to make a career out of touring in regards to long-term sustainability?

{DM} It's not a good place to bring a drug, alcohol, or emotional problem. If you're going to be on the road, those three items right there can be deal breakers for you. Treat it like it's a job. A lot of guys I know just couldn't distinguish this from being like recess in high school. It's like, what are you doing the other 22 hours of the day that you can't be on time for sound check or bus call? So people that have those issues, it usually exacerbates them on the road because there's a lot of down time. I did a lot of reading. I had my routine to where I would still get up as early as I could, usually around seven or eight, no matter what happened the night before. I'd get up, get off the bus, do my little routine, go work out, and do whatever I needed to do for my own sanity. Because, next thing you know you're just laying in a hotel room running up and down the channels. Can you do something constructive while you're out here? If it's working out, that's good. If it's reading, that's

Photo courtesy Danny Milliner

good. Playing, that's good. What else can you find to put in this amount of time where you can't do anything else really, what can you put in there that's going to be something good as opposed to something destructive?

{EN} So be prepared for the downtime.

{DM} Be prepared for the downtime and utilize it. Understand that, hey, I'm not doing anything else, I can go work out, I can play my guitar, I can write, I can read, I can get on the Internet. A lot of guys get out there and it's like they've been let out of prison. They get on the bus, drink two or three beers, and then start bitching about the free beer, how bad it tastes. I don't understand that. If you don't like the beer, don't drink it.

{EN} Perhaps, if you view it as a job, which is what it really is, and let the partying just happen a little bit, and not let that be the main focus...

{DM} Yeah, that's it. Every single night, I don't get it. At some point in time a little light goes on that goes, okay, you're done, you can go to sleep now. There's no reason to sit here until four or five o'clock in the morning and get so drunk you can't walk and then feel bad all day and then start the whole thing over. That's just stupid. Look at it with some maturity and understanding that it's a job, it's just in a different setting.

Steve Pope

Steve Pope has been a professional tour bus driver since 1989 and has logged hundreds of thousands of miles driving some of the biggest names in rock, pop, and country to concert destinations throughout the US and Canada. Included in this list of touring artists and bands are: Hank Williams Jr., Rascal Flatts, Faith Hill, Rod Stewart, Dave Matthews, Jeff Beck, Creed, The Other Ones, Jimmy Buffett, and many more.

A native of Bowling Green, Kentucky, Steve spent his younger years growing up in the rural countryside near the Tennessee border and eventually moved to Nashville for work. Retired from full-time driving, Steve is now an ASE certified mechanic and works for the Nashville based Prevost bus shop as a team leader/shift supervisor, where he works on, and oversees the repairs and maintenance of the Nashville Prevost fleet. He still enjoys driving part time, going out on weekend runs regularly.

{Eric Normand} How did you get into this line of work initially?

{Steve Pope} I was working at a bus garage in Nashville called Nixon custom coach back in the mid-80s, and we catered to the entertainment bus business, as a bumper-to-bumper service facility. I just got to know a lot of people that owned them and drove them. The first driving gig that I had was for Hank Williams Jr.; I knew his bus driver, and they needed someone to drive his crew bus one weekend. I took it, and one thing led to another.

I wound up working for Hank for about a year, year and a half. That was my first driving gig.

{EN} That's quite an artist to...

{SP} Cut your teeth on? Yeah. I did that for I guess about a year, year and a half maybe, just doing weekend stuff, fill-in stuff for Hank. And then the owner of a bus company back at that time, Curly Jones, owned Stagecoach VIP and he offered me a position driving full-time. I had been kind of planning it for a little while, I was kind of drawn into the life of travel, I got to see a lot of places that I had never had the opportunity to see before. That's how my life on the road got started.

What kind of training did you have to undergo to prepare for your CDL test to be able to drive?

{SP} Well, at that time you didn't have to have a CDL, all you had to have was a chauffer's license. So when the DOT changed its regulations for bus drivers to have CDL's, I was basically grandfathered into a commercial driver's license. Now you have to take a written test, and a driving test, and you have to have a passenger endorsement that's required by the DOT. Mine was by the school of hard knocks.

{EN} So you didn't actually have to take a course, somebody just taught you from the passenger's seat?

{SP} Yeah.

{EN} In the world of commercial driving, many drivers, include some who drive semis, delivery trucks, Greyhound buses, and city buses, aspire to drive entertainment coaches. Why does everyone want to drive an entertainer coach?

{SP} I think they all think it's a glamorous position to be out there on the road with some top name touring act, the draw of the prestige. It's just the simple fact of driving a very nice entertainer bus that's polished up and shiny. It just kind of draws them in.

{EN} What is different about how you approach driving an entertainer coach compared to these other types of commercial driving?

{SP} Well I've never driven a truck, but to drive a bus you just have to be smooth. Even though you're sitting in front, you have to put your head in the back to where the passengers are riding, and every move you make effects what's going on back there. You can't be rough on the breaks, hard on the brakes, rough on the in and out of parking lots. You can't make sudden and drastic moves unless absolutely necessary.

{EN} Many commercial drivers that aspire to drive entertainer coaches think they're qualified simply because they drive a large, heavy vehicle. In what ways are they not prepared?

{SP} Just sitting in the driver's seat and driving a bus isn't all of it. You have to be able to get along with the clients. Sometimes you're a maid, sometimes you're a babysitter, sometimes you're a plumber, an electrician. Driving's the easy part.

{EN} There's a little bit of a bigger picture.

Checking fluids on the XLII's 500 horsepower inline 6

{SP} Yeah. Years ago you'd get into some of these old buses, and you'd drive all night, work on them half the day, try to get three hours of sleep so you could do it all over again.

{EN} I'm sure there's still a few of those old buses out there.

{SP} There's still some of them out there…{laughs}.

{EN} Driving an entertainer coach, for the most part, requires a lot of driving between midnight and noon, as you are on a schedule that is opposite the band or artist. When you first started driving, was it difficult to get used to this grave yard shift?

{SP} Yes it was. Your body has to go through a whole change basically. You've got to get adjusted to sleeping during the day and staying up all night, just like any third shift worker.

{EN} When you were driving full-time, did you maintain this schedule even when you had weeks off, or did you let yourself get turned back around to normal sleeping hours?

{SP} Well that's the hard part. You go home and you try to get adjusted back to a normal schedule if you've got more than a few days at home. Once your home for a month or two, you get back into a normal schedule, being up in the day and sleeping at night. And then you go back on the road and you've got to change, your schedule changes all over again. You're constantly flip-flopping back and forth.

{EN} Anybody that drives full-time is probably going through a similar situation.

{SP} Oh yeah.

{EN} When you are driving in the wee hours of the night, several hours into your shift, how do you avoid getting sleepy? Do you use any mind tricks, caffeine beverages, or is it more like you just get into a groove with the road?

{SP} Mountain Dew is my caffeine fix. I never have been a coffee drinker. As far as your mind set, you've got to stay focused on the road and don't let your mind wander, 'cause if you do, you're going to have problems. But you do have a lot of time to think about things. Solve the world's problems, maybe create a few more...*{laughs}*.

{EN} Do you know of any tricks or methods that other drivers use?

{SP} I had one road manager tell me one time "If you get tired just yell". He said you would be surprised how quickly that would wake you up...*{laughs}*.

{EN} Having driven for many different artists and bands over the years, I'm sure you have dealt with varying degrees of hospitality from your bus riders. Best case scenario would be a group that treats you with respect and courtesy. Give me an example of what it's like to work on a tour where that's not the case (naming names is optional).

{SP} What exactly do you want to hear Eric? I don't want to blackball myself in this industry... *{laughs}*. I would say 95% of the artists out here, and bands and crew, are just regular folks, easy to get along with. There's that 5% that are a terror, not only for someone in my position, it seems like everybody that they're around can't please them for anything.

{EN} Walking on eggshells.

{SP} Yeah. Everybody's just kissed their ass for so long, they expect everyone to do and treat them in that way. I don't care to work for people like that. I left a couple tours because of it. When I see that that's the way the artist or crew is going to act, I take myself out of it.

{EN} That's really the exception; most of them are pretty decent?

{SP} Yeah. Most everybody that I've ever worked for, and there have been hundreds of them, are just regular folks.

{EN} In some ways, driving a tour bus is almost like being a party host. You remain sober and focused to skillfully guide the group to its next destination while, at times, a wild party is raging all around you. Does this get old, or do you feel like you're part of the party?

{SP} Well no, you're never really a part of the party. It does get old. If you're on a long tour, and the crew guys every night, or band or what have you, are either drunked up, coked up, or smoked up, there's no telling. I've had to stop several times to pick them up out of the stairwell...*{laughs}*. They can do what they want to on the bus, they're renting it, they're paying the lease on it, they're paying me, I don't care what they do. But, it does get a little bit old sometimes. But not all of them are like that. Those are few and far between.

{EN} More on a rock tour, or just any?

{SP} No, it can be any of them. Some of the bigger rock tours that you would think would be wild are actually some of the most calm ones to be on. It seems like, and I don't know this to be a fact, but the younger bands that are just getting started, they usually tend to be the wild ones. The ones that have been out there for a while have already been there and done it. I guess after doing it for 20 years, now they're into the health food stuff, and no drugs, and no drinking.

{EN} It's the only way to save themselves, save their bodies, because touring will wear you out.

{SP} Yeah. They've torn their body up for 20 years and now they're trying to put them back together.

{EN} Many high profile artists travel alone or with a couple of assistants on their tour bus, while a band or crew bus will typically have 8 to 12 passengers. What are the biggest differences between driving a star coach and a band or crew bus?

{SP} I guess when you're driving a star coach, you kind of mind your P's and Q's. Band and crew guys generally treat you different than a star will, especially if their management team is on there. You're on call all the time; they can call you in the middle of the afternoon. If an artist wants to go here, that bus is at their convenience, at their disposal 24 hours a day. On a band or crew bus, the driver's pretty much going either to the gig or hotel, and that's the end of their shift. On a star coach you're a chauffeur, you could be a nanny, a luggage carrier, the whole 9 yards.

{EN} I've heard some horror stories from different bus drivers about waiting long hours in hotel parking lots for artists gone missing. I'm been on some of these myself. From

Steve and a Roberts Brothers Prevost XLII

your experiences, is this common and how do you deal with it when it happens?

{SP} Not every artist is that way. It is quite common to have to wait on someone. Again, the bus is at their disposal. They don't feel like they're putting anyone else out if they are four or five hours late. Whether they had a crew or band waiting on them also, sometimes I don't think that matters, they're just going to do what they're going to do. As far as how you deal with it, there's really nothing you can do unless you leave the tour, or charge them an overdrive every three hours of waiting.

{EN} It's really part of the job.

{SP} Yeah, it is part of the job. I had one band that was pretty bad about being late. I just had a friend of mine finish a tour hauling an artist for a top rock 'n roll band, and he was pretty much on call, or sitting in the driver's seat 18 hours a day. And not all of that was driving. A lot of it was waiting for hours and hours on end for this artist. Sometimes he would show up, and sometimes he'd get a phone call that he wasn't leaving the hotel. It's either suck it up and keep your mouth shut and put the money in your pocket, or go home.

{EN} That case right there sounds like an extreme case.

{SP} ... *{whispers... "famous rock star" [name removed to protect the innocent]... laughs}.*

{EN} That's great. Can't we print that? {laughs}... He's not even in this market...{laughs}

{EN} Some bus drivers prefer to go right from the bus to the hotel when their shift ends. When you have down time after your shift, do you ever go out exploring interesting places if a situation lends itself, or do you like to go right to the hotel?

{SP} No actually, one thing I do miss about being on the road with, whether it be a top name artist or anyone for that matter, is free golf. I used to go play golf almost on a daily basis, which I haven't had the opportunity to do in years. I got to play some really, really nice courses across the country, generally for free. But yeah, I'll take a couple hours to unwind after driving; I can't just get out of the driver's seat and go straight to bed, whether it's have a beer, watch TV, or whatever.

{EN} If you occasionally play a place near the ocean or a scenic old town...

{SP} Yeah, if there is sightseeing stuff to do, or a historical marker, or just getting out and walking around in a downtown area.

{EN} You kind of get a little world history lesson.

{SP} Yeah. Like I said earlier, you get to see a lot of places that you would never otherwise have the opportunity to see. So take advantage of it while you can.

{EN} How many times have you heard the question "Where are we?" Or "Are we almost there yet?"

{SP} If I had a dollar for every time I've heard that, I could've retired years ago...*{laughs}*. *Or how much farther?*

{EN} What did you say about my father?...{laughs}...

{EN} It's no secret in the touring industry that good bus drivers are not only in demand, they are well paid. What is an average yearly income for a bus driver working on a busy tour?

{SP} You could easily make $100,000 a year. You could make as much as you want to be gone basically. If you don't mind being gone year-round, you're a single guy, no kids, and don't mind being on the road, you can easily make 100 grand or more. I never cared to be that guy even though I did work pretty hard. I think about 80 grand was the best year I had on the road. But that was taking the winter months off.

{EN} So that wasn't a full year of driving?

{SP} No. Not being gone 365 days a year. I had some breaks in between. I would say on average drivers are making anywhere from $60,000 to $80,000 a year, that would be an average. But like I said, a hundred thousand is not unheard of. But you're going to burn yourself out in about five years of doing that.

{EN} Being a tour bus driver, in some ways, is like being a touring musician, in the respect that you are on the road for long periods of time throughout the year. Did you find it difficult to balance a family life with the rigorous pace of touring?

{SP} When I started driving I was single. I had children when I was 33. When they were about six years old is when I came off the road. When I was single I didn't mind being gone.

{EN} Once you had the family thing happening, it was starting to cut into it?

{SP} Yeah. Once the kids were born it got harder and harder to leave each time, especially as they got a little older. When they were infants it wasn't so hard. But when they're hanging on to your pant legs as you're trying to leave the house carrying a suitcase, that's when it started to get tougher.

{EN} What do you love about being a bus driver?

{SP} What do I love about being a bus driver? Just the travel and the experience. Again, to go all over the United States and Canada, I don't think I would have gotten that opportunity with any other career that I would have chosen. And, meet some interesting people on the way.

What is one of the things you like least about being a bus driver?

{SP} It sounds contradictory but, being gone all the time. Yes, I enjoyed it, but when you're on the road for six months, it gets old, especially after doing it for years and years. When you've been to the same town, and the same venues, and the same hotels again and again and again, it's kind of like Groundhog Day.

{EN} I can relate to that.

{EN} Over the years you have driven for some of the biggest acts in music. What are some of the more memorable experiences you've had?

{SP} Well there is a lot of stuff that I can't talk about...*{laughs}*... due to confidentiality agreements that you have to sign.

{EN} Literally?

{SP} Literally! I do remember one time after leaving a venue, we were getting down the road about 200 miles and we discovered that some chick had come through the window in the back, and passed out in one of the bunks...*{laughs}*. We stopped at a truck stop and put her out. I hope that she's okay...*{laughs}*.

{EN} Have you ever seen the Grand Canyon?

"A big hole in the ground" (aka the Grand Canyon)

{SP} I did see the Grand Canyon. My experience at the Grand Canyon was just like Chevy Chase in Family Vacation. I walked to the edge of it and looked over and said, that's a damn big hole in the ground...*{laughs}*. I got on the bus, and took off. I was there for about five minutes. I was dead heading someplace and I said, you know what, I'm going to go to the Grand Canyon, I've never seen the Grand Canyon. Once I got there, I looked at it, that's a damn big hole in the ground...*{laughs}*.

{EN} You've probably seen the Rocky Mountains more than once?

{SP} Yeah. I've been to the Rocky Mountains. I drove a bus up to Pikes Peak one time, I think it was in the middle of July, and me and a couple of the crew guys had a snowball fight. Drove a bus one time up the Pacific Coast Highway from LA to Oregon, and then discovered that we weren't supposed to be on the Pacific Coast Highway...*{laughs}*. The regulations for the length of the bus. Actually it was about five buses, we all caravaned up there, dead heading from LA to Seattle. We stopped in state parks and campgrounds. Pretty interesting to see five half-million dollar buses sittin', $750,000 buses, sitting in a state park with just the drivers on them...*{laughs}*. It was just the drivers deadheading.

{EN} You've probably, I'm sure, been to every state.

{SP} Yeah. Hawaii and Alaska are the only two I haven't been to.

{EN} Pretty hard to take a bus to those two places.

{SP} Hopefully I'll make it to both of them before I die.

{EN} For people that are interested in driving an entertainer coach, are there any suggestions you could offer in regards to being prepared for this line of work?

{SP} Stay in school. Go to college. Get a degree.

{EN} Because there's a better line of work, or because they're eventually going to want to do something else?

{SP} It's a tough business. It's not as glamorous as you would think it is. Everybody that gets into it, it's kind of a catch 22. You start driving, you start making a bunch of money, and it's hard to get away from it. I know a lot of drivers that, especially during the winter months, these guys are delivering pizzas, they can't do anything else. Don't know anything else to do. You kind of get caught up in it.

{EN} Kind of like being a musician...{laughs}. Next thing you know, 20 years have gone by, and you're like, this isn't quite what I signed on for, but it's all I know how to do.

{EN} One last question, are we almost there yet?...{laughs}

{SP} 50 miles. We'll be there in less than an hour.

Mike Chapman

Photo courtesy Mike Chapman

Mike Chapman has been an A-list session bass player in Nashville since the 1980s. He has recorded with Garth Brooks, Martina McBride, Trisha Yearwood, LeAnn Rimes, Brooks and Dunn, Huey Lewis, Hank Williams Junior, Kathy Mattea, George Jones, Ray Price, Keith Whitley, and countless others. Mike has played bass on over 30 number 1 singles and the albums that he has played on have sold over 150 million copies.

Born in Athens, Alabama, Mike grew up playing all kinds of music. As a teenager he played guitar in rock bands, country bands, and soul bands. By his mid twenties, after a few years of steady nightclub work, he landed a road gig with Hank Williams, Jr. After a short stint with Bocephus, Mike decided to pursue his dream of being a studio musician and moved to the Muscle Shoals area of Alabama. After successfully inserting himself into the world renowned studio scene there, he worked sessions regularly for the next five years and eventually began getting calls to come to Nashville to record. This prompted a permanent move to Music City where he has worked and lived ever since.

{Eric Normand} Tell me about your upbringing and how you became a musician?

{Mike Chapman} I was born in 1952 in Athens, AL and grew up in the country in a rental house on a gravel road just a few miles outside of town. Both my grandfathers were sharecroppers and my parents were the first generation out of the fields. My Daddy worked in a textile mill and my Mama was a housewife who sometimes worked in factories. As a teenager, my Daddy had learned to play guitar and he loved country music. I have a sister who is eleven years older than me so when I was small, she was a teenager and she was listening to pop and rock and roll on the radio. Through my Daddy and my sister, I absorbed a lot of music and loved it all from the beginning. When the Beatles hit the scene in the early 60s, I got caught up in their popularity and decided I wanted to learn to play guitar and got a $35 acoustic for my 12th birthday. My Daddy taught me what he knew and I immediately became obsessed with music and couldn't get enough.

Photo Courtesy Mike Chapman

I played in different bands in high school and sometimes when we'd put a group together for a particular gig we'd be faced with the dilemma of having two guitar players available and no bass player...in those situations I'd usually volunteer to play bass. When I was still just playing around in local bands, a friend of mine who was a really good country singer got an offer to play in a nightclub in Huntsville, AL while the regular band was on vacation and he asked me to play with him. Since he was the only singer, he wanted some help on vocals (the drummer and I didn't sing) and he asked if I would be okay playing bass instead of lead guitar and he would hire an out of work professional night club musician who was a good guitar player and singer. The gig went well and about two months later that same guitar player called me and asked me to come and sub at a club he was working. He said the regular bass player was sick. I borrowed a bass and went to the club and after a couple of sets, I was told that the bass player wasn't really sick and that they wanted to hire me permanently....4 sets a night, 6 nights a week for more money than I had ever made doing anything else. Up to this point I had considered myself an amateur and I was worried that I wasn't good enough to work with pros but... I thought maybe if I tried really hard and practiced I could pull it off. That's how I became a professional musician and I'm still at it.

{EN} At what point of your career did you become interested in becoming a session player and what led you to this decision?

{MC} After playing the Huntsville, AL nightclubs six nights a week for about seven years, I started getting really burned out. I had gotten to the point where I was making the top money in town and I looked around and there were only 2 or 3 musicians that were past 40 years old and still playing in clubs. I knew I wanted more out of life and music and so I started dreaming of getting out of the nightclubs and doing something different. I had always had a tremendous amount of respect for the guys who played on records... the recording musicians...to me that was the big leagues...the ultimate. Milton Sledge (a great friend and drummer, Milton and I went to school together and played in teenage bands together and later we both wound up playing in the same nightclubs in Huntsville) felt the same way and he and I started trying to figure out how we could get out of the nightclubs of Huntsville and into doing recording sessions in Muscle Shoals...which was only about 35 miles or so from where we lived.

{EN} I understand your career as a session player began in Muscle Shoals, Alabama. How did your first professional recording session come about?

{MC} As Milton and I were planning our escape from the Huntsville nightclubs...he got a nightclub job on the Tennessee state line, up above Muscle Shoals. There was a guitar player in that band who told Milton he had free access to a small recording studio that wasn't being used much. He told Milton that he'd written some songs and asked if he'd be into playing drums on some demos of those tunes...for no money...just for fun. Milton jumped at the chance to get some studio experience. The next thing the guy asked Milton was if he knew anyone that was a good bass player who'd like to do the same thing and Milton told him about me.

{EN} What was it like to work in Muscle Shoals as a session player during the time period you were there?

{MC} Well...because it was all new to me and it was the start of what I hoped was a way out of the clubs...it was very exciting. But...the thing I didn't realize at first was that the recording business in Muscle Shoals was actually very slow at that time and because of that, some of the studio musicians had moved to Nashville to pursue work. That was good and bad for us. Because some musicians were gone, it left room for Milton and I to come in and start doing some work...the bad part was there just wasn't a lot of work to be done. Even though in the 60s and 70s Muscle Shoals was a busy place for recording pop and r&b, by the early 80's artists had almost completely quit coming to there to record. There were very few master sessions being recorded and when they were it was either at Muscle Shoals Sound (who had their own in-house band of fantastic musicians...The Swampers...who were the owners of the studio) or it was at FAME studios and producer/studio owner Rick Hall would call studio musicians from Nashville to play.

Milton and I were learning to work in the studios doing mostly songwriter demos and playing a lot of great pop and r&b with great musicians and singers and loving every minute of it. A couple of songwriters in Muscle Shoals had gotten some Alabama cuts (at that time, the group Alabama was the hottest thing in country music) and had a big hit single and so there started to be a lot of focus on Muscle Shoals songwriters trying to get their songs cut by artists in Nashville. People who had always primarily written pop and r&b began wanting to cut country music demos. There were country songs being written and there were pop and r&b songs being re-done with country style demos. The fact that Milton and I had experience playing country music, understood it and liked it...was a factor in our getting called for a lot of country music demos.

{EN} After a few years of working in Muscle Shoals, you began to get calls to come to Nashville and record. What prompted those initial calls?

{MC} After working with several great songwriters in Muscle Shoals, a couple of them (Donny Lowery and Russell Smith) signed publishing deals with big companies in Nashville. The publishing companies liked the sounds the writers had been getting on their demos in Muscle Shoals and told the writers to call their Muscle Shoals musicians to play on demos of their new songs in Nashville. Donny and Russell started bringing Milton and I and some other guys to Nashville to record. So, we starting driving to Nashville to do sessions...about 2 ½ hours each way. The last year I lived in Muscle Shoals, I actually made more money in the studios of Nashville than in the studios of Muscle Shoals and that told me it was time to move.

Photo courtesy Mike Chapman

{EN} Tell me about your first sessions in Nashville.

{MC} I loved it. It was fun recording with new people in new rooms, meeting new engineers, new songwriters, artists, musicians and learning new ways of doing things. It seemed like every time I did a session and met new people it led to more work. The musicians were awesome. It was a thrill getting to know and getting to play with guys that were legends to an album credit reader like me.

{EN} I understand you've played on most if not all of Garth Brooks recordings. What was he like to work for?

{MC} I love the man like a brother. He's a great guy, a wonderful human being. I met Garth when he didn't have two dimes to rub together and he's still basically the same down to earth guy that he was back then. I've witnessed some rags to riches stories with people I've worked with over the years but Garth has handled success better than anyone I've ever seen and that's pretty ironic when you consider the fact that he's the biggest star country music has ever had.

I met him at a songwriter demo session where I was the session leader and he was there to sing a song for the songwriter. It wasn't long after that I started seeing him more and more singing demos that I was playing on. We got to be friends and he started calling me to play on demos of songs that he'd written. About the same time I had started working with producer Allen Reynolds. When Garth got his record deal and sat down with Allen to talk about starting to record, Allen asked Garth if he had any musicians in mind that he wanted to work with and he said "Mike Chapman". Since Allen had already been working with me and we had a good relationship, he was agreeable and I got the call for the Garth sessions.

Garth's a lot of fun in the studio. He always comes in and hugs everybody, asks them how they and their family have been doing and he always has a brand new joke and kids around with everyone. It feels sort of like we're a ball team. It's like he's the quarterback and Allen's the coach and we're the rest of the team. Garth and Allen make us feel that our contributions…our opinions and musicianship… are very important and they treat us with the utmost respect…just like we're family. The first time Garth won album of the year, he called out each of our names from the podium…thanking each individual musician who played on his record….no one else has ever done that before or since….and he did it again a few years later. In all my years of watching award shows, I've only heard artists *collectively* thank the musicians a hand full of times but Garth called out each one of our names two different times.

When we start to work recording a song for Garth, most of the time, we won't listen to the demo. Sometimes Garth wrote the song or if not, Garth has lived with the song until he has learned it and knows how to play it on guitar. Typically, he'll ask to borrow an acoustic from Mark Casstevens and he'll sit down there in the studio and sing and play the song for us and everybody writes their own chart. Garth'll tell us what he wants to achieve with the song and we'll play it and add our own ideas to the arrangement. All along the process things are discussed and auditioned and some things are thrown out and some are included until we get it right. Allen oversees it all, making suggestions and editions. We don't record to a click track (we only used a click on one song… "Against The Grain") and no one is designated leader during the session (when we're paid the leader is alternated between musicians). When we're through, Garth helps us carry our gear to our cars…he's the only artist I've ever seen do that.

Garth has been very loyal to the seven musicians (Chris Leuzinger, Mark Casstevens, Bobby Wood, Milton Sledge, Bruce Bouton, Rob Hajacos and me) who started out playing on his first album and he's used the same guys on all his country studio albums…with very few exceptions. I think I've only missed playing on 3 or 4 songs. "The G-Men" (that's what we call ourselves) have been recording with Garth for 21 years now.

{EN} What is it like to play on a master scale session?

{MC} First off…you have a lot more time to work on each song on a master session than on a demo. When doing demos for publishing companies, it's a very limited budget and you're usually expected to do about 5 songs in a 3 hour session. When doing a master session…the budget is much bigger and therefore you can slow down and take more time and we usually get 1 or 2 songs per 3 hour session. You have time to really scope out your part…making sure it's the best thing to play and that you've played it absolutely the best you can. Secondly, there's the possibility that the song you're playing on will be a hit and while it's fun to hear yourself and your buddies on the radio…it also validates you as a successful musician and will help to make your phone ring with calls for other sessions… hopefully. Thirdly, we musicians all love to play on a master session because it pays really well. Scale for masters is twice what demo scale is and sometimes….we get double scale on masters which amounts to four times what a demo pays….and who doesn't like to make more money?

{EN} Do artists and producers exert a lot of control?

{MC} It varies from person to person. Usually the producer is the one really in control of the session but the artists can have a lot to say too. I'll just talk about producers here but everything I say can apply to artists as well.

Some producers are very hands on and have lots of ideas and have a real vision of what they want to accomplish….they might tell us to "just copy the demo exactly" or…they sort of play the song through us getting us to perform all their ideas…and that's fine. Other producers don't say much but they control the situation by the casting of the musicians… these producers hire musicians that they have confidence in and sit back and see where the musicians go with a song and then make creative and/or editorial decisions and this method works well. To me, the best producers are somewhere between those two examples… they give us some direction…but not too much… and then give us a lot of freedom to be creative and explore different paths.

Sometimes…we work with producers that absolutely don't know what they're doing when they're in the studio and it's up to us musicians to take the bull by the horns and record the songs with our own vision of what it should be. Truth is…the recording of many hit records were really produced by the studio musicians…but they just didn't get the credit.

{EN} Is there a lot of tension?

{MC} Usually the atmosphere at a session is a very up, positive type thing and everybody is in a good mood. Most people know that the best music is made when the ambiance is pleasant and everybody is happy. If there is tension…it is usually inside your own head. You may be struggling with playing a part as good as you want and feeling inferior or inadequate if you're having trouble…but…nobody is making you feel that way…

you're doing it to yourself....and maybe... hopefully...if you can present a cool exterior...then no one else will notice that you're having a hard time.

Starstruck Studios. Photo Courtesy Mike Chapman

{EN} Your recording credits read like a who's who of the country music industry's most celebrated artists. Which of your musical experiences do you find particularly memorable or meaningful?

{MC} Of course the zenith of my career has been playing on the Garth records. It's been a heck of a party and I'm glad I was invited. There's been many meaningful and memorable things connected with Garth. When we recorded "If Tomorrow Never Comes" my firstborn was just a few days old and I was still on the most emotional high I had ever experienced and I had pictures of my baby boy on my music stand. When we recorded the song, which is all about family and making sure the ones you love know that you love them, I had a really magical feeling...it seemed like everything about the performance was perfect and I told Garth "That's your first number one!" ....and I saved the chart and took it home. Well, I'm no fortune teller but...it was his first number one and I have that chart on my office wall. Other great memories with Garth: playing live with him a few times....him busing us studio musicians and our wives out to Dallas to see his concert at Texas stadium that was filmed for a TV special....him saying very nice things in public about me and my contributions to his records....the fact that he has sold more records than any single artist in the U.S. (currently about 123 million) and that he had the first country album to debut at #1 on the pop charts and the first single to debut at the top of the country charts. It has also been so cool sitting there in the studio as he sat two feet from me and played and sang those killer songs for us for the first time. He is such a great communicator, entertainer, singer, human being.

Memorable things with other artists: I absolutely loved being able to record with George Jones and Ray Price...two of the best country singers that ever lived...I'd been fans of theirs since I was a kid and it was an unbelievable, surreal experience hearing their voices through my headphones as I played bass. I met Martina McBride before she moved to Nashville and produced the demos on her that led to her getting a record deal and played on her first album...and she babysat for us once...she's a great singer and I'm really proud of her and what's she done with her career and family. Being on the first albums of artists like Joe Diffie, Blackhawk, LeAnn Rimes, and others was fun as I watched them morph from baby artists to big stars. Standing by Dolly Parton in a studio as she sang a song at the piano was a thrill...she sounded like an angel. Being in an Opry dressing room with Connie Smith while she was rehearsing with her band was a joy....what a voice! Recording with Trisha Yearwood...the best female singer I ever worked with in a

At the Opry Photo courtesy Mike Chapman

studio...an incredible vocalist who is always thoroughly prepared when she gets to the studio and therefore gives it 150% every time she steps up to the mic. Doing demos with great singer/songwriters like Robert Byrne, Mac McAnally, Tony Arata, Henry Gross, Deborah Allen, Audrey Wiggins and others was so good I should have paid them. Also, there is an artist who I was a very, very big fan of (I still am) and I also got to work for him for many years in the studio and although I never played on any of his records (they were all done before I met him) I've played on dozens of demos for him and we became friends. He is one of my all time favorite singers and it has always been a great pleasure playing bass for him and hearing him sing...Dave Loggins... as far as singers go...he's as good as they get.

{EN} I understand that throughout your career in Nashville you've also done some live performing and producing. How has wearing a lot of hats helped you survive in the often unpredictable and inconsistent music business?

{MC} Well, you've got to be versatile. I love music...but the music business is another thing altogether. It can be very fickle...so many times it's about who's new and hot. That pertains to not only artists but studio musicians as well. Just because you play on the records of the biggest star that country music has ever seen doesn't guarantee that other people are going to hire you too. The music business is always in a state of change and if you want to work and be a part of it you have to adapt as much as you can. I try to play live a lot and I do just about every session I get called for...no matter how big or small. I also enjoy producing records for independent artists.

{EN} There are many professional musicians in the world today who have spent the majority of their career performing live that feel they are ready for paid recording sessions. Does being a great live performer make you a good candidate for studio work and what are some common shortcomings that live players new to recording might have?

{MC} Every good studio musician was once a good live musician. So...yes... being a good live musician is a good place to start if you want to do studio work. But, not all good live musicians make good studio musicians. In order to work in the studio you have to learn a new set of skills. They are things that many live players don't worry about that in the studio you have to address. When you're playing live and the amp is pointed at your butt you can get away with being a little noisy...but in the studio when the speakers are strapped to your head (headphones) it's very crucial to eliminate things like strings buzzing, fret noise, etc. and learn to play clean. Also, playing live you might have trouble with playing that bridge in the 4th song every night so you just get through it even though you rush it every time you play it but...you get to try the same thing tomorrow night. In the studio you've got to be able to quickly perfect those difficult passages because people will be able to listen to it forever. Also, some really good live musicians are good at copying what other musicians play but not so good at creating something new, and in the studio it is essential to be creative.

{EN} In Nashville, there has been a lot of conversation over the years about how hard it is for new players to break into the recording scene. Some people have said that it is a somewhat exclusive club that one must be invited into. What are your thoughts on this?

{MC} I can understand how some people would view it like that. When you're on the outside looking in it seems almost impossible but...it can be done...I know because I did it and no one invited me. I just kept at it...doing everything I could the best I could do it. What some people don't realize is it's not just about being a good musician...it's so much more. First off, you've got to be a nice guy. There are so many musicians in Nashville that the first thing that gets weeded out is the jerks. Life if too short to put up with someone's bad attitude and when people are spending thousands of dollars on a recording session the last thing they want is for someone to say something that casts a chill over the session and everybody there. You also have to have a great work ethic. Get there early and stay late if necessary. If you're late to a session, you'll make everybody there mad at you. Be prepared...have extra guitar cords, batteries, strings, etc. Basically, you've got to bend over backwards to do everything you can to make the client happy and...he will call you again...and he'll tell his friends...and you've got a career. You have to remember that as a studio musician...you're in a service industry and the customer is always right. Yes, of course the client wants you to be creative but...ultimately he wants it like he wants it. If the client has a bad idea, tactfully offer an alternative way...if he likes your idea, you're a hero...if he doesn't like your idea, do it like he asked and you'll still be a hero. At the end of the day I take pleasure in knowing that I gave someone what they wanted and made them happy. I'll do pretty much anything to get a job done as long as it doesn't involve dishonesty or something illegal.

{EN} The digital revolution has greatly changed the recording industry and it seems there is less activity than there used to be for professional session players. Have you found this to be true and where do you think the future is heading for recording in Nashville?

{MC} The digital revolution has changed the recording industry and there is less work for session players…but I don't necessarily think the digital revolution is the main cause for the decrease in work for session players in Nashville. I think that's another story. But… it is to some degree because there are guys with home studios who will program drums and bass and other instruments for a little demo instead of calling musicians…but most of the music on successful demos and country records is played by real, live musicians. Now, if you think about how they record in New York and L.A., then the digital revolution has made a much bigger impact there. Nashville is almost the last place on earth where musicians still get together in the same room at the same time and record music. Record companies and artists and producers here still appreciate the talent and creativity of the musicians. They know 150 years of collective experience on the floor of a studio full of musicians always trumps 5 years of experience of one guy in his bedroom with a computer.

Where is the future headed for recording in Nashville? I'm not really sure. There are some trends I see starting that I believe will continue and get bigger. One thing that is in transition right now is how studios are used. The big studios in Nashville are hurting because people used to book them for a week or two weeks (or more) at a time to do a project. Now many times the big studio is booked for a day or two for the cutting of the tracks and then the project moves to the engineer's house for vocals, background vocals, overdubs, mixing and sometimes mastering. I think we'll see more big studios on Music Row disappear because of this.

I believe country music will always be somewhat about traditional country music but it'll continue to copy pop music because it always has and as time goes on will probably become more pop and less traditional. Because of this, we'll see more and more musicians who can't really play traditional country music but who are really good at pop and rock… be successful in the studios.

{EN} What advice would you give to musicians that are aspiring for a career as a session player?

{MC} Play in the studio every chance you get! Get there early and stay late if necessary. Be a nice guy. Have good equipment and extra supplies. Give people what they want. Go the extra mile. Don't leave any slop on the recording. Be the best musician you can be.

Listen to the radio because while asking you to play something, someone might reference a recent hit song. If you can't stand country radio…maybe you're in the wrong business. If you simply don't like country radio that's okay…maybe you can change it.

Bob Bullock

By the time he moved to Nashville in 1984, Bob Bullock, a native of Oakland, California, had already been working as a professional recording engineer in the Los Angeles area for well over a decade. The training he received under such notables as Humberto Gatica, Reggie Dozier, Barney Perkins, Roy Haley and Roger Nichols; helped him to become a top engineer himself, working with acts like The Tubes, Art Garfunkel, Seals and Crofts, Chic Corea, Crazy Horse and REO Speedwagon during his LA tenure. In 1981, while working with Kenny Rogers at Lionshare recording studio, he was approached by legendary producer Jimmy Bowen to engineer for Warner Bros. Records in Nashville. In 1984 he made a permanent move to Nashville after three years of regularly commuting back and forth for projects.

Photo courtesy Bob Bullock

Bob's Nashville engineering credits include over fifty gold and platinum albums, including Shania Twain, Reba McEntire, George Strait, Tanya Tucker, Patty Loveless, Waylon Jennings, John Anderson, Loretta Lynn, Hank Williams Jr., Jimmy Buffet and Suzy Boggus, among others. He has been written about in Sound On Sound, Mix and EQ magazines, and now also teaches engineering courses at Belmont University and the Art Institute in Tennessee, as well as hosting sound mixing and studio engineering workshops throughout the U.S.

{Eric Normand} Tell me about your first experience in a recording studio.

{Bob Bullock} My very first experience in a recording studio was at age 15, when I visited Sunset Sound Studios in Hollywood. I had a band and we wanted to see about recording a demo, so we visited Sunset Sound. That experience changed everything. The engineer (his name was Tom Harvey) let us walk in and see the room where they were setting up for the band the Moody Blues. They had just purchased an Ampex eight track machine. So what happened from that experience, I just shifted from playing guitar in bands, and thinking that's what I wanted to do, to wanting to learn more about the technical aspects and the audio production side of it.

{EN} How did you first learn the recording process?

{BB} Having gotten excited about the recording process, I set my sights on engineering and producing music, basically thinking at the time that I could produce and engineer my band's songs. So I found a way to get into recording studios all around Hollywood, North Hollywood, and Burbank. I was able to get into some doors where I could hang out and observe, trying to handle myself correctly, I suppose, so people would say *"Hey it's okay, you can come in and watch what we're doing."* My first real professional job was at a studio called Radio Recorders, which is still open in Hollywood. I went from there to working for ABC Records/ABC Studios in Hollywood. In that period of time, and before me, that was the only way you got into the audio engineering field. You would find a way to get in the door. It was very much a master and apprentice story. You assisted or apprenticed, we didn't really call it internship in those days.

A great read which kind of tells the story of probably most everyone my age and older would be Geoff Emerick's book *Here, There, and Everywhere, My Life Recording the Beatles.* That book would pretty much sum up the engineering career. Emerick's story was very similar to what mine would later be, although his career of working with the Beatles was really quite amazing and I feel humbled making that comparison, but at 15 years old, he interviewed at EMI Studios, became hired as an apprentice working under Norman Smith and others, and literally started the same day the Beatles auditioned. It's his whole career, being apprentice, and then becoming the first engineer, that's how you did it. One thing that was good about it was that it was a natural filtering system. Someone had to be pretty dedicated to do what we did. And everybody that I know, all my peers in my age group or older, has a similar story. Bob Clearmountain started in New York, I started in LA, someone else started in Detroit, Chicago or San Francisco, and basically we all have the same story. If you really weren't dedicated to it, you probably would realize that it was way too unpredictable, just not secure. I guess the good thing was, because it filtered out so many people, if you really were dedicated you probably would make it work, and we did.

{EN} So you spent the first part of your career working in LA. How did this evolve into your relocation to Nashville?

{BB} I had been working on staff in various studios and freelance in LA, but I was really trying to move up to Northern California. Although I was very busy in LA, it was a pretty thriving industry in the 70s, I just wanted a change, and the bay area seemed like it would be a good fit for me. I was working freelance at Fantasy Studios in Berkley California with several members of The Doobie Brothers on a Tim Goodman project for CBS, when I got a call to come back to work on staff with Kenny Rogers at the studios that he purchased (later to be called Lionshare Studios), which originally had been ABC Studios. I had a lot of background there and a friend of mine who was chief engineer, Jay Antista, called to see if I would take the staff position, which I did because I loved the facility and knew some of the people that were already there. So that kept me in LA a few more years. Working with Kenny led me to visit Nashville. Through Kenny Rogers and his connections, I had people from Nashville calling me to come here and work. The first couple of years I was commuting, making several trips to work with people in Nashville, it was very thriving back then. I finally moved to Nashville in 1984.There was a point in the 80s, throughout the early 90s, that I had to turn down so much work that I probably could have been three or four people. I literally had to book myself out for vacations. There was not only a lot of work; there was also a lot of volume. Many of the artists I was working with were doing two albums a year. That employs a lot of people, it helps a lot of songwriters, it employs a lot of musicians, and it employs a lot of studios and engineers, and the fans were buying the records, so we were staying pretty busy. Now, even though there are still people making records, we're seeing the volume of albums be more like one every three years, or every five years. We're still making albums, and some acts are doing really well, but there are fewer people that are being employed.

{EN} The whole process has been slimmed down.

{BB} Yeah. There are fewer acts selling the big numbers so it's a very different industry now. I suppose if I were a young person starting out, I'd have the tenacity to still insist on making it work even in today's environment. Just maybe more like what you are doing now. Maybe it would be a little music and also have another field, not just solely the guitar player in the band, maybe I'm cutting some demos at home too, and I'm the tour manager. That just seems to be the current way of surviving.

{EN} Wearing a lot of hats is now essential in the music business.

{BB} I'm teaching, I enjoy it, but it's also another stream of income. Fifteen years ago, if you would have said, *"Bob, would you consider teaching some classes?"* I would have said, *"I'd love to, but I don't have time because I'm working all the time"*. Now, I have more downtime, and teaching is also a way to pick up some extra income. But I do also get gratification out of it, because this is the only way that people like myself that have had experience can pass it on to new people in the industry, as they don't necessarily have that many recording facilities where they can be an apprentice and learn from somebody that's been doing it. That is really a loss to me, because most all of us that ended up having careers, it was basically handed down to us by great producer/engineers.

{EN} Kind of passed down generational...

{BB} Yeah, it really was. I worked under people who are still active and still fantastic like Al Schmitt, Reggie Dozier, Roger Nichols, and Humberto Gatica to name a few, they were all the best of the best, and they handed that down as they got into production and other things. I still think that's important, but most people today that are out there engineering records really don't get that information passed down. They have Pro Tools, Cubase, Logic or some other DAW and they read magazine articles and watch some tutoring videos... that's all they get. It's kind of a shame because there's a lot more to it.

{EN} I've learned a lot of what I know about recording and engineering in that way, but some of the most valuable stuff I have learned has been just sitting in a room with someone that knows more than me. Sometimes it might be just two little moves, and it's like, "Oh, what was that, what did you just do?" You can read for hours and not learn some of those things.

{BB} Right, precisely. But it still just comes down to, most of us now; we are all wearing several hats. For me, it's sort of between producing, engineering, and teaching. I'm still just as excited about it; it's just what we do has taken on a different look. We were talking about one of our great musician friends selling real estate on the side. When he comes in to do a session, he's just as excited about doing it and is as great as ever, but on the downtime he's got another income source too. That's kind of the way it's more different than it used to be. The music industry is maybe more like some of us are hobbyists now, but the hobbyist still has a chance to make something happen, and then be able to turn it into something bigger.

{EN} It's the same way for me as a guitar player. I might do a month of gigs, recordings when they happen. But to create enough work to make a living just from playing guitar in Nashville, that's very difficult.

{BB} I know exactly what you mean. You could probably talk to a few engineers today that are busier than I am, but then you could have talked to a few engineers a few years ago that weren't as busy as I was. It really depends on who you're talking to, but I think it's fairly safe to say, that even with the people that are busy and successful, there are fewer numbers.

{EN} This is just all the stuff that people who haven't been here, or people that just get here, they don't quite understand all of this until they work in it for a little while.

{BB} It's such a bad notion; if you think about the companies that you can move up in, have benefits, retirement plans. As much as I enjoy it, and as much as I love passing information on to new people in the industry, I do really believe that, unless this is the only way that you're going to be happy, I would say do something else. I don't think it's logical to say, "I'm going to have a career in the music industry."

{EN} There's a lot to be said for just picking a career with something that you enjoy doing, and playing music because you enjoy playing music.

{BB} Yeah, I think for most people that's how it should probably be and will be. There's a great quote from a famous producer that goes something like "The development of the technology, being Pro Tools, Logic, and Garage Band, etc., has made it so a lot of people are creating music that probably should be in other trades or careers." It's really a hobby for those people, because it's very affordable. Everybody that has a Mac laptop has garage band, has loops, can get on MySpace for free, they can create something, they can put it out there, and it may be a fine little outlet for them. There's just so much product that's out every day now, but a lot of it is really non-professional. I can take pictures and put them up on Facebook, but I'm not a photographer. So I think that blurs the industry a little bit too, there's not so much separation between what would be considered semi-pro and pro.

{EN} When working on a major album project, how do you approach the recording process, in broad terms?

{BB} My approach is really never any different. I've always said to people that I've worked with, that to me demos are unreleased masters. But if I'm doing something for a major label, hopefully, it means there is a major product to be released, and that the people would like to give us the opportunity to do something competitive, or above competitive to help raise the bar. So the only thing that would be different is, typically, we would have a bigger budget, more time to work, be able to use better tools, and the artist can hopefully bring more to the table. So it's not that my approach is very different, hopefully in those situations, I can do what I do in a better way.

{EN} In those situations, does the producer usually call all the shots, or can the engineer have input in terms of production, mixing concepts, etc.?

{BB} I've always felt I've had input on every project. I think, most always, the engineer is probably somewhat of a co-producer, even if you're not called a co-producer. That's always been okay for me, because what it really says to me is that you have to be a team player. To really play well with others in the music industry I think it's important that you're open-minded. So as an engineer, when I'm producing, I always feel comfortable with anybody I work with to offer suggestions, to say this is what I think sounds good. And if they say *"Well no it's not really what I was thinking*", then I just basically erase that and go, *"Okay, what do we need to do? What do you want?"* I think that's important. I think you're going to find that more so than not, you're going to be able to contribute, but it's probably not just going to be your show.

{EN} Having a good vibe during a recording session is a crucial element for all involved. How can the audio engineer help to create and sustain a good vibe during sessions?

{BB} That may be the single most important element to the recording process, and an engineer can really be a good vehicle or conduit for that. When I'm engineering a project, there may be producers, artists, other musicians, and arrangers involved, and there's a lot of tension in the creative process. I think the better quality you're going for, the more passionate people are, and the more vulnerable your intentions are. There's been many times in the studio that I had to be a calming force. Maybe there's a musician who's just kind of struggling to give the artist what they're looking for. There's a producer who is feeling some tension because the artist is now unhappy. So a lot of times the engineer has to be the one to try to keep everybody up and cool. I think it's probably more of the producers' role to kind of maintain the vibe, but they're also usually in a closer relationship with the record company, or whoever's managing, and with the artist. So I think the engineer has a very important role helping to maintain the vibe.

{EN} The recording world has changed greatly over the past 40 years. What are some of the biggest differences between recording in the pre-digital era to the post digital era, and have these changes affected the demand for skilled engineers?

{BB} It seems that now we're expected to be playing in a band, tour managing, and have a studio. I don't think many of us really prefer that, I certainly don't. We're kind of forced into that. I've had conversations with other producer friends of mine, and they've said, *"I really wish I could get bigger budgets so I could just produce, hire you to engineer, and go to a studio where if something breaks down they take care of it."* We're given so little money to do these projects now that I've got to be many people in the process. I don't really think of engineering as being the same career anymore. Fifteen years ago, if you wanted to produce a project, you we're going to call me, or someone like me, but now you have your own studio. You're not an isolated case, you're like 90%. So there is no real career for audio engineering as it used to be, you become kind of an engineer through doing other things. Now, I teach it, but I teach to people of all different backgrounds and interest; songwriters, guitar players, drummers, and audiophile types. I teach them how to mix and how to record, but they're not necessarily able to specialize in that one thing unless they go into maybe film, television, and things of that sort. Most of them are doing this while they're doing something else. But I want to say here that we are talking about comparisons of what engineers like me used to do and I don't think it's all bad now, in fact

I believe there are many new opportunities in creating music for picture (film, television, broadcast, etc.) To make it sound like no one can earn a living doing this is not fair, I am only pointing out that the way I have seen audio engineering change as a craft has made it very different now.

{EN} When do you think this transition away from the traditional way of doing things first began, and why?

{BB} When I was 17 or 18 years old I started getting into studios. Prior to that, the only recording studios were owned by the record companies. You either didn't record or, you sang live in front of somebody and auditioned, or, you were at a record company that had a studio and a staff of engineers, and that's how it was. Then when some studio engineers started building studios and going independent, the record companies said "You know what, we don't really need to have our own studio. We have to pay these guys union scale; it's a big overhead and everything. Why don't we just go book time at so-and-so's studio?" That was kind of the beginning of when it started to change. But still, for a long time, if you were going to professionally record, you had to be in one of those professional environments. So there was always a little bit of a haven for the studio musicians, the Muscle Shoals rhythm section, or the Wrecking Crew in LA and all that. And the same thing with engineers, there were house and staff engineers that did lots of projects. So it's just been a transition through all these years.

{EN} Are we entering an age where engineers also need to be studio owners to earn a living?

{BB} Yes. I would prefer not to have my own home studio, to be honest with you. But the reason that I do, just as I'm sure the reason you do, is in order to take some projects, there's just not going to be a lot of money, and it's not going to be enough money to pay me, and to book time at another studio. So you hire me and my gear for one price.

{EN} What are some of the advantages and disadvantages in owning a home studio?

{BB} The good part is, when I am mixing a project, I can make my own hours. The part that I'm not so keen on is that it does isolate you. There used to be a difference in going to work, going to a studio, running into other peers. I used to pick up a lot of work by being at a facility with three or four studios there. I would be working, and somebody in the other room would say "We've got to add another week but my engineer is going to Australia to work on a project. Hey Bob, can you work next week?" That kind of stuff changes with the home studio. I also don't really care to be so responsible for having to upgrade, fix gear, and deal with all that, because it constantly changes. It's quite an investment to have your own studio, because it's an ongoing investment.

{EN} Are you seeing, or are you a part of many projects that are conducted mainly through the Internet via FTP sites?

{BB} Yes, with the exception of maybe projects I produce. People send me their files, FTP, U-sendit, I'll send them mixes, and then they'll review the mixes. If they have some things for revisions, I'll do the revisions. They'll either get it mastered, or I will get it mastered. I prefer it if I can get it mastered, because I feel like I have a bit of a call on seeing my work through to the end. But most of the time now, it's online and I don't meet the clients.

{EN} Sometimes you don't even speak to the client, it's a lot of e-mails?

{BB} I usually try to make a point to talk to them on the phone, at least a couple of times. But it's mostly e-mail correspondence.

{EN} Are there any specific tendencies or ways of doing things that are unique to the Nashville recording community?

{BB} The one thing that might still be a little unique to Nashville is that, the nature of country music, and that's still the biggest part of Nashville, country music, is to record with a roomful of musicians. I'm certainly not saying that I think it's not that way in New York or LA, but with Nashville being a small music community, there's probably more old-school stuff going on here than other places. When someone says "I'd like to come to Nashville to do an album with you guys; can you put together a band?" I think what they're feeling is that we're still very comfortable working that way.

{EN} As opposed to someone recording the guitar solo on the other side of the country...

{BB} I think if someone's thinking, *"I'm just going to call up somebody, a saxophone player in Detroit that I like, and have him play sax for me"*, that goes on all over the world now, and it is kind of exciting in some ways. But you don't have that in the room camaraderie, and the discussions of things that go on. I think that Nashville probably still has a little more of that going on than other music communities.

{EN} I think that's a good thing.

{BB} I do think it's a good thing, I think it's one reason that's kept me here too, because even though it doesn't happen on a day-to-day basis for me like it used to, it still happens here.

{EN} That's where most of the best music comes from, the old-school approach. Most of my favorite recordings were done that way.

{BB} I did a tracking date the other day, we cut a couple of songs, and we had a great band. I came home thinking, while I enjoy the other stuff I do, that's really my element, and that's what I grew up doing, being in the studio with a bunch of musicians. We all have mutual respect for each other, we spend a lot of time together, there's discussion, there's vibe, that's really truly my element, that's what I used to do every day. All of the other stuff is a little bit more of an adjustment. But it does still go on, I thank God it does.

{EN For musicians and songwriters new to Nashville, networking in the nightclubs remains a good way to slowly build relationships that will lead to work. Does this apply to recording engineers as well, or is a different approach needed?

{BB} To some extent I think it's the same, I think there is a real parallel between engineers and musicians. You play guitar so your instrument is obvious. My instrument is a console, a tape machine, Pro Tools. To me, engineers are musicians; I think it's really the same for an engineer. You get out, you visit people, you go to the number one parties, you go to the clubs, you do the things you can.

{EN} What kind of pay scales for freelance audio engineering are you seeing today?

{BB} Well, for engineers, sadly, it's really gotten all over the place, and what used to be considered customary is now a wider gap. Roughly speaking, assistant engineers are probably making $10 to $25 an hour. But sometimes it might be $100 a day, which is more like $5 dollars an hour because they're probably working 20 hours a day. First engineers, or chief engineers, are probably on average making $30 to $100 an hour depending on what they can command. There are mixers out there that make several thousand dollars per song to mix, and there are some that make $150 for the day.

{EN} So there's really no standard pay scale for engineers?

{BB} Unfortunately, it is whatever you can get, and that's really been a problem. When I was making the correlation between engineers and other musicians, engineers really are listed as part of the musicians union, but very few people exercise that. Engineers went independent and separated from that back in the mid to late 60s, early 70s, and I don't think there was a lot of forward thinking involved. Luckily, I'm in a position where, because of my background, I can usually command a little bit more money. But, if I'm too stern about that, I end up passing on a lot of work too, I can price myself out pretty easily, compared to the people that get more desperate and say, *"I'll do it for less."*

{EN} What advice would you have to offer to those who are just getting started as engineers?

{BB} Realize that everybody that has a home studio and has Logic or Protools, technically, is to some extent engineering for themselves. The career isn't quite so protected. But if someone really specializes, which is what I try to do, and puts all their effort into engineering, then hopefully what happens is, someone like yourself who gets a really important project says *"I really just want to produce this and play guitar. Bob, would you cut the tracks for me? You've been doing this for a long time now."* Hopefully, there is still work for specialized engineers in that way. You've just got to seek out your clients. I'd say the other bit of advice is, if you specialize in engineering, you probably need to not only have your own studio, you should be out there looking for acts. Maybe you'll discover an act that you can help forge. So I don't think that it's impossible, but there's no doubt that a lot of people can do some engineering on their own without the pro engineers.

{EN} So even though we all have to wear a lot of hats now, it's still a good idea to have at least one specialty?

{BB} If you want to stand out, try to offer something that's above the person that's doing three other things. My studio is really specialized for mixing, and the gear is the best I can find for mixing. A lot of people that have their own studios to record, call me to mix, because not only do they hopefully think that my experience brings something to the table, but that I have specialized my studio and gear for mixing. So try to find a niche that way. That's the way that I've made the transition. I used to call myself a recording engineer, but now I'm more focused on mixing because, including yourself, most of my musician friends are able to engineer enough to do their demos, but they get a little nervous about the mixing process. So that's where I still have some work, and a couple of my mastering engineer friends, it's the same thing, they're still pretty busy mastering because, even the home studio people say *"Let's spend a few bucks and let this guy master it, because if he masters it, he'll probably bring a little bit more out of it"*. So I guess, even I am constantly on the lookout for what can I do to stand out.

{EN} What are some of your favorite projects you have worked on?

{BB} There have been so many I don't even know where to begin. I was in a restaurant the other day and a song from the seventies came on, *You Don't Have to be a Star*, by Marilyn McCoo and Billy Davis. A music business friend I was having lunch with *said "I wish we had more music that felt like that today"*. I said I had worked on that record assisting Reggie Dozier, and from his reaction I realized how lucky I was to have been part of so much of the music of that time, or at least be around at that time. My discography can give you a slight glimpse into some of those times, maybe in more recent years being able to work with Mutt Lange and Shania Twain would be a high point. It was exciting to travel anywhere in Europe or the States and hear those songs being played on the radio, in airports, restaurants, etc. The most fun part for me has always been having a visual of what took place while we were making that music. It's like carving a sculpture and then finally you unveil it to the world. You hope they like it, but just completing it, and the excitement of that, is so much of it. I love working on a project and finally getting to listen to it as one complete finished work. That makes everything it took to get there worth it! So on all of those recordings I have a visual memory of what was going on in the studio to make that happen. Some very exciting times and great memories!

Photo courtesy Bob Bullock

Rhett Akins

Country music artist and hit songwriter, Rhett Akins was born and raised in Valdosta, Georgia, and it was on the back roads, dusty trails, and river banks of this corner of the rural South where a young Rhett first fell in love with American roots music. Music by artists like Hank Jr., Waylon Jennings, the Allman Brothers and Lynyrd Skynyrd would become a formidable backdrop, eventually inspiring him to become a singer and songwriter himself. But long before he would ever dream of a career in music, football was at the center of his life, and his involvement in the sport during his early childhood would eventually lead to the role of quarterback on the Junior varsity team at the University of Georgia.

But somewhere during his freshman year he realized that playing football wasn't going to take him much further, and opted out. It wasn't long before his passion for music would lead a 21-year-old Rhett to Nashville, TN where he began singing on demos and eventually landed his own publishing deal. This helped lead to a recording contract with Decca Records in 1994 which yielded three albums, several top 40 hits, a world tour with Reba McEntire, and the introduction of his signature song "That Ain't My Truck". Rhett built a loyal cult following and continued touring throughout the 90's and early 2000's, eventually signing a new record deal with BNA in 2005 which yielded his fifth studio album, "People like Me". Despite some new radio success with the controversial single "Kiss My Country Ass", the recently fragmented record industry failed to see the project through, and the album was self released in 2007.

Re-focusing his efforts on songwriting, Rhett signed a new publishing deal with EMI in 2008 and teamed up with Dallas Davidson and Ben Haslip to form what would become the red-hot songwriting team known as the "Peach Picker's". Together, the trio has penned numerous radio hits, including three number ones - Josh Turner's "All over Me", Blake Shelton's "All about Tonight", and Joe Nichols' "Gimme' That Girl".

An avid outdoorsman and hunter, 2010 would see the dawn of Rhett's first self produced album, "Bone Collector", a collection of hunting songs resulting from a joint effort with Dallas Davidson and hunting show personality Michael Waddell. Despite his new wave of songwriting success, Rhett hasn't lost his love for the stage and continues to tour, performing between 30 to 50 concert dates a year for his loyal fans.

{Eric Normand} Describe a standard publishing deal for a non-established, newly signed writer?

{Rhett Akins} It's usually a three-year deal with one-year options. It's the publishing company's decision after each year to keep you for the next year *(option)*. That's whether you are a new artist, a new writer, or an established writer. For a three-year deal with options you might receive anywhere from $15,000-$30,000 (annually) depending on your family situation, what you need to survive, and how enthusiastic the publishing company is about you. That money will be considered an advance and is recoupable.

Most of the time, a first-time writer won't retain any publishing. The publishing company will always be able to make the decisions of what happens to the songs. They can sell them to another publishing company, use them in movies or whatever form they decide and the writer will have no say. The writer will receive performance royalties (from BMI, ASCAP, or SESAC, according to who you are with) and money from album sales, but they won't receive any money from publishing.

{EN} How does the writer receive this advance? Is it all up front, installments?

{RA} It all just depends on your deal. It could be all up front, monthly installments, or half up front and the rest in installments.

{EN} Is there a monthly or yearly quota for completed songs?

{RA} It's usually 12 whole songs (per year). That's not just 12 songs, its 12 complete songs. It's either 12 songs written completely by you, 24 co-writes, or 36 three-ways. They might state that the first six must be done within the first six months of the year, but no publisher has ever asked me, or told me *'Hey, you're two songs behind on your quota.'* I've never once counted the songs that I've written during the year, and no publisher has ever asked me for a total, even though it's written in the contract as a pretty big deal.

{EN} I wonder if that's different for a newly signed writer, if the publishing company would be more on top of them.

{RA} Yeah, I would say the publishing company would be more interested in keeping up with them. But most people that get a writing deal in this town are so enthusiastic about writing songs that there's usually never a reason to ask because they're going to write at least 50 to 100 partial songs and wind up with at least 20 total songs a year. If you're only writing 12 songs a year, you're not doing a lot of writing in my opinion. I would say most people write one to five songs a week. Even if you wrote one a week, that's 52 songs a year, or parts of songs. I write at least three days a week minimum. I would say I write 3 to 5 songs a week. So the quota is never an issue.

{EN} What are some other factors and variables writers should understand about publishing deals?

{RA} They'll usually charge you half of the demo costs. If a demo costs $1000, you are charged half of it, and that cost is added to your advance.

If you're just a writer, with no aspirations of being an artist, there probably won't be any incentives or bonuses. If you are an artist/writer, maybe they will own all of your publishing until you get a record deal. And then once you get a record deal you might have a third to half ownership in the publishing of the songs you recorded yourself.

What you should strive for in a publishing deal is to own as much of the publishing as you can, which is usually about 50%. That's about the max unless you have a lot of clout. If you're a successful writer and they really want to keep you bad, they may give you more than half of the publishing, but probably with less advance money.

{EN} What would be different about a publishing deal for an established writer?

{RA} An established writer will usually get a bigger yearly draw, more money per year to write, which is still recoupable. So you get more money, more publishing, and at least co-writer status. If you own half of your publishing you're making $.75 out of every dollar and the publishing company is making $.25. If you don't own any publishing, it's 50-50. So a co-pub would be at least a $50,000 minimum on the advance. With a minimum/maximum deal where according to the earnings you made last year, your next year's advance would be up to 75% of what you earned last year. The base salary might be $50,000 and according to what you made last year, they will pay you up to $100,000 per year. So if last year you made $100,000 in royalties, instead of making $50,000 next year, you'll make $75,000. But there's usually a ceiling and a floor. You can't go below $50,000, and you can't go above $150,000. And that would all be negotiable.

{EN} When you say recoupable, you mean the publishing company needs to be paid back from the earnings of your songs?

EMI Publishing house on Music Row, Nashville

RA} Yes. But you'll usually get your BMI or ASCAP money. Let's say they paid you $50,000 in advances, and your portion of demos is another $20,000. So you owe them $70,000 for that year. If your portion of royalties from a song that was on the radio were $100,000, you'll get your $100,000 from BMI, ASCAP, SESAC, or whoever you are affiliated with, let's just say EMI, that's who I have my deal with. BMI will also send a check for $100,000. So the writer gets half and the publisher gets half. So out of $200,000, as a writer, I get $100,000, and as a publisher I get $50,000, because I got $50,000 and EMI gets $50,000. But EMI will take my $50,000, and put that towards the $70,000 that I owe them. So I still owe them $20,000. I won't get the publishing side of my money until the $70,000 is recouped. They take it from my publishing side of performances, and all of the mechanical royalties that I get (record sales). I don't receive any of the money that the labels pay EMI for albums that have sold until that $70,000, or whatever that number is, is recouped. So the only money that I will definitely get is my $50,000 advance, and whatever performance money was collected by EMI.

The writer can often end up in a better situation than the publisher. If you're making $50,000, and you owe them $70,000 to $100,000 you pretty much have to have one hit song per year to keep that kind of deal going. Especially nowadays, most songs are three ways or at least co-writes. So the more people that are involved in the co-writing, obviously the more songs you have to produce to be successful. It's kind of a tricky deal, you want as much money as you can get to live on, but the more money you get, the more you have to produce to keep the deal. Ultimately, the less money you can live on from the publishing company, the better off you are in the long run. You kind of hedge your bet that you will have hit songs this year, but if you don't, and you put out a couple of songs that go to, say the 50s to mid-30s on the charts, hopefully that's going to earn enough money to keep you at the publishing company because you didn't take as much of an advance.

{EN} In Nashville, many of the songs that become successful are written by two or more writers. Why is that?

{RA} It's kind of weird, but I think it's just become the norm. I think that 80 or 100 years ago most people wrote songs by themselves. I don't think anyone just decided one day that 'Hey, I need to write this with another person'. I think it just kind of evolved that way.

{EN} What might be some of the pros and cons to working with cowriters?

{RA} Sometimes my publisher might know of another songwriter that he thinks I might click with. Sometimes two heads are better than one. One writer might be strictly a lyricist and another might be strictly music. You would then also have two different publishing companies pitching the song. You've got my publisher, plus my co-writer's publisher ganging up together on a record label exec, producer, or artist, just really hyping the song or whatever. There are more avenues. Maybe my publisher doesn't know an artist, but my co-writer does. Obviously the publisher just wants songs that are going to get cut and hopefully be hits.

There are a lot of benefits to co-writing, but obviously, the more people that are involved in a song will decrease the amount of money that you and the publisher make, so most of the time it doesn't go beyond three writers. There are occasions where four or five people write a song together and I think that usually happens because two or three writers began a song that they didn't finish and somewhere down the road two other people got involved and finished it. But I don't think six people usually get together to write a song.

I think a lot of artists write songs by themselves more so than strictly writers do. Toby Keith has written a lot of songs by himself. Taylor Swift has written a lot of songs by herself. But most writers have 3 to 5 other people that they really click with and they usually get together weekly.

[EN] What is a songplugger and how important is it to work with one?

{RA} It's pretty important. Unless you are already a very successful songwriter, and very, very connected, you will need a songplugger even if you own your own publishing company. Most people who don't write for a major publishing company, like EMI, Sony, or Universal, still have to hire someone. You don't really have enough hours in the day to write songs, demo songs, and then try to get them into the right hands. And you just won't have all the connections you'll need to have your song heard, placed, and end up in the right circles.

It's like any other business. It's nearly impossible to run any business as a one-man show. Somebody's got to produce and somebody's got to sell. Your job is to be creative, write a song, record the best demo you can on it, and then put it in the hands of your publisher who pretty much knows all the key people at every record label, the producers, and a lot of times the artists themselves. It's their job to find the best possible way of getting this in the hands of the potential artist.

Most of the time they'll play it for the A&R person at a label who then decides whether they think it's good enough to be passed on down the line. And obviously a lot of times the artist will never hear the song that was intended for their ears, because the publisher couldn't get it past the A&R person, the producer, or the manager. Whoever is the gatekeeper of the artist's CD player is a lot of times in control of what happens. There's been plenty of times in my career where somebody said *'I sent you a song, did you ever listen to it?'* And I'm like 'I've never in my life heard the song.' That's because my producer, the record label exec, or whoever decided that they didn't like it, or they didn't think I would like it. So it's very important to have a publisher that maybe has multiple avenues of getting your song heard.

{EN} So the songplugger usually works for the publishing company?

{RA} Yes. You can hire independent songpluggers if you own your own publishing company, but most of the time they work for a particular publishing company. Obviously they can't like every song that they promote. Basically they are salesmen, and although they go in there and try their best to convince, hopefully the song sells itself. I think they do hype a lot of people, and they might say '*This song was written by such and such writer. You know his last three songs have been number ones, and this artist has recorded his songs before and really likes his stuff.'* They're basically salesmen; they're just selling creative pieces of work instead of shoes or cell phones.

{EN} So if you get a publishing deal that's part of what they're going to do?

{RA} There's usually 2 to 4 songpluggers that work for a given publishing company. Another part of their job is to be looking for potential ways for you to write with an artist. Maybe they have a really good relationship with an artist, an artist's manager, or producer, and they sell that artist on the fact that 'You really need to write with my writer. Why listen to all these other songs if you could be participating in the creation of the song *and* earning more money yourself? I think you should write with my guy.' When you write with an artist, it allows you to skip a lot of steps. Obviously, you don't have to play that song for the artist to hear it; he's part of the creation of it. So that's also the publisher's job, making the right connections with artists so you can skip all of the middlemen.

[EN] How do you go about the songwriting process? Do you start with a melody, story, title?

{RA} The majority of the time I start with the title or an idea. The music and the words for me have always come at the same time. Sometimes we start out with a lick or a groove on the guitar or piano. But at a typical writing session, we all might have 2 to 10 titles in our cell phone, computer, or notebook, and we throw them out there until we land on one that everyone thinks is worth pursuing. Somebody grabs a guitar or piano and starts banging around. Next thing you know your spittin' out words. It usually all flows together with me, at least in all of my co-writing situations.

{EN} Do you have to write stuff down as your doing it so you don't forget it?

{RA} Today, with computers and garage band, you don't have to write anything down. It used to be that a song would take two or three pages in my notebook because I'd keep scratching out lines. But now, people type so fast that as soon as you say something, they type it, and if you change it they'll just erase it and type it again. Most songwriters today are writing on their computers. I don't, I still write in a notebook, one reason being because I can't type...*{laughs}*...I can one finger peck. But there's always somebody there that can type really fast. We also use Garage Band to record everything we need to.

The Peach Pickers: Dallas Davidson, Ben Haslip, Rhett Akins
Photo courtesy Alanna Conaway

{EN} So you record a lot of these writing sessions?

{RA} Not necessarily the whole session, but when we've got two or three lines or a melody going we'll make sure to put the melody down so we don't forget it. Usually by the end of the day I'm looking at somebody's computer and writing the lyrics down in my notebook. Sometimes we might just put our computers together and hit the record button and record a work tape. Or someone will e-mail you the work tape later on in the day or that night, and that's what we send to the demo players, the studio musicians. The band leader will get a work tape and he will chart the song based on that recording.

[EN] How many songs do you write to come up with one great one?

{RA} That depends on your definition of a great song. I've written a lot of songs that I thought were great that were never cut, and I've written a lot of songs that I thought were mediocre or average that got cut. The meaning of great is subjective. I remember at one point in time I had been getting a lot of songs recorded, and they were mostly up-tempo, fun party songs, not a lot of meaning behind them. And I told one of my publishers 'I promise you that I have a good song in me, like 'The Dance', or 'God Bless the Broken Road', a song that I would consider a great lyric, a great story. And he looked at me and said *'Don't you dare write a good song. I have a basement full of great songs, and I don't need another one.'...{laughs}...*

He was obviously kidding, but publishers aren't in the business to care whether or not a song is critically great or not. Success to them is; did it make it onto a CD, did that CD sell, and did that song become a hit on the radio? The song could be horrible, I could name you hundreds of songs that I consider horrible that made millions of dollars, and songs that I think are fantastic that didn't see the light of day.

So when you ask me how many songs do I have to write to write a great one, I would say I don't know. But how many songs do I have to write for one to succeed? I would say 1 out of 20 to 50. It's like a batting average I guess. It could be 1 out of 20; it could be one out of 50, or even one out of 100.

{EN} But out of those 20, 50, or 100, there are a lot of songs that you would consider to be good songs.

{RA} Oh yeah, there's a lot of songs that I consider good songs.

{EN} Why do you think some of these good songs don't make it through?

A lot of it depends on whether or not you 'hook the demo'. Sometimes the demo just comes out very different than what you envisioned; maybe other people aren't seeing your vision. I think a lot of artists like or dislike songs based on who sings the demo. If they don't like the sound of the voice coming out of the speakers it can be hard for a lot of people, even A&R people, to hear the songs potential. I think that's one reason a song might not get passed on to the artists. They hear only the negative, and they can't get past it. So that's why a lot of publishing companies and writers are adamant about having a certain singer singing a demo.

{EN} What kind of pay can an in demand demo singer earn?

A lot of demo singers in this town make $100,000 plus a year singing demos. They'll do four to six songs a day, 5 to 6 days a week, and they probably get paid between $100 and $200 per song. Harmony singers are also working all day long and making a boatload of money. So when you find a singer that people seem to be reacting to, and all their songs are getting cut with their voice on it, that singer suddenly starts getting a lot of work. Jamey Johnson made a killing one year singing demos, before his record deal. And that can also propel somebody to get a record deal. A&R people get used to hearing the same people singing demos, and then the songs that they're singing become hits, and they're like *'God, this guy should have a record deal'*. That's how I got my record deal; my very first record deal was through me singing demos, and a producer hearing my voice. That has a lot to do with the success of your song.

{EN} So a good demo singer is a big part of selling the song. Are there exceptions to this rule?

There are a couple of songwriters in town that are extremely successful even though they have the worst vocals ever. They sing their own demos, and sometimes it's almost unintelligible. But I think that they've established themselves so much that it kind of becomes a Bob Dylan effect. 99 out of 100 people would say Bob Dylan has a terrible voice, and he's not a singer, but he is a character. Bob Dylan could sing a song, then you could have a Mariah Carey sing the same song, but you believe Bob Dylan's version of the song more than Mariah Carey's, even though her version is vocally better. There are a couple of songwriters in town that have become so successful with what they do, that singers want to hear their version of the demo, even though vocally it's not good. They have a way of selling the story and making it more believable even though the vocal is terrible.

{EN} There's more emotional content.

{RA} Yeah, it's more emotional. And a lot of guys are getting songs cut with just a guitar. They just sit in their basement and put it on tape, it's terrible, it's out of tune, but the singer somehow feels it and believes it more than a perfected demo. There's absolutely no way to tell why anything in this town works. You can throw something with the most glue and mud on it and it will not stick to the wall. And you could throw a rubber ball with grease on it and it sticks. There is absolutely no rhyme or reason as to why, who, when, where, anybody writes a song, records a song that it becomes a hit.

{EN} I guess the good news is that it gives everybody a chance.

{RA} Yeah, it does. That's why I think that if you're not a quitter, and you're very passionate about what you do, you will succeed at some point in time in this town. Just don't quit. Because one day what you do will be popular. At some point, and there's no reason why...*{laughs}*...

{EN} Before you became a successful songwriter, I assume you wrote songs for the fun of it. Now that you are doing it for a living, is it still fun?

{RA} Yes and no. A lot of it depends on who you're writing with. Sometimes, when I look at my calendar and see the names of certain people, I just automatically dread that I have to write with them. Not because they're not a good writer, sometimes personalities

don't mix. Maybe they have a bad attitude, or they're downers, or too hyper. Some people are fun to write with but we don't get anything done. With some people we get a lot done, but the mood is just terrible. It really depends on who it is.

I think that's why a lot of people start out writing with everybody, it doesn't matter who it is, they want to write, it's like *'Yeah, hook me up, book me with them. Let's write.'* Then after a year or two of that you start figuring out who's more enjoyable to write with, who you write better songs with, who's more fun. So I've kind of started narrowing it down to where I'm writing with people that I enjoy writing with. I don't know if it makes the song any better, but it seems like it does. It seems like there's less pressure, the process is more enjoyable, and when it's more enjoyable I think your mind opens up to be more creative. When you're under pressure, and your writing with somebody that you don't really care to write with, you focus so much on the song, that you kind of kill the creative vibe in the room.

{EN} So you still love the art of songwriting.

{RA} I love the art of writing songs. Every day that I go to write, I go in there thinking 'How in the world are we going to make up something up today?' We go in there with a blank sheet of paper, and come out of there with a song, and it's something that you never even thought of the day before. It's like 'Where did this idea come from? Where did this melody come from? I never would have guessed in 1 million years that we would be coming out of here with what we just wrote.' That's pretty fun. And then months later, or however long it takes, you go somewhere like to California or New York and see people singing the song that it took you hours or days to create. And they're just singing it, walking around humming it, or at a concert you watch them singing all the words, like that song was meant to be. It's almost like that song has always been around, it never was created, it's just always been here.

{EN} Kind of like you just plucked it out of the air...{laughs}...

Out of all the songs you have written, which ones are you most proud of?

{RA} Some people would want me to say the songs that were number ones, or the biggest hits, but they aren't. This might not be the best song I've ever written, but I'm proud of

'Friday Night in Dixie' because I actually got to write it with Charlie Daniels. Ever since I was a kid, I grew up loving Hank Williams Junior, Waylon, Charlie Daniels, you know the outlaws, sort of redneck artists. To be a kid in South Georgia you're like 'I will never meet Hank Williams Jr. or Charlie Daniels, I will never meet anybody that is famous'. So 20 years later to be sitting at their house writing a song with him, that makes a song more special.

I'm also really proud of 'Kiss My Country Ass', even though some people might laugh, I mean it is what it is. But I'm proud of it because that song changed the way I write songs, and it changed the way that I look at the music business. That's the first song that Dallas Davidson and me ever wrote together. And Dallas and I have had more success with each other than we have had with anybody else in Nashville. That song kind of set the tone for 'We're going to write, play, and sing what we want to, and we're not going to try to fit radio, or these boundaries that Nashville seems to have. I believed in that song so much that I told record labels, other artists, other songwriters, I told them 'You need to trust me, this song strikes a nerve with people because we didn't care what we said in the song. We said exactly what we wanted to say and didn't care if a radio station ever played it, or if a record company ever believed in it.' When we get on stage and play it live, people react to this song more than they do to 'That Ain't My Truck', more than they do to 'Don't Get Me Started', and more than they do to songs that they've heard a million times. You play it one time and by the second chorus people are going crazy for the song. I've seen people lined up at the merch table buying T-shirts and CDs and they've never heard this song before in their life. To me, that song on that level is the song that I'm most proud of. Obviously you might think 'That Ain't My Truck' because it's been played 3 million times, I made a lot of money on it, people everywhere know that song, and I *am* proud of that song. But that song became popular because it was heard so many times. 'Kiss My Country Ass' is popular the first time you hear it and that means a lot to me. Dallas and I started this little songwriting team on a 'We don't care, we're just going to do what we want to do' basis. And that's why I'm really proud of that song.

And also, to give you guys credit, because my band played on it. And then I recorded it again with studio musicians, and then Blake Shelton recorded it again last year for his Sixpack album 'Hillbilly Bone '. But every comment I've ever heard from other people, and on the Internet, was that what I call the 'demo version', basically what me, my band, and Bobby Pinson did in the studio when Hank Jr. came in, that's their favorite version of the song. Every time I look on YouTube, I never hear the album version of that song. It's always our demo version that people play. It's rawer, it's not as in tune, it's not perfect, but people for some reason believe in that version of the song more than any other.

{EN} I'm proud of that one too.

[EN] How does an unknown songwriter just starting out in Nashville go about establishing a name or reputation for themselves?

{RA} I would say coming here completely blind is tough. If you don't know anybody in the music business and you move here from Russia, or wherever, and you just want to be a country music writer, you should join the NSAI (Nashville Songwriters Association International), and BMI, ASCAP, or SESAC. They will be willing to help you get connected with somebody, at least to start. You should go to Broadway, Tootsies, the Stage, Legends, the Fiddle and Steel, all of those places. And don't be shy, just say 'Hey man, I'm so-and-so, I came to town to write songs'. They're probably going to laugh at you and say *'So did everybody in this bar. So did the waitress, so did the bouncer.'* But who cares. If you came here to write songs, come on in and throw your flag in the ground. Just get out there and ask.

I knew one songwriter when I moved to Nashville. I didn't even know him, he was a contact. I really did my homework too, because I'm a songwriter fan, and every CD I ever bought, the first thing I did was to open up the package and look at who wrote the songs. So when I came to Nashville, if I was at lunch someday and somebody said *'Hey, that's Paul Overstreet over there.'* I knew every song he ever wrote. I wasn't afraid to go up to him and say 'Hey Paul, I'm sorry to bother you, but my name is Rhett Akins and I'm a huge fan of this song, this song, and this song. And I'm especially a huge fan of the album cut that was on so-and-so's record that was never even a single. That's my favorite song you wrote.'

If you try this, sometimes they might be a jerk, but most of the time they're really nice, and they're really appreciative that you know their stuff. They might not write with you, but they might say *'Call this guy, he's my publisher.'* Or *'Call this guy, he's a buddy of mine. Tell him who you are and what you're doing, and maybe he can help you out.'*

I just think if you come to town and you really want to do it, hit the streets, go to BMI, ASCAP, SESAC, NSAI, go to the Bluebird Café, go to Douglas Corner, go to other places where they have songwriter nights every night. Don't be afraid to go and tell them who you are and ask for a hand, or ask them what you can do for them. You can't go anywhere in this town and not meet a songwriter. Maybe the first 50 songwriters you meet will be horrible, but they will lead you somewhere. One of them knows somebody. The music community is extremely small and everybody knows everybody.

[EN] How important is it for an unknown songwriter to have a likable personality?

{RA} It's very important. You might be the happiest person in the world and have a great attitude, but there is a type of person, as you mention in your book, that we call a 'gherm', and they are basically an annoying person. When you see a gherm coming you might think *'Oh god, here comes so-and-so.'*, you won't want to help them out. You'll dive into a bathroom, you'll pretend like you're on the phone. I think for a lot of people, the stereotype of Nashville or the music industry in general is sleaziness. It's a lying, dark, underground business where everything is shady. And to me, I don't see much of that at all. Be on the up and up, don't try to slide in the back door, just be honest, be nice, be respectable, and just tell somebody 'I want to write songs.' You don't want to walk down the street and have somebody say *'Oh God, here comes that guy, and I guarantee you he is going to slip a CD into my hand.'* Or he's going to say *'Hey man, when are we going to write?'* You have to have some kind of restraint. Obviously everyone in this town knows what you want. They know you want to write, they know you have a song, but there's tactful ways of presenting that. Don't be shady, and don't associate yourself with people that don't have good reputations and you'll be fine.

{EN} Be a good person.

{RA} Just be a good person and don't annoy people. Here's a good example. If you run into an artist, and artists are all over Nashville, you can go to Tootsies on any given night and see Hank Williams Jr., or Eric Church, they're around; Toby Keith might be sitting in somewhere like The Fiddle and Steel. Do not go up to Toby Keith and hand him a CD. Do not go up to Toby Keith and say *'Hey man I would like to write with you.'* You might go up to Toby Keith and say *'Hey, I'd like to introduce myself, I'm so-and-so, and I'm from so-and-so Kansas, and I really love your music.'* And you're probably going to get a *'Thanks'* and that's it. And then walk away.

Artists, record producers, publishers, they know what you want, they know what you got, so don't bother them with it. Introduce yourself if you want to, and tell them you're a fan of their work, and maybe they will open the door from there and say *'Really, well give me a card.'*, or *'Do you have a CD? Bring it over to my office one day.'* Do that one time and after that, quit. Because the next time they see you, they'll run out the back door. *'Here's that kid again with the annoying CDs.'*

{EN} A lot of people don't know this. These are the basic do's and don'ts...[laughs]... Aside from publishing deals, what other avenues can songwriters pursue to earn income from their songs?

{RA} I don't really know of any other avenues. You would have to be very lucky and fortunate to know somebody that could get your song into a movie or something like that. If you don't have a publishing deal, it's going to be pretty much a miracle for Garth Brooks or any major act to cut your song, unless God smiled on you that day. Your songs just can't get into the right hands; they have to go through the channels. It's very rare that something happens out of the norm.

I will say this, I give credit to Garth Brooks on this, Jarrod Nieman is a friend of mine, and he has a buddy named Richie. Richie sat outside of a studio one day where he knew Garth Brooks was recording. He set out there for like five or six hours. And Garth walked out of the door, and Richie approached him like I'm telling everybody not to, and said *'I'm a big fan and I've been sitting here for six hours to meet you and I would love for you to listen to my songs.'* Garth did, and called him, and now they're friends and he's written a few songs for some of Garths albums. That never happens.

{EN} Except that time.

{RA} Yeah, that time it happened, but the majority of the time it doesn't happen. I would say try anything once, but if they slam the door in your face, don't do it again. There is a difference between being persistent and confident, and being absolutely annoying. Because once you get the reputation that you are an annoying songwriter or musician, people just don't want to hear what you have to say. I think that people in this town are extremely nice. Nashville seems to have an open door policy if you're an honest person and aren't out to do shady things. Somebody's always willing to help you, or at least guide you in some direction.

The Peach Pickers *Photo courtesy Alanna Conaway*

Colt Ford

Hailing from a small town just outside of Athens Georgia, Colt Ford has made a recent splash in the music world with his unique blend of southern country with hip-hop, rock, and R&B influences. His interesting journey has taken him into some unsuspecting worlds which collide to make this bigger than life "average Joe" a one-of-a-kind artist and entertainer. Before his recent arrival on the Nashville scene, Colt had spent some years as a professional golfer and had already invested a lifetime into his passion for songwriting.

Photo by Heather Brand

He discovered his knack for songwriting while in high school, when he wrote a rap for a friend, and soon after this discovery he began working with acclaimed producer Jermaine Dupri (Mariah Carey, Usher). After recording a hip-hop album with Dupri, Colt would spend the next six years as a professional golfer before returning to his musical pursuits. His recently re-focused efforts have yielded him a wave of success as his self released country album "Ride Through The Country" sold nearly 150,000 copies within a year of its release. Without any help from radio or TV, this album has made it to the hot 200 albums chart through word-of-mouth and a rigorous touring schedule (200 dates in 2009).

His recent songwriting credentials include country music songwriter and recording artist Jamey Johnson, songwriter/guitarist Jeremy Popoff of the alt rock band Lit, and hip-hop writer Attitude. Other musical contributions include country artist John Michael Montgomery, hip hop artists Bone Crusher and Sunny Ledfurd, and No Doubt's Adrian Young.

{Eric Normand} Tell me a little bit about your younger days. What was it like growing up near Athens Georgia?

{Colt Ford} Athens is a great town, University of Georgia....I've lived there my whole life. My dad's from Hart County which is a small country town, and my mama's from Anderson South Carolina, so I was raised country, and country music and stuff I learned. Growing up there, I did a lot of hunting and fishing, and before I was as fat as I am now, I was a pretty good athlete (*...laughs*). I played a lot of sports, was pretty gifted as an athlete and had a lot of baseball scholarships and golf. I ended up playing college golf and then I played professional golf for living. Just a great town, hard to leave Athens.

{EN} Who were your musical idols and influences back then?

{CF} I've never been like, specific one thing or one genre. Music from all different styles has always interested me. If it's something I just like, I just like it whether it be Run DMC or Johnny Cash or Waylon Jennings or Lynyrd Skynyrd. All that stuff I listened to, and still continue to listen to. If you picked up my iPod you'd go, wow this dude's got such a wide range of stuff. The Commodores and the Barkays to a lot of the old country stuff, and Kenny Rogers or a lot of the new country stuff.

On stage with DMC *Photo by Lisa Carpenter*

{EN} A pretty wide variety, even in your early days.

{CF} Yeah, always has been, I've always been like that.

{EN} I understand that you discovered your knack for lyric writing while in high school, at which point you wrote a rap for a friend. How did this come about?

{CF} Yes, just a buddy of mine, I think I was a freshman in high school and we had a song. He was wanting to be in this contest and he was having a hard time writing it. When I was little, I used to sit in the front seat and rhyme words together. I would beat on the dash. I've played drums since I was real little and I guess the rhythm and the patterns have always kind of intrigued me. I just wrote something for him and he went in the contest and won. And I was like, man, well maybe I should just do it (*...laughs*). I got into that, it was different; it was like a movie for me. Hip-hop was really taking off then and I certainly didn't know about most of the stuff I was talking about. Back when I was into it, hip-hop wasn't bashing women or as violent, it was more about fun and party kind of stuff.

{EN} Just good stories.

{CF} Yeah, stories, fun, party kind of stuff, that's what really intrigued me. A lot of the new stuff doesn't move me very much, most of them don't really put any thought in to the lyrical content.

{EN} It's kind of strayed.

{CF} Yeah, I've got a 14-year-old daughter, and I'm married… I'm not interested in hearing you tear women down and all the violence there. When you put that to a kid's ear, if they hear it over and over again, that's potentially dangerous, as the world has shown.

{EN} Upon your discovery of your songwriting abilities back then, did you ever consider the possibility of pursuing it as a career?

{CF} Yes, I kind of always wanted to. There's two things that I always wanted to do and that was music and golf and I've done both of those (*…laughs).* I kind of set out to do both of those and have been really lucky and blessed and given a lot of opportunities; you don't do anything like that on your own. First of all, you're given a gift; God's blessed you to be able to do something. These people that go, you know I've made it and I've worked hard, well no, somebody helped you along the way, that's the way it is. So I've been lucky to have a lot of people to help me. I mean my parents never stifled me, being a white kid in the middle 80s and being really good at rap in Athens Georgia was a little bit different (*…laughs…)* a little bit different. So I was just a big outcast, it was like, wow, that dude, what's wrong with him.

{EN} But your parents were behind you.

{CF} Yeah they never stopped supporting me; it's as much their dream as it was mine I guess.

{EN} Early on in your career, you recorded a hip-hop album with Jermaine Dupri. Can you tell me a little bit about what it was like to work with him on that project?

{CF} Truthfully, Jermaine Dupri is the most talented producer maybe ever in the Hip-Hop and R&B world of things. They can say whatever they want to, I know Timbaland is fantastic, and Dr. J, and Puffy, a lot of those guys are fantastic, but if you put them all in a room they cannot do what he can do. He can play just about every instrument, he writes songs, he can write a rap song, he has written songs for Mariah Carey and Usher and Madonna, he's just unbelievably talented. Jermaine, I met when he was only 16 or 17 and he had just done his first record, produced his first record then for a girl rap group on Geffen records. We met and hit it off and started working together. But I'm glad it didn't work out because it led me to where I am now and it led me to being myself instead of being something, you know, that whole career, although it could have been great and it could have made me a lot of money, it wouldn't not been very real or very honest and I'm kind of glad that it all ended up where it did.

{EN} Things happen for a reason.

{CF} Sure, absolutely.

{EN} After that project you put music on the back burner for a while and spent several years as a professional golfer. How did you wind up in that profession?

{CF} Golf, like I said, I played college golf. I was all American College and I've always been gifted at that, and I was lucky, and I was good enough to go play for a living, and make a living playing for a long time.

{EN} You went right from college to playing professionally?

{CF} I did, and I was doing music at the same time so it was very weird. In music, I'm going to bed, when in golf I should be getting up. *Right, (laughs...)* It is very different. It doesn't seem weird to me because it's what I've always done, but to everybody else, they think I'm a pretty weird guy, which is all right. It's what I am, it's always been me, I've always had fun and I've always known what I wanted to do.

{EN} So you made a good living with that for a while.

{CF} Yeah, I played on a tour, I played professional golf, I made my living playing 25, 35 weeks a year, playing around the world, playing golf. It was fun, you learn a lot from that, and that's other things I've applied to that and my music.

{EN} About six years into your career as a golfer you decided to make another attempt at music. What led you to this decision?

Photo by Lisa Carpenter

{CF} When music, when it's in you, cause there's many people when I started out trying to do something else, especially in the country world of things that are like, what are you doing dude, you're crazy, this won't work, you can't, and you're too old, and you're too fat. And I'm like, the bottom line is it's about the song, they can say whatever they want, I don't give a shit what you make these dudes look like, and the pants and the clothes you put em' on, it is still about the music. And, I think if you make good music, people could care less where it comes from. If you make something that's real and honest, there are people that will dig that. You just can't turn it off; you can't make it go away. So it never stopped. I always wrote, I always did stuff; I always chased it at some form or fashion, although I was doing something else. I had to pay the bills; I have a wife and kids, so golf was paying the bills. But, my wife said look, just go try one more time, and I'm lucky, because most people don't have that, they don't have a wife that says, I'm going to quit my job that I'm making pretty good money at and go try to do country music, and I'm about twice as old as most of the guys that are coming out, and by the way I'm also going to do something that's never been done before (*...laughs)*. So she still said I dig it, and I think it will work, so, I'm really lucky.

{EN} Much of your songwriting seems to pull from your life experiences and people seem to relate to this kind of honesty. Tell me a little about how you approach the songwriting process.

{CF} I think I just write about stuff that I know and stuff that I've seen. People ask me all the time, where do you come up with an idea? And I'm like, you know, walking around Wal-Mart.

{EN} So your song ideas begin with a lyric?

{CF} Yeah, I think so. It's a very different process in the hip-hop world of things versus the country world of things. In the hip-hop world of things the track is already made, the music is already made. You don't write anything until you hear that, and then you write the song. In country, it's the exact opposite of that. The lyrics take the music where to go; you get a guitar riff and then write it around that. It's the exact very opposite, but both are equally cool and very challenging. Like I said, if you're real and honest, it will be all right no matter what you're doing.

{EN} Your path to success has been unlike most in the music world. You've built your success from the ground up through hard work and networking and without the help of a major label record company. Did you have a certain business approach or plan in mind when you embarked on this wave of your career and if so, can you tell me some specifics about it?

{CF} What I had, if you look at it, it was a little bit similar to the way that Interscope records started. You had a guy that had the ability to run a record label in Jimmy Iovine, you had an artist, and you had a guy with some money, that said, all right, I'll give you the money to go do it, and that's pretty much what we had. Myself and my partner Shannon Houchins who runs the label and is also a producer, and Zach Mackeroy who had the money and believed in me as an artist and believed in Shannon, that he could run it. Our philosophy on our record label stuff, we don't subscribe to what most labels, especially

Nashville, the way it's going, we do things very differently. I've always thought there's plenty of money in the music business, you don't have to rob people to make it. There's plenty of room for the artist to make money and the label to make money, just don't spend a lot of frivolous money on dumb bullshit that nobody cares about just to look cool (…*laughs*…) and we don't do that. You can want it to be grassroots all you want, you can't make it that, the music has to make it that, and that's what a few of them really fail to understand. The music has to make it do that, it can't be what you want to do, you can promote it all you want to, but if people don't like it they ain't gonna buy it. I'm amazed when people go, hey; our song is number 10 on the charts. And it's like, yeah, but you're selling 300 records a week, okay. I don't have a song on the charts, but I'm selling 5,000 a week, I'll take that. It's a business. I'm not here to look cool, and go around and slap each other on the back and go hey we got a top 10 record. I'm here to sell records, and sell shows, and sell tickets, and sell t-shirts, and make songs that people like.

{EN} So write good songs and they'll come.

{CF} I promise you it is. If you find the right songs and write good songs and are honest, and if you let the artist be who the artist is. That's a little bit of a problem I see. Some of these artists, I see them, and it's like, wow, that's not really who you are dude, or girl, or whatever, that's who they're trying to make you be with it, and sooner or later people get tired of that, and they'll know that it's not real and go, okay, I've seen that, whatever, it's the same 10 songs that I heard the other 10 guys sing.

{EN} In what ways have used the Internet to help build and maintain your following?

{CF} Huge, that's been huge for me. It's been MySpace, and I still to this day answer every message myself on MySpace. I don't have anybody answer them for me, I don't like people talking for me anyway. It's been huge, and I think some of the big record label people have failed to understand a little bit. And it doesn't do any good for you to have five people sit in an office and send out friend requests. A lot of times people just accept them, but they still don't know who you are, that doesn't do any good. When our numbers started coming together there were plenty of people that questioned it, and said, oh it's made up. And it's like, no; I need that for real data. If I'm going to Baton Rouge Louisiana, I need to know how many fans I have there for real so I can know what I can do when I go do a show there. I've never requested anybody as a friend on MySpace, it's been organic, and they tell their friends, and that's the way I need to be, because I need it to be real data, not made-up data. So, I spend a ton of time on there. Radio is not what it used to be. I have a 14-year-old daughter, and she could care less what you play on the radio. I hear songs from her all the time; she finds it on the Internet, that's where it's at now. And it ain't just 14-year-olds, it's a lot of people, they don't need radio like that anymore.

{EN} The Internet has become part of the new grassroots.

{CF} It's been very much a big part. It's certainly been a huge, huge part. I think it's been the same for artists like Taylor Swift. I think it's brilliant and I think more artists should take time to answer their fans. I know most of them, and ain't none of them near as busy as they make it sound like they are. I know they're busy and I know you get tired and worn out, but we aint digging a ditch, we're not curing cancer, we're playing music. So some of them need to get over themselves a little bit and just go play and realize that the reason you're playing is because people sent you messages. It don't take but a little while. Sit down for a couple hours and send out, you know, a couple hundred of them, it will make somebody's day.

Covington, GA   Photo by Lisa Carpenter

{EN} Your career has some major ties to the Nashville scene while your success has been largely achieved without the help of the big music industry side of Nashville. What aspects of the Nashville music scene are you currently involved in?

{CF} I want to be more and more involved in Nashville. Nashville is an amazing, brilliant place. In that little square mile, whatever radius you do around Nashville, there's nowhere in the world that has more talent than that. And when it comes to singer songwriters and musicians it's just literally the best of the best. There's certainly good people in other places but musician wise and everything you just can't go anywhere and find those kind of players and singers and songwriters. I'm trying to get more involved, it's been tougher for me because I'm an outsider and coming in from doing something a little different. But I think I've gotten a lot more and more accepted. People after meeting me, they're like, this dude really is what he says, and he's real, he's not some slick, polished up something that was made up in the studio. He's really just a fat dude from Georgia that's got his own style and is pretty good at songwriting. I try to be good guy and I try to be nice to everybody, treat people the way they ought to be treated. I think if you do that, you'll be all right. They're starting to let me in a little bit.

{EN} You're starting to do some co-writing with other artists.

{CF} Yeah, I wrote with Rhett Akins, and Dallas Davidson, and Ben Haslip. I've written with Jamey Johnson, Noah Gordon, Bobby Pinson, these are some of the absolute best of the best songwriters in Nashville. Being able to write with those guys is amazing, and it's changed the way I've written songs a little bit in certain things, which is a great thing. I mean, you've got to grow. I wrote most of the first album myself, but I wanted to expand

and see what else I could come up with. I don't got all the ideas (*...laughs*). There's a reason these other guys have hit songs, so I'm honored to be able to sit down and write with them.

{EN} Your eight-piece touring band is made up of many veteran Nashville players and I understand some of these players are also involved in your recordings. This somewhat breaks the traditional Nashville approach of using only A-team session players for a major project. What are some advantages you have found in involving the players from your own band on your recordings?

{CF} I think more artists should honestly spend a little more time and get the best players that they can get. I didn't want it to be something hokey or goofy. A lot of people in Nashville were like, you should get a DJ, and you should get matching outfits, and a midget, and a goat. And I'm like, haven't you all seen that before? That looks like some sideshow shit. I'm not trying to be funny, this is for real. I wanted the best players I could get, and I worked hard to find them. I feel like I got A-list players that play in my band, so why can't they play on the record. I think they know me, and know who I am and what I'm trying to do. I think that's a little bit of the problem on some of the records. Some of these A-list session players are the greatest I've ever seen. I love hearing Kevin Grant play bass, you know what I mean, but I love hearing Paul Chapman who plays for me, play bass. All those guys are fantastic, but a lot of times they're not let out of the box to be anything, and that's why some of the stuff sounds the same to me. If I hire Rob Hajacos to play fiddle, which he has on every one of my songs, what the hell am I going to tell him? He's the greatest fiddle player in the history of Nashville. What am I going to tell him? What's a producer, what are you going to tell Rob Hajacos. Just shut up, push the red button, and say go ahead my friend. That's why you're in here. I don't get it. I've had the best of the best session players play on my stuff, as well as my guys, they don't play on everything but they play on a good bit of it. When they come in there, and Kevin Grant is playing bass, and he's like, what do you want me to do, I'm like, just swine out, just do your thing. That's why I brought you here, to do your deal. Play it how you feel it.

{EN} Do you think involving your touring band with your recordings gives them a bigger sense of belonging?

{CF} I think that's hugely important. I'm not trying to blow my horn, I just do stuff the way I am, I'm not going to change that, I don't care what a manager says, or anybody says. I do it the way I do it, and that's what it is. So when I hear them go, oh, when I played in this band they would never let me do that. I'm like, why? I want my band to shine. Every night I play, and unless it's a limited set where I can't do something, every one of my players does a solo, because I want people in that audience to go, wow, Jayson Chance is a fantastic guitar player. I want them to see that, that doesn't bother me; I'm not threatened by that. I'm plenty secure in what I'm doing. I want people to think that these guys are really good,

Photo by Lisa Carpenter

and I want people to know that when they leave. Wow, that band was really good, I think it's important.

{EN} In 2009 you played about 210 shows, and touring at that pace is obviously a part of your recent success. How do you balance such a hectic touring schedule with your family life?

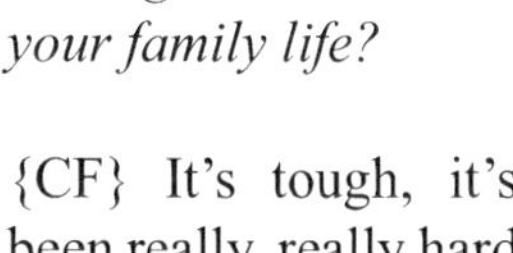

{CF} It's tough, it's been really, really hard to be gone that much but like I said, I'm really blessed. I married a girl, Jessica, that's just a strong, strong lady that can handle it. We got my family there, my parents, and her parents, and I'm just really lucky, just really lucky to have the opportunity to go do that. You can't do that on your own, unless you're a single guy, that's fine. But being married, with two kids, it's tough and it's tough to be gone, but I'm just lucky to have that kind of support system and to be able to go do it. And it's hard. There are plenty of times when I'm on the road and it's like, God, I'd give anything to be home. My little boy is becoming a great athlete, and I'm missing a baseball game or something. But at the same token, you got to put food on the table too, and this is what's doing it.

{EN} What advice would you give to aspiring singers and songwriters that are trying to build a career in music?

{CF} First of all, in relation to the songwriters and the players and stuff, that's the backbone of the music, and I think a lot of them kind of forget that. Even with players, go spend time with other players. If you want to be a good guitar player, then go find your Brent Mason's, or you, and find the people that have been playing for years, that are fantastic, and talk to them. Most of them, I have found, if they see that you really want to learn or work, are more than willing to take some time with you. Go find those guys, and go seek out these songwriters and check your ego over there at the table and sit down and listen and see what you can learn. There is something every day. I don't give a shit how many hit songs you wrote, or how good you are, there's somebody that's just as good or better than you. So go find those people and talk to them and spend as much time. The bottom line is you need to be honest. If you want to have a career, you better be real and honest about who you are.

Because if you're doing something that's not, it's going to be short, and people will figure it out, and they'll go, I'm done with this dude or group or whoever. I think you better be real and honest about what you're doing, so that you can stand behind it and go, this is who I am.

I hear a lot of songs today and I'm just going, wow, I know that person, that's not them. A lot of it is labels, the problem is they try to, they think they can build an artist, like you just go in there and design it and build it, like, all right I'm going to put them in these jeans, and give them this thousand dollar pair of boots, and this right there, and he's good-looking and everything, and he can sing alright. That don't mean people are going to like it. And it ain't gonna last long when that is. I need you to be who you are, man. Again, at the end of the day, it's all about the song. They can say anything they want. For a fat guy like me, the same girls that scream for those good-looking boys scream for me. When you're on stage is totally different.

So have good songs, man, have good songs. Some of these artists need to work harder to find them. Don't let them make you cut something. If you really don't feel like you dig it man, you just got to say, hey. And a lot of them are just stuck, they're like, well, I'm on this label, and I feel like I have to. And that's a shame. I've talked to quite a few artists this year that have said, well, I had to cut this, this, this, this, and this, cause that's what they made me, and I'm like, wow, that must suck. That's why we did our own thing. I don't have to do that, if I like it, I cut it, if I don't, I don't. It's pretty simple.

Photo by Lisa Carpenter

I conducted this interview with Colt in January of 2010, just one year after he began his meteoric rise in the music world. Since that interview, "Ride Through The Country" and his 2010 release "Chicken and Biscuits" have gone on to sell over 370,000 copies and 470,000 downloaded tracks collectively, Colt made his first appearance on the Grand Ole Opry, and in 2011 he would receive his first ever ACM awards nomination in the Vocal Event of the Year category for his collaborative single "Cold Beer" with friend Jamey Johnson. He continues to tour with a rigorous schedule showing no sign of slowing down any time soon.

EJ Bernas

EJ Bernas was raised in North Tonawanda, New York, and already enjoying a successful career as a college soccer coach when he was offered a job at UMG (Universal Music Group) as director of secondary promotions. Growing up in a rural community halfway between Buffalo, New York and Niagara Falls, he always had a passion for music, being introduced to the songs of Willie Nelson, Johnny Paycheck, and Kenny Rogers by his father at a young age.

Never having envisioned a career in the music business prior to being approached by UMG, his story is a unique one, and his "abduction" into the record industry the direct result of long-term friendships and relationships he had formed over the years. He is currently the Senior Director Southwest Region UMG.

{EN} How did you first begin working in the recording industry?

{EJ} My college roommate in Brockport New York, just outside of Rochester, was a communications major and he was working at the college AM radio station at night. He got me doing an on-air shift; they let me do whatever I wanted to do, kind of just "*Go have fun*". Music wasn't a dominating passion of mine, I don't play an instrument, I listen to music, I love music, but it's not like I was telling about album cuts from Pink Floyd's third record.

We became friends, built a relationship and I was the best man in his wedding. Damon Moberly, who is currently the vice president of national promotion for Mercury records, was the Northeast director of promotions for Mercury at the time, and was in attendance because he was their radio guy. He met me at the wedding, I was just being EJ and having fun, and he was like *"You're a pretty good dude"*. So every couple of months when he came back to Buffalo, we were out of college at that point, I was included in Terri Clark's dinner with the radio guy because I was Damon's friend. Then three or four years later they said we have this position opening up at Universal, the bosses at the time had met me at an event, we hung out, and they just thought I was this outgoing, easy to get along with kind of guy. They said we have a position that we would like to see if you would be interested in interviewing for.

At the time I was coaching soccer in Buffalo, working for Canisius College, a Division One School. I ran an 80,000 square foot athletic facility and was one of the head coaches of the premier football and soccer club in Buffalo. I was very intertwined in my coaching career and worked for the national team and the Olympic fundamental program, so it was some pretty elite stuff that I was climbing the coaching ladder on. I came down for the interview, and needless to say they wanted to hire me. I moved to Nashville in April of 2003 after coaching my last soccer tournament the weekend before. I was hired as the director of secondary promotions for Universal Music Group. So basically every Erie Pennsylvania College Station, Texas, Peoria Illinois, College Station Texas ,the markets that are big enough to have Wal-Marts and airplay and sell records with really big radio stations, they weren't really being focused on if you weren't on the billboard or media-based chart. So they had me, I was their rep. With very little budget to travel, and meeting very few of them, I built relationships over the phone. Basically, they let me learn how to work records.

EN} So you were kind of abducted by the record industry?

{EJ} I've met so many people that move to town that so badly want my job, there's probably 10 people that want my job, and I didn't go looking for it, it found me. It's been one of the greatest things in my life, period. Coaching is a different level of satisfaction and a different kind of reward. Working music, being in the business and working with all these talented people, and being a part of Josh Turner's career from the beginning is something I'll never, ever forget. I'm also on the tail end of George Strait's career; I mean I've had the last eight number ones on George Strait. Pretty Incredible!

{EN} What does your job as senior director of Southwest region for Universal group entail?

{EJ} I cover Nashville, Memphis, New Orleans, Kansas City, Albuquerque and everything in the middle including Oklahoma, Texas and Louisiana. There are 24 radio stations in that region that report to media base and R&R. There are two stations in Houston Texas, two in Dallas, Tulsa has a station, Oklahoma City has two, I work those radio stations. I have relationships with the program directors, the promotions director's, the DJs, the morning shows, and I'm the relationship between the artist and the radio stations. I have George Strait, Gary Allen, Josh Turner, Lee Ann Womack, Vince Gill, David Nail, Mallory Hope, the Randy Rogers Band, and Josh Kelley. We set up a schedule when we are coming out with singles, we choose a single off an album and then we work that to radio to try to get that single up the charts. For instance Gary Allen's 'Kiss Me When I'm Down' single is going for airplay on September 27th. So we're going to ask radio to start playing this record then. If everyone gets the same time frame, that's how the song climbs the charts. The longer the song is on the air and climbing the charts, the more commercials we have to sell records.

The ultimate goal in promotion is getting a number one record. Some artists might have a song on the charts for 40 weeks, or sometimes you have an artist whose song is added right away and then in four weeks it goes number one. Taylor Swift got a number one record last year in one week and that's never been done before.

So basically a radio station will commit to playing a record. To start it off, it plays three to five times a week roughly. Then it goes into a light rotation which would be like 8 to 10 times a week and it might stay there for a couple weeks. If it continues to go well, it will go up to medium rotation which would be 10 to 25 times per week. And then if it's overwhelming that people want to hear it more, it goes to a heavy rotation of as many as 40 times a week, some stations even playing it 50 times.

{EN} So listener response is part of what drives this.

{EJ} Yes. There are phones, there's research, they have these new things called PPM meters, in some markets, people used to fill in little diaries, ratings diaries, and there's only a handful of people that have them, but those are some of the many ways radio conducts its research. Our research we get every week is in Sound Scan. A radio guy might say, "Boy, you had 400 plays on Josh Turner this week and we're up 18% in sales in your city." And then the next week we might have 800 plays on Josh Turner and were up 22% in sales. You can see that. As soon as the fans are hearing it and starting to hear it more they want to buy it, that's how we know we have a hit.

The radio world and the record world, as much as we have to work together, have two different lines of thought. When you start turning your radio station off when a song comes on, they don't want that. So they have to figure out what song made you turn it off, and if it made you turn it off, then how many other people turned it off at the same time.

It's very formulated and calculated; you're going to hear George Strait's 'The Chair', that's a strong gold record. There's a handful. Any Brooks & Dunn hit, any Toby hit, any Tim McGraw hit; those are always rotating.

{EN} Even if they're five years old?

{EJ} Even if they're five years old. To get to a gold category means they're probably going to spin anywhere from 3 to 15 times a week no matter what. 15 times a week could mean at 2:00 in the morning on Monday, 4:00 in the afternoon on Tuesday, 6:00 PM on Friday, and then twice on Saturday, and so on. It's part of my job to monitor all that. For a current record, which is a song that is currently climbing the charts, each radio station has a percentage of their playlist that is dedicated to current music. In the day of the iPod, most people tune in to hear local news, weather, traffic and new music. They want to know and hear what's new. And when they start to hear their favorite song, that song is probably in heavy rotation and probably spins around six or seven times a day - 1:00, 3:15, 6:30, 10:00, and so on. Sometimes when you get in your car and you're like "I just heard this two hours ago." it's probably because it's in heavy demand.

{EN} If people are tuning in, in the day of the iPod, to hear new music, why does all that older stuff still occupy the airwaves so much?

{EJ} That is a very fascinating question. Because it researched! There's a percentage of the current country listener, the P1, P1 means the Top, dedicated listeners. "*The only thing on in my truck is country music, I don't listen to anything else, I won't even flip stations.*" that's an example of a P1 listener. They might occasionally flip stations, but their diehard country fans. So when they hear an old George Strait song every once in a while they might think "God, I love that song." But if most people's reaction is "I can't believe they're playing that song." chances are that's not going to be in rotation in a couple weeks.

{EN} So they just play whatever they think will keep you listening.

{EJ} Radio wants to keep you listening to the next four minutes, that's a goal. Sometimes now you'll even hear something like "Tim McGraw, and boy he got into *trouble; I'm going to tell you in the next three minutes and 30 seconds, stay tuned.*" Time spent listening is a huge tool for radio and one of the tools they use to be able to sell advertising. The average listener listens to x-amount, they need time spent listening to WSIX or WKVM, and they need to increase that constantly. So in the day of the iPod, for example Garth Brooks' "*The Dance*", you have that on your iPod and it's probably in your favorite songs playlist, you have access to listen to that whenever you want. The listener may choose to flip to see what else is on, I love Garth I wouldn't, but someone else might.

So it is changing, it is evolving. Radio is figuring out how to do this, record labels are figuring out what the consumer wants, and all of that big jumbled mess is me talking to some radio guy and trying to figure it out.

{EN} So you have to try to get these radio stations to keep experimenting with new artists and new songs amidst the old staples. Sounds challenging.

{EJ} I'm one of five people for MCA records in promotion that do this, there are five people for Mercury records, and we have the four vice presidents in promotions. This team of us is in contact daily with radio about what's coming up and what's happening. I have a Josh Turner song sitting at number four on the chart right now that most of my stations have in heavy rotation, I have one station that's not spinning it in heavy. As soon as he goes into heavy that's another 20 spins a week and still increasing. As soon as that record stops increasing, or people move it back, we're in trouble. If the record loses spins two weeks in a row, meaning you're minus 28 spins, you're in trouble. Every Monday is your report card. So I have from Sunday at midnight till Saturday at midnight to increase my spins on my stations. And if it's not, that's one week, or un-bulleted. If we lose it again, that song can no longer climb the charts, it's over.

{Note: The Josh Turner song EJ was using for an example here was "(All Over Me" and did eventually make it to number one!}

{EN} So you work weekends… {Laughs}…

{EJ} I work weekends. I send e-mails on Saturdays and Sundays and make phone calls to try and make sure my records are spinning the same or greater than the week before.

{EN} Here's a question from one of my readers. So much of today's popular music has become formulaic. Many of the song arrangements, production, and artists all have a similar sound. Why is there so little diversity in popular music today?

{EJ} It's fascinating, because, obviously we are exposed to a lot of different types of music. There's a bluegrass band called 'Steel Drivers' that we love, and we listen to in town. Could we get that on country radio? Is the guy in Peoria, Illinois, or the guy in Buffalo, New York, or the program director in LA, are they going to relate to that? I think what happens, for instance, there's really only been one Gary Allen. Do they say that Chris Young sounds like Tim McGraw? Do they say that Terri Clark and Sarah Evans sound alike? They are different. There's not really anyone that's been a long like Shania. We can't just sit around and go "*Dierks Bentley is huge. I can't wait to find another Dirks Bentley.*"

But in the same vein a lot of the songwriters, a lot of the same sounds, and the same types of songs all come from here. So when you find something that's working, the tendency is to stick with it. How many songs are we going to hear about whiskey? A gazillion, but it works, I don't know why. We're always talking about a dirt road, or a clay road, you know, the people in rural America.

Radio tends to like to play up tempo songs more than ballads; it's hard playing a lot of ballads, they want to keep the listener entertained and upbeat. Typically, there are only a couple of slow songs a year that will get to number one. Radio is looking to keep people in a good mood, and to keep you listening to the radio. If you're playing a 'death song', maybe death song is a little harsh, or a song that's very deep in meaning and is maybe a slower tempo, and people want to change the station because they don't want to hear that right now, that's not good, radio's most likely is not going to play that. So it *seems* like there is a mass Nashville formula about music. But basically, radio is always looking for a good song, something that people can relate to.

There is an interesting thing I hear in town, because there are so many songwriters and publishers here, it's seems like whoever is hot right now. "Craig Wiseman just wrote a song today, you guys have got to hear this" or "Lee Brice just wrote a song today with Jerrod Nieman", and those songs get passed around. But there's still another 40,000 songs in the catalog that somebody has to listen to and figure out if so-and-so can cut it. That Jerrod Nieman song "Lover Lover" is 16 years old I think, and he cut it. It's a huge hit right now.

{EN} So there are a lot of factors...

{EJ} A lot of factors. And obviously what seems to be working is what radio is looking for. There was nothing like Jamey Johnson's "In Color". It's probably been said before, but never like that. But it was so different that there was a lot of resistance towards that record from radio. "Oh, it's so slow. I don't really like his voice." While some people heard it like "This is amazing". But that song just kept growing. They almost lost that record twice. Like at number 34 on the chart. There was a week where people were making phone calls on a Sunday to try to get the radio station programmers to call in and give it a spin to save it. They almost lost that record, and it never would have been as big of a hit as it is if it lost its chart position.

There's so many tools that we have to monitor, I can pull up Media Base right now and tell you what my station in Dallas did in the last two minutes, how many spins I'm up with Josh Turner to the minute. So we monitor all that, we have a grasp of that, we run it, but as far as the sound, I don't think I really have anybody that sounds like anybody else in our group. And Capitol records doesn't think that they have people like that in their group. And Sony/BMG doesn't think that they have the same artists over and over, they don't have a George Strait in their building, we don't have a Kenny Chesney in this building, and we don't have a Lady Antebellum either. And those are artists that are on each one of those respective labels, . Actually, we do have one Comparison; Easton Corbin is being compared to George Strait. They may sound a little alike, but Easton is from Florida, and while this is a huge compliment to him, he's not trying to be George Strait.

{EN} Singers can sound different, songs can be different, but maybe one of the things that makes a lot of country music sound the same, is possibly the fact the recordings are made by the same session players in the same studios.

{EJ} And I didn't understand that process. It blows me away how those guys will chart the music of a song and just make amazing music. And the session players are so good!

{EN} But the fact that it's the same A-list session players that have been doing this for a few decades, that might be part of the sameness that some people hear. Now lyrically speaking, that's a whole different situation.

{EJ} The thing about country music that people make fun of, it's about somebody's dog dying, it's about some old truck, and whiskey, or trying to get over you, or trying to get you out of my mind, but for some reason it still hits home for a lot of people in different ways.

{EN} There are only so many things that happen in your life.

{EJ} *There are* only so many things that happen, and everybody's been through a breakup, somebody knows about driving that old truck and breaking down. When we start talking about my twitter account didn't work and I can't believe my iPad's broke, when we start getting into that element of songs…{laughs}… where they're relating to a lot of the stuff today…"My new F150 Blackhawk edition broke down, sons of bitches." However you would come up with some sort of song like that.

{EN} They will at some point.

{EJ} Well you know, Brad Paisley touches on that a little bit with "Online", he seems to have somewhat more of a novelty feel, with songs like "Water" and "Waiting on a Woman" *and* "Mud on the Tires." He has such a big fan base and following, and he's keeping it fresh. There is a good example of that. My Favorite Brad Song is "Whiskey Lullaby," it's simply amazing.

{EN} Today, it seems like most newly signed artists get one shot at success, and if they don't take off the label drops them. Whatever happened to the days where record labels developed an artist's or band's careers over a series of album releases?

{EJ} Times are changing, period. We don't sign somebody and then put a record out on them next month. David Nail has been on this label since 2005, 2006. We released his first song in 2008. So there is a developmental period, it's handled by the A&R department (artist and repertoire). They're building the record, they're building the sound, they're putting him with better writers; it's actually a process of developing the artist. We're not selling records like we used to, the return on investment has changed. There is a lot of time and money spent on our artists.

Let's say that I'm a new artist and my first single is just hitting radio. *"This is EJ Bernas, he's a brand-new artist on MCA records. Boy this guy is really great, God I like his music!"* Then the song dies at 44. But radio wants to buy into me; they believe in me, they're giving me my shot. The label is going to help to try to get it played. They're going to find people that believe in me, they're going to find people to play my music, and I'm going to go out and tour the country, meet everybody, play in conference rooms, and try to create excitement about my music. Meanwhile, I'm taking up a spot on that radio station. And as much as you like me, that song doesn't work, and then it's on to the next song and maybe that doesn't work. And by the way, it's my first record deal, these are probably the best 10 songs I've ever heard or wrote in my life.

One of the Best things you can buy is someone's first album. That's why they talk about the sophomore album being a little bit of a letdown in some cases. There's so much time and thought that's going into that first collection of music. These are the best 10 songs we can put on this record. This is what we're going to blow this country wide open with. "EJ *Bernas, you are a great singer, you have a great personality, you're a little chubby, you could lose some weight, but radio is going to love you, these songs are hits. We're going to do a photo shoot on you, we're going to get you some clothes, we're going to get you some interviews, and we're going to work this record real hard. Let's get you on the road, let's get you two players to come and play with you at these radio stations. Here's our first song, we're really excited about it, we really think we have something. My friend, Eric, loves the record; this guy over here loves it.*" And then the song dies at 44 on the chart, kind of a letdown. And by the way, typically we like to release an album when a song is sitting higher on the song charts, ideally, we want that song in the top 10 when that album comes out, so that there is a buzz and people want to buy it.

And by the way, in some cases the process takes two years for that first song to come out, and that song was on the charts, or working, for 18 weeks, before it died at 44. So now were going to regroup and try to do another song. I know that the first song didn't work, but I know you really like EJ, so now we're going to try this song, and this is actually a better song. Then that song dies. So now what do we do? Do we regroup? We just put together the best 10 songs that we think we have with this artist, songs that showcase the artist's talent and should've blown us wide open. And we just failed twice. "God, I love EJ *Bernas, I love him to death. He's so talented; he blows me away when he sings. Why didn't this work?"* I don't know.

EJ in the UMG offices on Commerce Street, downtown Nashville

EN} So a lot of effort is made before a signed artist reaches a point that he or she might be dropped.

{EJ} Since I've been here, there have been two artists on MCA records that I can think of that have been released. Jedd Hughes and a band called Hannah McEwen *(Jamey Hannah, and Jonathan McEwen)*. Jamey Hannah and Jonathan McEwen, their father's were the founding members of the Nitty Gritty Dirt Band. They married twin sisters, so their sons were cousins. It's hard to find a story about an act with any more musical heritage than that. They were arguably two of the most talented people I've ever been around. But it just didn't work for radio. It was almost too cool. Jed Hughes is one of the top guitar players in town, songwriter, in that Keith Urban vein, still plays around town and blows people away. I don't know why that didn't work either.

So we don't look at it like *"Well, time to give up on them, he has no talent,"* it doesn't happen like that. There's a lot of personal and emotional attachment that happens with these artists. You get to know their families. Sometimes it just comes down to simple numbers and economics. We can regroup, and redo, which happens, but some things just don't work. There's a term that was floating around that I heard a while ago, it's called "the spaghetti theory". *"Let's throw out three or four artists, throw 'em against the wall, and see what sticks. Where are we going to hit the lottery, hit the jackpot?*" That just doesn't happen. The days of selling a million records are almost gone. Platinum selling artists used to be more common. Now they're only a handful; artists like Taylor Swift, Lady Antebellum, Kenny Chesney, George Strait, and Brad Paisley usually sell a million. But those numbers used to be three and four million, and now they're barely a million.

{EN} It's a whole new ballgame.

{EJ} In the age of the iPod and iTunes, with the lower return on investment, our market plan has changed drastically. We have a whole department, called new media, which handles all the websites and the digital world, and that's now as important as any other piece of the puzzle here. So it's not like we don't want to give it a shot, it's not as simple as "Hey we got this song, let's put it out there", the whole process has to be done. Because if that song starts romping up the charts and you don't have an album ready to sell, it's suicide because you have a hot song and people may want to buy the album.

So the timing of that has to coincide with everything else. Lee Brice is now on his fifth single with the song "That's Crazy". It finally got to number two, and was on the charts for something like 50 weeks, I mean it's insane. I've worked two of those records, long records, but 50 weeks? I don't think his four other songs ever got into the top 30, but the record label believed in him. They never released an album. So he starts touring and builds a fan base. It's not sometimes as simple as one or two attempts, they may have had two or three other songs, and you just never heard them. Lee has been working hard, building and growing.

{EN} Unless you had a record deal and had it fail you wouldn't really know this.

Here is another question from one of my readers. In this day and age, with 360° deals, low budgets for new artists, and all the control a major label wants, what incentive is there for a developing artist to sign with a major label?

{EJ} That's a misconception. That sounds like somebody who is trying to be an artist, somebody that's out somewhere doing something and has figured out a way to work that. 360 deals aren't so new; we don't have any artists on 360 deals.

{EN} What is a 360 deal?

{EJ} When we invest into developing new artists, we only make money off of album sales. So when you go on tour and someone books you, and they pay you $22,000 to play the Bridgestone Arena in Nashville, and the Arena goes and sells tickets, we don't get any of that touring money. And when you sell $5000 worth of T-shirts and posters, we don't get any of that either. And when you're asked to go on another major tour, and you're being paid to be on that tour, we don't get a piece of that either. The touring life of the artist is their own financial group. The record label only makes money from album sales period.

So a 360 deal means that we're going to take you, grow you, and build you, working as partners. We're going to take 15% of your merch, we're going to take so much of your ticket sales, and make it a 360 deal, we get a piece of all of it. Some artists do that. There are a lot of artists that will say that's crazy.

I don't know the negative side of it. Everybody thinks that the record label benefits and controls each artist's career. If you want to go out and be a jackhole and just make mistakes in life, we're not in control of you; you're the one that's hurting you. And if you want to be rude to people and not meet your fans, maybe you're tired and would rather go right to the bus instead of standing at the merch table selling merch, that's on you, and if we don't sell records we lose out. You may have three top 10 hits, but nobody's buying your records.

We don't have the major control over artists that people think we do. When you're on your radio tour, radio is the number one partner for country music. That is our number one major way of exposing our artists. Not CMT, GAC, or Sirius radio, I mean they're all important, don't get me wrong. Being on Oprah, at some point it takes a way to get you to Oprah, or David Letterman. That stuff is all amazing, but country radio is our biggest add space for commercials. And if we don't sell records, we don't make a dime off you. WE have a marketing department, a finance department, a new media department, a publicity department, and a promotion department all devoted to making artists succeed. It's all a working machine.

{EN} It can still work like that.

{EJ} It can.

{EN} What are three key elements of an artist that you look at right off the bat when they approach you for a record deal?

{EJ} They don't approach us. We don't solicit. There's nobody walking in the front door with a guitar saying "I want to play for you." It just doesn't happen. Some artists start out as songwriters or playing in someone's band, just trying to make a living. Sugarland is from Atlanta, Jamey Johnson is from Alabama, he was kind of in town and had a deal, but he wasn't playing at Tootsies or the Stage.

{EN} He had a writing deal at first.

{EJ} He had a writing deal, he wrote Honky Tonk Badonkadonk. A lot of these people are actually songwriters that write hits for other people. That's one thing that happens. Being a songwriter is not necessarily the most important thing, but it's a huge component. Kenny

Chesney writes music, but he doesn't write all of his music. George Strait doesn't write his hits. So there are a lot of different formulas, but I don't know if there are three equally important things.

There seems to be a lot of really attractive female country singers. If you put a list of these people today against people from 15 years ago and looked at their press photos, it would be night and day. In the age of YouTube, Twitter, Facebook, videos, and constant media overload, obviously the more attractive sometimes wins through. I don't know why. Sometimes I see someone as beautiful for the music they're singing, that makes them beautiful to me.

So, songwriting helps, and, obviously, you've got to be able to sing.

{EN} With the sheer numbers of uber-talented people that move here every year, even having those skills doesn't guarantee you anything.

{EJ} Countless people move to town because this is where they come to become a star. "My dream is to become a country singer and get a major record deal." And while you hear about some people's dreams coming true, there is a gazillion dreams that don't come true. Everybody that's a country artist has gone through their version of American Idol, where it just doesn't happen. And everyone one that has a record deal right now, or a song on the charts, will tell you that they're blessed, and that it's amazing that they finally got to this point.

Some people come in and they say "I'm going to move to town and sing." If you are singing in a bar in Nashville, I would be willing to bet that there are four people in that bar drinking that can sing better than you and don't even want to be stars. So it's one thing to have your mom, dad, aunt, and grandma say "You're one of the best *singers I've ever heard in my life."* It's another thing to get to that point in reality. There is nobody in this town that I've seen or heard that thinks that they're the best thing in country music, its genuine and authentic to each artist in their own way. They are fans like everyone else.

{EN} So how do record labels find their talent? You could say that you kind of hear about them, but you don't actually walk into a bar in town.

{EJ} Here's one example. I took Josh Turner down to Muscle Shoals, Alabama to play a radio show on WXFL, "Muscle Shoals to Music Row Live", a songwriter event that the radio station set up. I was working that radio station; it's just a small market. They sent a limo to Nashville, brought him to Muscle Shoals, put him up in a hotel, and fed him, everything that is completely different than the norm for this kind of thing, all so he could sing his songs for the listeners live on the radio for two hours. At the time, Josh had 'Long Black Train' out, and Muscle Shoals Alabama was one of the leaders of the nation in buying that single. Their Wal-Mart was selling more than anywhere else. It costs a lot of money for our travel, his travel, or his guitar players. So I went to my bosses and said "This radio station wants to do this event, they want to promote our artist, and it's the number one thing. I would like to go down to meet them and I would like to bring Josh." And they said "You know what, we can't say no to that, if Josh's management will agree to it, fine."

They agreed to do it and we rode down there. Singing on the show with him was a guy from Muscle Shoals by the name of Gary Nicholls, who actually got signed to Universal years later. He had a real bluesy voice, raspy voice, sick guitar player too. So he did the show with Josh. They did it like a songwriter round, back and forth. After hearing this kid and meeting him I was blown away. Josh Turner liked him too. After I got back I was listening to the show on my computer and one of the guys from A&R walked by and heard him and said "I love this dude". I was the new kid, it was like my third month of the label, and sure enough, a year and a half later he played one of my charity events that I put on in town, and he ended up getting a record deal. Now it didn't work out with us, Mercury records, but he got that deal from that one event.

If you're out playing music in your local bar, and you're in knee-deep woods, Minnesota, you never know who's sitting in the room. I've been to places with artists where we just go in to have lunch when we're on the road. I've got my senior vice president with me and we walk into a club with our artist, who has his hat on so you can't really tell who he is. There's someone on stage singing and we're there for an hour. We've made the comment ourselves "They have no idea who is in this room right now and what could possibly happen."

If you're going to go on stage and you want to be a star, you need to act like one and *be* a star. If you want to wear your hat backwards because you've had a bad hair day and you're hung-over, god bless you, but that may not be a great first impression, because you get one chance to make that first impression. I know that's a cliché and everybody says it, but boy it is absolutely the truth. If you're wearing the worst god awful shirt because you had no laundry, and you're wearing these flip-flops and you would normally wear boots, maybe you'll never know if someone's watching. People pass through, it happens.

It's one thing to go play because you love doing it. You want to hone your craft, you want to practice, you've got to be on stage, you've got to be able to take requests, you've got to be able to handle this and that. But it's another thing to think "I'm a country singer, I'm going to go to Nashville and light them on fire." Either way, you need to bring it every time you're on stage.

{EN} So it sounds like you never go looking for talent in the bars of Nashville.

{EJ} Here's what happens. To make a living in Nashville, you're singing a three-hour shift. Our artists that we take on the road sing three or four songs. For one thing, nobody knows the music. So around here, you'll have to sing something that's familiar, and relatable. You're covering Alan Jackson, George Strait, Lady Antebellum, or Jamey Johnson songs when you play in Nashville. You're a cover band. And that gets said more often than not. Most can't separate. The really talented people can. More often than not, we're not going to go watch somebody sing six cover songs. We want to know what kind of artist you are, in what direction you are going, what you sing about, what you like. If it's a Mac Davis song from one of his albums from 1970 that nobody knows, but it's something that means something to you, that means something. If you want to sing Lady Antebellum's 'Need You Now' because everybody in the crowd wants to hear it, that's great, you're making a living, but in the same vein it's not who you are.

So it's very hard to separate that. There are people that have deals from being in town. I have a story about a girl that I've really come to like. She moved to town, was here for a couple of years, has friends, she was networking in town, I met her through some friends. So we're friends. She knows I work at a record label. I see her out, we hang out, we're in the same group, I had no idea she was a singer. I didn't even really know what she did. She never told me. I was at a hockey game and she sang the national anthem and blew me away. I respect that more than somebody that's trying to get to know me, or somebody that's in town because they're trying to be an artist. Everybody has a different way of doing it. And not being tainted by some of the stuff in Nashville is a good way to go.

I have someone high in my office right now that says if you're an aspiring country singer *do not* move to Nashville. That's his belief. Hone your craft and start touring. Drive 60 miles to a bar in another town and start playing there, then drive 60 miles to the town past that, and then keep going in a circle. Build a fan base. Play your music. You're going to have to play music that other people like, but then you slip in your own songs here and there, and then sure enough those songs become familiar.

There's a kid that plays in town at the Tin Roof, he plays four hours a night. I go to watch him play. He sings covers. He's very Joe Cockerish, just very smooth. He's got songs that he sings of his own that people know. I played one of his songs for somebody and they said "*Yeah I know that song.*" It was his song; he's just played it so much that people think it's familiar.

So there is many different ways to do it.

{EN} But A&R guys aren't scouring the bars of Nashville looking for talent.

{EJ} There is a dude that plays down at Roberts Western world, he plays guitar on Thursday and Friday nights, he plays the 6 to 10 shift, and he's the sickest guitar player anybody's ever seen. Everybody wants to take him on tour, Keith Urban wanted to take him, Brooks & Dunn wanted to take him. He's just playing in a three-piece band in town because that's what he wants to do. We go and watch him. So there are people that play down here because they love playing down here. He doesn't want to go on the road.

{EN} And there's a lot to be said for that too.

{EJ} He doesn't want to travel 248 days a year. He likes playing around here. He makes his own money. So I'm not taking anything away from anybody that plays on Broadway at all. They're all amazingly talented. Anybody can get up on stage and do something, but that's not the formula. If you're sitting somewhere in rural America and want to make it big, moving to Nashville without being prepared for it is probably the wrong move. "But, nobody's going to find me. I'm in Wilmington, Delaware. They're not going to find me here." Yeah, they might be surprised when nobody finds them even when they're two blocks away.

View of downtown Nashville from the UMG conference room overlooking the rooftop of the Ryman Auditorium below, Lower Broadway, and the Bridgestone Arena.

{EN} Regarding the signing of new talent, is there a specific age group record labels are looking for, or is age inconsequential?

{EJ} I'm 6 foot two and 310 pounds; I'm probably not the prototype of what they're looking for. But it goes without saying you've got artists that are over 40, you've got artists that are mid-20s, you've got some that are in their late 30s just starting out, you've got some that are in their early 30s that are having their first chart success.

{EN} It probably applies a little more to females than males?

{EJ} You could probably say that. Some people look timeless; it's all about who you can relate to. Our country listener, the number one demographic is females 24 to 54, those are the people that listen to country music and buy records, somewhat of our target audience. They're the ones who are judging more so than the guys are.

{EN} Are solo artists more attractive to labels than bands?

{EJ} The solo stuff seems to work easier. We have the Randy Rogers band, there's the Zach Brown Band, and Lady Antebellum. Just an example, a small one but still an example, When you take three people on the road because they're a band, it's harder to focus during interviews, who talks, and who doesn't. We don't look for solos, there's just not an awful lot of the band stuff, there's a lot of duos, there's Brooks & Dunn, Sugarland. I think it just comes down to the music. Gary Allen has had the same band members for five years, but it's still Gary Allen. He knows how important they are to him. But as far as anybody else is concerned, I'm taking Gary Allen to the interview.

{EN} *I would think that legally it's simpler for the record company to sign an individual.*

{EJ} They're all set up as corporations anyway, so it's probably easier to handle schematically, but normally you're dealing with the managers anyway. The Randy Rogers band is set up as their own Corporation. Randy Rogers is the lead singer, but they're a band. They split the money evenly. But Randy is kind of the spokesperson. *"Sure, you do the 7 AM interview. Go ahead Randy!"* I think they kind of have fun with it. What other band do we have? We don't, it's kind of funny.

{EN} Where do you see the recording industry 10 years from now?

{EJ} I'll be in the bar business, easily… {Laughs}… I just think there's going to be changes. There's evolution, figuring out what the next step in this process is. There's always going to be music, and there's always going to be a need for music. You and I could go to your house, and I can pretty much guarantee this even though I've never been to your house, we could go to your house and put an album together in your studio, because you have one in your house.

{EN} You're right, I do.

{EJ} And I know that you can probably play every instrument... {Laughs}...

{EN} Most of them...

{EJ} We could lay down a track, and put something on the Internet tomorrow.

{EN} Millions of people can do this now.

{EJ} There's so much overload. But there are people that grow. The Zach Brown band had a following before they got their deal; they had a big following in Georgia. The Randy Rogers band does 200+ dates a year, I'm not going to say how many millions, but they do multiple millions of dollars a year touring. They have not had a song higher than the top 40 on the charts. We struggled getting some of their songs on the radio, but in the Southwest, they'll sell out 21,000 in Dallas. Sell it out! They had 6000 people at Cowboys in San Antonio three weeks ago for their album release party. And then we could go somewhere up north and maybe do two or three hundred and that's fine, they've got to grow their fan base in the north, and they understand that and they do it. But they're making their money touring.

{EN} That's less crucial then it was 10 years ago.

{EJ} You look at all the different media outlets, and all of the TV channels, and all of the music genre formats, how do you make it happen? The record label? I can tell you the return on investment is not there. In 2009 we sold 50% less CDs and we did in 2002, as an industry. It's dying. Album sales that is, NOT the business of artists. Touring is up. Exposure is up. The number of people making records, making money, and going on the road is climbing. But capturing the money it takes to get that artist to that level is diminishing. It's much less what it was.

Lady Antebellum is having a huge amount of success right now; they're selling a ton of records. If you take that number, let's say they sold 100,000 records. They're going to be millionaires from touring. They're selling out arenas right out. So the record labels, there's always going to be a need for them, I just don't know how big that need will be. We bring you the artists. There's nobody that has a song that's an independent artist that's in the top 20 that I can think of. People have record deals. They're not selling three or four hundred thousand records out of the trunks of their cars, there has to be distribution deals, that's what the labels bring. We're going to have the product, and you exposed out there, and media and all of that wrapped in, we're going to provide that, we're going to get your airplay, we're going to find the best way to get you exposed, and we're going to figure that out together. We know how you want to write. Let me see if I can pair you up with someone writing over here. There's so many different ways to do it.

{EN} There still might be a place for record companies 10 years from now.

{EJ} I think there's always going to be a place; I just don't know how it's all going to factor out. Before, when we had a hit record, on an album sale we used to make about six dollars. Now if we have a hit with an artist, take "Pretty Good at Drinking Beer" by Billy Currington for example, people are buying the single. And then they're going and buying the single they like from Dierks Bentley. And then they're going and buying the single they like from Lady Antebellum, and so on. And they're taking that $10 and spreading it out over four artists. Where before, when you wanted to own that Billy Currington song "Pretty Good at Drinking Beer" you bought the album, and you bought the rest of the album, which you liked and listened to.

{EN} Maybe that's one of the biggest differences between this generation and the previous. When I was growing up, if I heard a song on the radio that I liked, I bought the album, on vinyl…{Laughs}… I took a chance that I'd like the rest of it, but I liked that one song enough and the only way that I could get it was to buy the album.

{EJ} We all used to pirate. I'm 39 years old; I used to sit and listen to the countdown shows with my radio and a tape player and try to record a song. Next week I would come back because I wanted the song before the next one, so I recorded the top 10 song, and I made my own little mix tapes. We would hit record and copy shows so we could listen to the song whenever we wanted to. The idea hasn't changed it's just that now that technology has caught up. I would say it seems like we may have underestimated the power of the

Internet in the beginning, I'm talking 2002 or 2003. It's actually cool to buy music now. In 2003 the attitude was "I'm not paying $.99 for a song. I'm not buying a song." They didn't realize that you weren't paying Shania Twain because you wanted her song, you are paying the 10 people that played on the record, the producer, the publisher who spends money to get the songs played, there's a lot that people didn't understand.

From the Napster days, there's a generation of people that feel like "I'm never paying for music again. Why would *I, I can get it for free. You want me to pay for it?"* You remember when bottled water came out and nobody wanted to buy bottled water? And now we all buy it by the case. People have more diversity regarding what they can get. You used to walk into your local record store and they would have the new albums out, there were four or five to choose from, plus all the other albums. Now there's hundreds and hundreds on iTunes. Are you the featured artist on iTunes this week? Are you the hot selling artist on iTunes this week?

{EN} Do you think that technology has helped the recording industry in anyway?

{EJ} It's exposed artists, its exposed people that would probably never have gotten exposure. You're going to find naysayers; people are believers and nonbelievers on either side. Ultimately I think it hurts the record labels the most.

{EN} Maybe it's helping artists more...

{EJ} It's helping artists, but in the same vein, the money that we spent to launch that artist has to be paid back. So we have to make X amount of money before you're going to start getting your album money. If you get dropped, you don't have to pay us back the money we invested in you. That's our loss. The amount of money that it takes to do that is insane.

{EN} What advice would you offer artists who desire success in the recording industry?

{EJ} I think you have to figure out, in reality, what your desired success level is. What is success for you, what does that mean? Standing up there and receiving your award for new artist of the year? Is it having a song on the charts? Having a song that goes top 30? Is it that you want to sell a million records? Plus it's all changed. Things have changed since I've been here. The Randy Rogers band can't get a song in the top 40, but they just sold 28,000 records last week, in their first week with no song on the air. That was a huge first week. Blake Shelton sold 39k. If you said Randy Rogers and Blake Shelton in the same sentence, well naturally you would think it would be Blake Shelton. So there are different levels of success.

And that's why I keep coming back to saying that I'm really lucky, I understand the gift that I've been given to do what I do and to be in this business. To be on the road last week with Josh Kelley and going in to a Subway in Tacoma, Oklahoma, because we just needed to get something to eat while driving to the next town. I know how important this is to him, I know that I get to share that with him and that I'm his relationship to introduce him to radio. It's my relationships "Josh, this is Mike Kennedy from Kansas City." "Mike, Josh Kelley." "*I've heard so much about you, this is great.*" I get to share that. I don't know what it's like to sit on the street and try to figure out "How can I get in?" I'm very lucky.

There are a million people that will say they're lucky. We've got kids that are coming out of Vanderbilt that are sitting in a mailroom working. They've graduated from Vanderbilt with a 200 and something thousand dollar education, and they're starting at ground level to work their way up in the industry. So I'm very humbled and very appreciative. As far as being an artist? Sometimes I go home to Buffalo to see my family and I walk into a bar and I hear someone singing and think "Man, that person is really, really good. Do they know how good they are? Do they want to go be a star?" I don't know. There's no formula. Everybody's done it the right way. If it was so easy, we wouldn't be here, there would just be a handbook. This is essentially what you're doing. It almost needs to be dos and don'ts.

{EN} Are there some things that people ***shouldn't*** *do if they want to become successful?*

{EJ} There are some things that people should understand and consider. I was picking somebody up on music Row from lunch the other day and I saw a girl wearing a western shirt, boots, jeans, and blond hair, with what looks like her mother, I saw them walk into one record label with a guitar, and then I saw them walk out. The people in the car with me said "They're going door-to-door to try to get a record deal." They walked into the next building, which was WHA, the one next to CURB, it's like a little radio station, and it's not really a record label or a radio station I don't think. She was literally walking door-to-door to try to sing. Definitely don't ever do that! There was a kid that sat out in front of Sony Tree Publishing for three weeks straight, from eight in the morning till five in a lawn chair, singing songs because he wanted to be a writer. Well that's a little nuts. That isn't going to work.

So how do you do it? How do you network? How do you come to be a songwriter? There are songwriter nights all over town nightly. Go and listen to people sing. Go listen to what people write. Writing your own songs and having them appreciated is a huge reward, and maybe even having an artist cut a song. The fact that you want to sing your own songs someday, is probably a pretty good way to come lick your chops. There are three songwriter events tonight in multiple bars. Those are posted all over. The Bluebird is the most famous one. But there are little bars close to songwriter nights, you want to go up and sing two songs, great. You're just going to have to find a way to make a living to do that.

{EN} The thing you said a minute ago about defining your success is such a simple statement, but that really is it. What is really important to you? What are you trying to get out of this?

{EJ} I was friends with The Randy Rogers guys before they were on the label. I was on a bus riding with them when I lived in Dallas and with MCA records and they weren't on any record label. So I've been with those guys. They will play in front of 21,000 people, set records, set beer records, they sold $50,000 worth of beer in a 3000 person venue, they play so many nights a week and they make money. They want to be on the charts. They want to be global. "Hey guys, you just made a ton of money tonight. That's a pretty good night." "Man, we want a hit."

So everybody's got their own goals. Some people may just want to ride the bus, and live that life. Some people might be happy to hear that Tim McGraw is cutting their song. Randy Rogers had a cut on a Kenny Chesney record a while back, Kenny cut one of his songs. There are so many different levels of defining success, but be realistic about it. Everybody's going to tell you "Pick a goal, and you can achieve it if you just dream it." Well there is a lot of luck involved in all of this stuff. When you see someone at an award show and they say "I have wanted to do this since I was a kid, *and I'm finally standing here."* and they're receiving their award and crying, that's genuine, that's not manufactured. But in the same vein, there are 150,000 others that have a worse story than that. Go play music, if you are happy being onstage and making money, then just build it and grow it.

{EN} Maybe create your own little industry and don't worry so much about signing with a major label even.

{EJ} Yeah. I have to be kind of, not political in how I say it, there's independent labels that open and close every week here. Somebody says "I've got $5 million, let's go start a record label. And were committed to bringing the music to the people, we're going to show you the way to do this. We have very smart people with a lot of money. People that have degrees from major universities that want to start a record label and bring you an artist." Well if the music's not there it's not going to work. And then the money runs out. Toby went off and started his own label 'Show Dog'. He tried to do his own thing. He spent his money to try and do it his way, good for him. There is a point when business comes into play. He sunk a lot of money into opening that label. It made sense to partner with Universal again.

It takes a lot of money to run a record label. And we're not here doing it because we want to fail. And we're not still successful because we are failing. There are people that need to be on the right path. Scott Borchetta left a major label and started 'Big Machine Records, found a girl named 'Taylor Swift'. She was 15 years old and five foot 11, and all of a sudden, he's arguably one of the brightest record labels and town. He's got Taylor Swift, Rascal Flats, Jimmy Wayne, Justin Moore, who's had some great success on the charts early on, and he got a couple that haven't worked out. They opened a second label 'Valerie', they now have Reba.

Scott Borchetta left to do his own thing. So there are opportunities to not be at a major record label and work and be successful. It's been proven, but there are a million of those that have failed as well.

"But I'm not going to get any bigger sitting in Buffalo. I've played in front of 800 people, there's no more room." Okay, I get that. Get your website going; go to the next town over, figure out how to start building it there. And then go to the next town. If you're going to move to Nashville, great, but it's going to take a while once you get here. Kenny Chesney was in town for 10 years before anybody would talk to him. 10 years. He's the biggest star on the planet right now next to Taylor Swift, as far as our world is concerned.

Chapter 4

Nashville Institutions

"The hallmark of our age is the tension between aspirations and sluggish institutions." — John W. Gardner

To better understand the Nashville music industry, it is important to understand some of the long-standing institutions that are unique to this place. The Grand Ole Opry, the A-Team, the Musicians' Union, BMI and ASCAP, and the Good Ol' Boy network are among the most influential and powerful forces that impact the lives of many in Music City. If you plan to become successful working as a musician in Nashville, it is important to understand a little about these organizations and the impact they have.

While the Grand Ole Opry, ASCAP, BMI, and the Musicians' Union are obvious and visible corporate entities, the A-Team and the Good Ol' Boy network are much less obvious and essentially invisible on the surface. All of these institutions have been around for decades and play an important role in the Nashville music industry.

Rhett Akins on the Opry, 2006 *Opry photos courtesy Kelly Normand*

The Grand Ole Opry

"The band kicked off a song, and I tried to take the microphone off the stand. In my nervous frenzy, I couldn't get it off. That was enough to make me explode in a fit of anger. I took the mike stand, threw it down, then dragged it along the edge of the stage. There were 52 lights, and I wanted to break all 52, which I did." — Johnny Cash, on the night he was asked not to return to the Grand Ole Opry, 1993

For many, The Grand Ole Opry is perhaps one of the most prestigious and desirable places at which to perform in the world. It has been written about in countless books, mentioned in numerous songs, co-starred in many movies, and remains an inspiration to millions of country music aficionados. For artists and musicians, it remains an intimidating stage to ever set foot upon.

I have met many singers and aspiring artists whose biggest goal in life was to perform at The Grand Ole Opry. Dreaming this is one thing; getting to actually do it is another. While it is not an impossible feat to accomplish, getting to play at the Opry is not something that performers choose to do, for it is the Opry that does the choosing.

There are two locations for the Grand Ole Opry - the world famous Ryman Auditorium located on Fifth Avenue in downtown Nashville, and its modern counterpart the Grand Ole Opry House, located at the Opryland complex northeast of downtown on Briley Parkway. From 1943 to 1974 the Ryman Auditorium was home to the Grand Ole Opry, although musical performances have been happening there since shortly after the building was constructed in 1892. In 1974, the Opry moved to its current location in the Grand Ole Opry House at Opryland. Since 1999, during the winter months, the Opry has returned to the Ryman.

The artists and repertoire of the Opry have helped define American country music in many ways over the years, as hundreds of new stars, superstars, and legends have graced her stages. The Opry's live radio broadcast on WSM radio in Nashville, Tennessee, is the oldest continuous radio program in the United States, having been broadcast regularly since November, 1925. Many artists are made official members of the Opry, and this grants them exclusivity in what is perhaps country music's most elite club.

There is a staff band of A-list players that back most of the artists performing at the Opry. The current lineup of veteran Nashville musicians features:

Eddie Bayers and Mark Beckett - drums
Larry Paxton - bass
Kerry Marx - electric guitar
Jimmy Capps - acoustic guitar
Mark Casstevens - acoustic guitar
Tim Atwood - piano
Tommy White - steel guitar
Hoot Hester – fiddle
The Carol Lee Singers – harmony vocals: Carol Lee Cooper, Norah Lee Allen, Rod Fletcher, Dennis McCall

As is preferred by the Opry, many artists will use this house band to back their performance, while some will bring a couple of key musicians from their own bands and add them to the core band of staff Opry players. If an artist has enough popularity or clout, they may be allowed to bring in their entire band if they desire, and use no Opry players. Most artists' performances at the Opry are limited to two or three songs, as they will be sandwiched between several other artists on any given show.

For an artist to perform at the Opry, they must be requested to do so by the Opry. For a musician that isn't a part of the staff band to be able to perform at the Opry, they must be working for an artist that is requested to play the Opry. If you're an aspiring artist and it is your dream to perform at the Opry, you'll have to wait until your career gets you there, as there are no Saturday afternoon talent shows on this stage. For musicians it might be a slightly more reasonable goal, as there are many artists who regularly perform on the Opry whom players could potentially be employed by.

Opry dressing room before a performance

From my experiences, the most intimidating part about playing the Opry has always been performing with the A-team players more so than for the audience of 4400 or so out front. For the most part, the audience is comprised of tourists who won't notice a mistake or two. That's not the case with the A-Team guys. If you even break wind they'll likely hear it.

Playing the Opry for the first time can be one of the most nerve-racking experiences musicians and artists will ever have. There are no sound checks or rehearsals for about 90% of the performances; it is typically "throw and go." A typical Opry performance slot goes something like this.

Artists and musicians wait side stage prior to their performance slot. The artist currently performing finishes his or her last song and walks off during the applause. During this applause, the next artist and band members will be walking out to their spots. While the MC is making a few brief announcements, the players will have about 20 or 30 seconds to plug in to the provided backline and get situated. They often won't even have enough time to ask for a monitor level adjustment and will sometimes convey their needs to the monitor engineer via subtle hand signals after the song has begun. Before they know it, their two songs are over before they even started.

If you ever get to play the Opry, regardless of how well (or poorly) your performance is received, you will be granted one of the highest orders of bragging rights in the music world. For you will be forever able to begin a story or two with "When I played the Opry...."

One time, when I played the Opry....

Thomas Ryman – Revival Of A Steamboat Captain

Thomas Green Ryman was born south of Nashville, Tennessee, on October 12, 1841, and grew up learning about river life in the steamboat era by fishing with his father. After his father's death in 1880, he became the main provider for his mother, brother, and three sisters. Although he could barely read and write, he had became a successful businessman over the years, eventually owning a fleet of steamboats and riverfront saloons.

By 1885 his fleet of steamboats had grown to 35, whiskey had become his main cargo (you could buy a glass of it for a nickel on one of his leased out riverboat bars), and riverboat gambling rounded out his lucrative enterprises. Although his character has been defined by some as tough and shrewd, he was also known to show compassion as well, often helping the needy by providing them with coal. He was even known to pay for his employees' funerals and take care of their families.

While Captain Ryman was getting rich from his steamboat and riverfront bar endeavors, traveling evangelists were doing their part to disrupt these kinds of operations. In May of 1885 one of these traveling evangelists, Samuel Porter Jones from Cartersville Georgia, held a weekly tent revival in Nashville. On May 10th Jones was holding one of these revivals when Ryman stopped in with some of his friends intending to heckle the preacher, as these evangelists were ultimately bad for business. Captain Ryman was apparently deeply affected by this sermon and was "converted" by the end of the service. In fact he was so moved by this evangelist that he decided to construct a building for Jones' revivals to have a more permanent home.

The story goes that from that day on Tom Ryman became a very religious man, never to sell liquor again, and made "saving souls" and cleaning up Nashville his life's mission. In 1889 construction began on what would be called the Union Gospel Tabernacle and the project was finished by 1892. The huge auditorium cost $100,000 and boasted excellent sound quality and unique architecture, quickly becoming the most iconic building in Nashville.

Captain Tom Ryman died on December 23, 1904, and his funeral was held in the great Tabernacle he had created. It was suggested during the service by none other than Sam

Jones that the great Union Gospel Tabernacle be renamed in honor of Captain Ryman, and to a standing ovation "The Ryman Auditorium" was born.

A variety of musical concerts had already taken place in the auditorium by the time of Ryman's passing and its reputation of being a great performance hall was growing. By 1943 the Grand Ole Opry weekly concert and radio broadcast had outgrown its previous location and would begin its 31 year reign at the Ryman. Even though the Opry program had been well established prior to this point, it was, perhaps, Thomas Ryman's vision to build this great structure for the community he loved that would ultimately create the environment in which the roots of country music would flourish.

Statue of Thomas Ryman at the main entrance to the Ryman Auditorium

The House That Tom Built

RYMAN AUDITORIUM

3A 209
BIRTH OF BLUEGRASS
In December 1945, Grand Ole Opry star Bill Monroe and his mandolin brought to the Ryman Auditorium stage a band that created a new American musical form. With the banjo style of Earl Scruggs and the guitar of Lester Flatt, the new musical genre became known as "Bluegrass." Augmented by the fiddle of Chubby Wise and the bass of Howard Watts (also known as Cedric Rainwater), this ensemble became known as "The Original Bluegrass Band," which became the prototype for groups that followed.
TENNESSEE HISTORICAL COMMISSION

RCA
THE RCA RECORDS LABEL
BMG
RCA
07863-67462-2
ELVIS' GOLDEN RECORDS
ELVIS PRESLEY

The A-Team

"We had absolutely no idea that we were making history. We were just doing a job." — Bob Moore

When you hear someone referring to the A-Team in Nashville, they are referring to a group of 60 or so A-list session players that play on the majority of the recordings that come out of Music City. Whether you listen to a recording by Alan Jackson, George Strait, Shania Twain, or Sugarland, more often than not, you are essentially listening to the same band. The roots of this band can be traced back to a collective of studio aces whose various different groupings have been largely responsible for the Nashville sound since the 50s. Today, modern day A-team players like Brent Mason, Michael Rhodes, and Eddie Bayers are continuing this tradition, and while they may be household names within the Nashville music industry, they remain basically obscure to the countless millions who have bought the albums on which they have played.

The roots of the modern day A-Team began way back in 1947 when Castle Studios became Nashville's first established recording studio. During this time period, Chet Atkins became the main producer for RCA Records, while Owen Bradley was the head producer at Decca. These prolific producers sought out musicians who were highly skilled and extremely adaptable to play on the records they produced. Many of the musicians they chose had previously worked on the road with country artists of the day.

The cast of the original A-Team included bassist Bob Moore; guitarists Hank Garland, Grady Martin, Harold Bradley, and Ray Edenton; drummer Buddy Harman; pianists Hargus "Pig" Robbins and Floyd Kramer; fiddler Tommy Jackson; steel guitarist Pete Drake; saxophonist Boots Randolph; harmonica player Charlie McCoy; and vocal groups the Jordanaires, the Anita Kerr Singers, the Leah Jane Singers, The Nashville Edition (who were also the staff group on Hee Haw), and the Cherry Sisters. These musicians quickly found that studio work was much more lucrative and often more exciting than touring. One session could be with Patsy Cline, another might be with Elvis Presley, George Jones, Roy Orbison, and the list goes on.

They worked a four session day, 5 to 6 days a week. The 3 to 4 hour session blocks began at 10:00 AM, 2:00 PM, 6:00 PM and 10:00 PM with this same basic schedule being followed today (although typically without the 10:00 PM slot). There were many musical innovations and contributions to the Nashville sound made by the A-Team such as the tic-tac bass, the use of pedal steel guitar, and the invention of the Nashville number system by Jordanaires member Neal Matthews. This musical shorthand system is based on traditional Western harmony and assigns numbers to chords, allowing musicians to transpose keys and learn new songs quickly. Upon its introduction it spread quickly throughout Nashville and beyond.

Over the next several decades this original A-Team slowly morphed into a modern day version, with a few of its original members still involved in recording. While this is not an official list, and there are certainly other session players in Nashville that play on major recordings, the following list comprises the bulk of the modern day A-Team.

Drummers:
Eddie Bayers
Lonnie Wilson
Greg Morrow
Paul Leim
Chris McHugh
Shannon Forrest
Nick Buda
Brian Fullen

Bassists:
Michael Rhodes
Glenn Worf
Kevin Grantt
Mike Brignardello
Jimmie Lee Sloas
Mike Chapman

Fiddlers:
Rob Hajacos
Glen Duncan
Stuart Duncan
Aubrey Haynie
Larry Franklin
Joe Spivey

Guitarists:
Brent Mason
Brent Rowan
JT Corenflos
Tom Bucovac
Troy Lancaster
Jimmy Capps
Larry Beaird
Adam Shoenfeld
Jeff King
Kerry Marx
Chris Leuzinger

Keyboardists:
Gordon Mote
John Hobbs
Gary Prim
Steve Nathan
Michael Rojas
Katherine Styron
Tim Acres

Steel Guitarists:
Paul Franklin
Michael Douchette
Mike Johnson
Bruce Bouton
Dan Dugmore
Sonny Garrish
Robby Turner

Harmony Singers:
John Wesley Ryles
Wes Hightower
Judy Rodman
Michael Black
Thom Flora
Chip Davis
Perry Coleman
Jennifer O'Brien
Vicki Hampton

A-Team list disclaimer: I was hesitant to create this list at all as I feared it would be impossible to determine all of the players who deserve to be on it. It is simply a starting point of reference for all the album credit readers of the world. If you are an A-Team musician and I have left you out, please accept my apologies.

There is also a short list of A-list musicians that play less commonly used instruments, such as dobro, mandolin, percussion, banjo, harmonica, saxophone, and tuba, etc. (Okay, maybe not the tuba.)

During the 1990s the Nashville music industry experienced a recording boom which kept the A-Team players busy day and night, year round. In the early 2000s, this pace slowed as the digital download craze cut into album sales resulting in fewer high budget major-label recordings. Even with a diminished pace, most of these highly skilled players are still in demand. If you research the performance credits on most modern Country, Gospel, Christian, and Pop recordings made in Nashville, you will find that it is the A-Team session players who played on the tracks.

Owen Bradley became vice president of Decca Records in 1958 and handpicked many of Nashville's original "A-Team." In a "Quonset hut" attached to a house he owned on 16th Avenue South, the birth of a more commercial style of country music took place. Bradley and his A -Team produced recordings that helped launch country artists such as Patsy Cline, Loretta Lynn, and Conway Twitty, among others. A park in his honor can be visited on Demonbreun Street, at the northern end of Music Row.

Nashville Association of Musicians

The Musicians' Union

Jake: My name is Jacob Stein. I'm from the American Federation of Music. I've been sent to see if you gentlemen are carrying your permits.
Tucker McElroy: Our what?
Jake: Your union cards. May I see your cards please?
Tucker McElroy: Well, suppose we ain't got no union cards and go in there and start playin' anyway? Whatcha gonna do about that? You gonna stop us, Stein? Ha. You're gonna look pretty funny tryin' to eat corn on the cob with no fuckin' teeth! — from the movie 'The Blues Brothers'

The American Federation of Musicians was founded in 1896 and is an international union organized in the United States and Canada with 90,000 current members. The Nashville Association of Musicians, or AFM Local 257, was founded in 1902 and is a part of that union. As stated on their website, they are "currently representing over 2600 of Music City's finest musicians, including the Nashville Symphony, studio players, road musicians, singer/songwriters, arrangers, and producers."

The AFM's main website lists many benefits of being a member, stating that the union "can negotiate agreements and administer contracts, procure valuable benefits and achieve legislative goals". Their services include negotiating wages and working conditions to maintain minimum standards for AFM members involved in recording, TV shows, music videos, commercials, films, video games and traveling theatrical productions. Members may also earn credits toward retirement, and, in some situations, health care is also available. There is also a referral service offered.

The Musicians' Union, like many unions, can be a source of great debate. While some would argue that the union helps protect musicians' rights, ensuring they are paid properly for recording sessions and TV appearances, others would argue that while in many cases this may be true, in general, the union only helps those in the upper echelon of the music industry and does virtually nothing for the majority of musicians who never reach that level. If you are working a union controlled or "on the card" recording session, as are most major-label sessions, the union ensures that you will be paid union scale wages (see the chapter on studio musicians for a breakdown). If you are performing on the Opry or a televised event, they will make sure you are paid union scale for these performances as well.

The state of Tennessee is a "right to work" state (there is a state law that prohibits required union membership of workers); therefore you do not need to belong to the union to work in the Nashville music industry. However, if you are living and working here as a professional musician and plan on being here for the long haul, there can be some long-term benefits to becoming a member, such as the health care benefits and pension plan.

As stated in previous chapters, the pay scale for musicians working in the Nashville nightclubs is often less than that of other cities, and this area is essentially outside the realm of the union at the present time. An oversaturation of musicians has created a supply and demand problem that works in favor of the nightclubs. As long as hungry, work starved musicians are willing to work for low wages, the nightclub owners will take advantage of this fact. If enough musicians could organize and boycott performing at these clubs that pay poorly, the wage standard *could* improve. To take this a step further, if enough musicians could make this stand *and* join the union, the union could negotiate on their behalf. There is strength in numbers. Just one more person joining the union isn't going to change this, but if more musicians were to join and become proactive with issues such as this, things might improve long-term.

One of the biggest problems for musicians just starting out in Nashville can be a lack of income. Currently the annual membership fee for the musician union is around $300, and this is paid every January. That's a lot of money for poor, struggling musicians to come up with during the slow time of year, and this fact will ultimately prevent a lot of musicians from ever joining. 2600 union members from a city that has potentially many thousands of working musicians is a fairly small number. If the union's membership can ever increase substantially, it will potentially be in a better position to improve the working conditions and wages for *all* of the musicians working within the Nashville music industry.

The PROs (Performance Rights Organizations)

"Music is everybody's possession. It's only publishers who think that people own it." — John Lennon

ASCAP, BMI and SESAC are the three Performance Rights Organizations in America, more commonly referred to as P.R.O.s. These organizations represent many American songwriters and music publishers regarding the licensing of copyrighted musical works. They are responsible for the collection and payment of performance royalties. To understand the finer points of how this works, it is necessary to understand the difference between the different types of royalties collected for copyrighted musical works.

Performance royalties are royalties that are paid when a song is played on the radio, television, satellite or Internet radio; used as background music for businesses such as hotels, bars, restaurants, etc; used by DJs in clubs as dance music; or performed live in clubs, concert halls, and other venues by musical groups - essentially, any time music is performed publicly. (Copyright law explains what is meant by "publicly", and most situations where music is used to enhance a business.)

Mechanical royalties are royalties paid from the sale of music in a physical medium such as CDs and DVDs, digital mediums such as downloads, and subscription services (like Rhapsody) that offer on-demand streaming and limited downloads. The majority of these royalties is collected by the Harry Fox Agency, while a smaller portion is collected by the American Mechanical Rights Society (AMRA).

Royalties And Licensing For Film, Television, And Other Situations That Pair Music With A Visual Medium

Note: While song licensing for TV and film does not always necessarily pertain to the PROs, as it is related, I felt it is still pertinent enough to be addressed here.

Not all music that is used in TV shows or films are paid royalties. Some situations pay performance royalties, some offer buyouts, while some offer an upfront fee plus royalties. Everything is negotiable via contracts, and your contract will determine what your back end results will be (if there is a back end involved). If your contract states that you will be receiving performance royalties if the film is played on TV (broadcast, cable, or satellite) or in international cinemas, then this is handled by the PROs. (No performance royalties are paid from films played in U.S. cinemas.)

Licensing Of Music For TV And Film Involves Two Different Kinds Of Licenses And Fees:

Synch Licenses And Synch Fees

TV shows, films, media entities, and any situation that pairs music with a visual medium will acquire the right to use a song with the purchase of a **synch license** (music synchronization license). The synch license will cover a specific period of time and will stipulate how long the song can be used. **A synchronization fee** is a flat fee that is paid to the owner of the PUBLISHING of the song who must first agree to this fee and the terms set forth in the synch license in order to grant the right to synchronize the song to picture.

Master Licenses And Master Fees

The Master fee is paid to the owner of the MASTER version of the song. There are a lot of different versions of a given song, but this is the fee paid to the owner of the MASTER. For example – if a record label paid for the recording of the song, then the record label has to agree on the amount and the terms in the license in order to grant the right to use that version of the song in the film/tv show, etc.

If one of these two companies does not agree, the deal is off the table.

The PROs collect performance royalties by negotiating blanket licenses with all entities that perform music publicly, whether for profit or not (even nonprofits have to pay this). These fees can range from a couple of hundred dollars for small businesses to millions of dollars for big broadcasting companies. Radio and television broadcasts are then monitored by the P.R.O.s to determine the amount of "plays" a given song receives, which then determines how much to pay the publishers and songwriters. There are other mechanisms in place to monitor what is played in live venues.

ASCAP (American Society of Composers, Authors and Publishers) is a not-for-profit member owned performing rights organization which is controlled by composers, lyricists, songwriters and music publishers. Anyone can join, and writers and publishers can apply for a membership online. There is a one-time application fee of $35.

BMI (Broadcast Music Inc.) is also a not-for-profit performing rights organization and will also allow anyone to join. Membership is free, and writers and publishers can apply online. ASCAP and BMI control the vast majority of songs, with SESAC controlling the rest.

SESAC (Society of European Stage Authors & Composers) handles a smaller share and operates differently. They typically choose fewer and bigger writers and go after their royalties more aggressively.

If you join a PRO, you must sign a contract that states you won't affiliate with the other two PROs; however, by doing so, you are not bound for life and can switch PROs in the future. These organizations offer different services for their writers and publishers which vary from one PRO to the next, such as showcases, songwriter workshops, instrument insurance, and consultations. If you are a new writer, they *will* talk to you and help point you in the right direction.

Song Ownership

It is noteworthy to mention that songwriters don't have to have a publishing deal to belong to these organizations. Many writers set up their own publishing companies. Also, you own your entire song until you give it a way or sign with a publishing company. The standard model for most writers and publishers is a 50/50 split. (For more on how this works read the chapter on songwriters on page 81, or the Rhett Akins interview on page 219.) Until you sign a contract you own 100% of your song. Some successful writers that are affiliated with the PROs don't have a publishing deal at all, though it is pretty rare. Also, literally every songwriter who expects to ever get paid public performance royalties belongs to one of the PROs.

Song Registration

Once you are a member of one of the PROs you can begin to register your songs with them which will allow you to collect performance royalties if and when any of your material starts to circulate (registering with the copyright office is a separate activity). One of the biggest problems the PROs have regarding paying writers and publishers is inaccurate documentation (song registration). Regardless of having a publishing deal or not, you can and should register your songs to ensure you will get paid for your work, and this can be done online. Publishers don't register every song they deal with, so it will be in your best interest to make sure all the bases are covered.

If you are a songwriter and plan to earn a living from your craft, understanding the mechanics of these organizations, and joining one will help ensure that one day you might be paid for your work. You should also take some time to research and understand the current copyright laws.

BMI building at the northern end of Music Row, downtown Nashville

The Good Ol' Boy Network & The Buddy System

"What's the difference between a good ol' boy and a redneck? Jeff Foxworthy is a good ol' boy, Larry the Cable Guy is a redneck." - Anonymous

Historically speaking, "the good ol' boy network" has been a broadly used phrase used to describe a system of social networking that exists among certain communities and social groups. Many will argue that the term has its roots in the American South; however, these networks can be found almost anywhere within the Western world. The term has endured some negative connotations over the years, as the traditional stereotype implied the inclusion of white Anglo Saxon males and the exclusion of all others. In some places it is believed that this network still exists, exerting influence over local government, business, and law enforcement, in order to preserve traditional power structures.

I believe there are many variations of the good ol' boy network, and that the term is no longer limited to race or gender. The term can mean different things to different people and does not always have to imply negative connotations. As a musician living and working in Nashville, I have found that the good ol' boy network is a more loosely defined term that pertains to the different networks or "cliques" in which most working musicians belong.

Within the Nashville music industry there is a clique or group of cliques within each facet of the industry. There is a studio musician clique, a road band clique, a songwriter clique, etc., and there are many cliques within each of those cliques. If you're a touring musician, you are probably close to some, if not all of the members on that tour. You are in that clique and, along with everybody else in it, can benefit from those relationships. If you're a songwriter you probably work with a co-writer or group of co-writers on a regular basis.

In whatever working situation you are involved with, there is likely a group of coworkers with whom you share some common ground. When you need help with a project, a referral or advice, etc., you are most likely to turn to the people you work with every day. This network, or clique, is *your* good ol' boy network. You can look at the Nashville music industry as one huge network comprised of many smaller networks within it. These smaller networks are all separate entities, yet many of them are also interconnected.

For musicians, your clique or network is often like an extended family. You will tend to look out for your family, and they will in turn look out for you. If you hear of some work being offered that you can't do, you might first offer it to someone within your group. The others in your clique will usually do the same for you. A sense of protectionism can often exist in these situations. For instance, if someone within your group hears that another within that group is about to be fired, or that somebody is trying to steal his gig, he will usually pass that information along to warn his cohort of the imminent danger. This sense of protectionism can also sometimes create exclusion. For instance, A-Team session players will want to maintain control over their accounts, therefore being less likely to invite newcomers into their clique. If a group of players has some regular time slots at a club on Broadway, they will do their best to hold that spot as long as possible. They don't want anybody else to take their gig.

There is one more thing about these networks in Nashville; you can fall out of a clique just as fast if not faster than you can get into one. So whatever you do, don't screw up!

Women in the Nashville Music Business - By Judy Rodman

With the connotations associated with 'chick singer', the 'good ol' boy' network can indeed feel, well, 'boy'centric. Of course, there have always been female 'good ol' boys'. These women, such as Connie Bradley, Leah Jane Berinati, Dolly Parton and Francis Preston, learned to work within the reality of the male network and became legends. However, from what I've seen and experienced, being female in the Nashville music business usually means you work with a feeling of isolation and a sense of always having a career in a precarious position. New chick singers have regularly been told by the good ol' boy doorkeepers holding the major label keys that only male singers sell. Hmm. Now we have Taylor Swift on an "Indie" label and the demise of one major label after another. The times, they are a-changing.

Now women in leadership positions of the Nashville music industry are forming true community. With female business groups (songplugger group "Chicks With Hits" comes to mind) and equality-respecting groups like "Indie Connect", women are creating their own cliques that are male-inclusive but female-respecting. There is less tolerance for dismissive patronizing. For instance, when I produce I tend to use musicians and singers who know what I can do and for whom I no longer need to 'audition' my production skills. Now more than ever it's possible that a woman could make or break you in Nashville's music business. If you want to do well, be a respectful and trustworthy buddy to her... she could be the best 'good ol' boy' you'll ever meet.

Judy is a vocal coach, an award-winning recording artist, stage and television performer, hit songwriter, top session singer, producer and vocal consultant. www.judyrodman.com

Chapter 4

Nashville Specifics

"I like to sing. I write music. Country songs. You have to if you're in Nashville. It's part of the lease. You sign a lease that says, I will write country songs and pay my rent on time." — Jim Varney

If you are a musician and considering moving to Nashville, there are a lot of things you should know and consider in order to make your move successful and the experience of relocating as painless as possible.

Nashville is a big city. The Metropolitan area currently has a population of about 1.5 million people and covers an area of 533 square miles making it the nation's second-largest city in terms of landmass. It has a massive and often confusing network of roads which can make it difficult for many newcomers to get around.

The culture is unique as this place is a melting pot of a constant influx of people migrating here from all over the world. The music business centered here combined with a low cost of living makes Music City an attractive destination for many.

The climate can be harsh as the city is located in a valley which causes excessive humidity during the long summer months. Some locals refer to the Nashville metro area as "the valley of sickness" as the humidity and stagnant air can cause many people to develop sinus and allergy problems. As we are located on the outside edge of the ever expanding tornado alley, additional hazards from extreme weather are periodically a factor. We are also located right in the middle of the Bible belt.

All of this you will learn from experience once you are here and the perspective will be different for everyone. One of the biggest hurdles you will need to overcome is the mere process of relocating. If you are moving here from far away, many of you will be leaving your friends, family, job, and peers behind. You might feel like a fish out of water. It will be like starting a whole new life.

In this part of the book we will explore some specifics for musicians regarding relocating, adjusting, living, working, and getting around in Music City. Nashville is a unique and interesting place, and if you are considering moving here, I highly recommend a visit first.

Statue at the "Roundabout" on Demonbreun Street, Nashville

Culture Shock

"I believe in a long, prolonged, derangement of the senses in order to obtain the unknown." — Jim Morrison

For me, relocating to Nashville was like starting a new life, and this is the case for many. I spent my first 35 years living and working in New England, and all of my friends and family, literally everyone I knew, lived there. My decision to move to Nashville was solely based on my music career aspirations. I knew I would miss New England and all of the people I knew there once I was gone, but I didn't realize to what extent until much later. You never realize what you have until it's gone.

I was fortunate enough to have a support cast come with me, as my wife and son were a part of this relocation. We packed up all of our belongings, said our goodbyes, and began to drive away from our native land in a U-Haul truck packed to the gills. Many emotions ran through me like waves as we began to put miles between ourselves and our old home - fear, sadness, excitement, anxiety, accompanied by a sense of mystery and adventure. Driving off that day, I felt like my life was a novel, and I had just finished reading the last pages. I then immediately grabbed a new book but when I opened it there was nothing but blank pages. I knew very little about Nashville and what the future would hold for me there, and the feeling was both unsettling and empowering.

The early days of living in Nashville for my family and I were the toughest to endure. Gone was all familiarity as the people and daily scenery I had grown up with were now absent. The familiar backdrop of life that I had grown so accustomed to was now replaced with a new landscape and nothing but strangers everywhere. My daily routines, once taken for granted and almost comforting, now had to be completely reinvented.

This town that would be our new home in our new life was called Gallatin, a suburb of Nashville located about 30 miles to the north of the city. It's a medium-sized town not unlike many towns across the land. It has stores, businesses, schools, people, and its own set of problems just like any place else. Missing from this town was familiar faces, a street name that I recognized, or a way of life that I yet understood. I felt this sense of confusion and isolation on an even greater scale when I made weekly trips to downtown Nashville to solicit work.

Over time, I slowly began to learn this place. I got a map and just drove around for a couple of days to try to get a sense of where things were. My wife and I went out on the town at night to make new friends and begin my insertion into the music scene. We quickly found that downtown Nashville at night was a flurry of activity, with nightclubs lining both sides of Broadway, a few more on Second Avenue, and yet even more on Printers' Alley where we quickly became regulars at the Fiddle and Steel Guitar Bar. We were relieved and encouraged to find that most people in this new musician world were friendly and easy to talk to. Most of the other musicians living and working in Nashville are also transplants, and this fact combined with a desire to earn a living in the music industry gives almost all musicians some common ground. Ever so slowly Nashville was beginning to feel like home.

The culture and pace of life in middle Tennessee is much different than that of my native New England. Life in New England is very fast-paced. Everybody drives too fast, people can be overly aggressive and pushy, and an overall sense of hurry up and wait exists just beneath the surface. Life in Nashville and especially the Nashville music industry *seems* to go at a much slower pace. People drive slower (although sometimes not particularly well), and there is a more laid back way of life here in general as there is throughout much of the south. For the most part, people are outwardly friendly and will gladly engage in conversation, and some folks will actually help you without expecting something in return. At the same time there is an extreme sense of competition for those involved in the music industry, and *this* always exists just beneath the surface. At first glance it can seem as if life may be happening in slow motion. Don't be fooled; although many people's careers might be stuck in slow motion, life is still zipping by.

For musicians working or hanging around in the Nashville nightclubs, there can be a sense that you are on a permanent job interview, and a unique set of social behaviors exists because of this fact. One of the first things I noticed when I first moved to town was that the only people who ever dance in the nightclubs are tourists, with a few exceptions of course. Most musicians (regardless of gender) just don't dance, even if it's their night off. Perhaps they think it will harm the image they are trying to put forth to prospective employers. In the Northeast, it wasn't uncommon to see girls dancing with each other to a band or jukebox in a local nightclub. In the mainstream Nashville nightclubs this is much less common. In the Northeast encountering someone who was rude, arrogant, loudmouthed, or boisterous in a nightclub setting was often par for the course. If you are a musician trying to fit into the Nashville music scene, this kind of behavior won't get you very far.

In many other cities and small towns across America, musicians are the exception not the rule. Here in Nashville everybody's a musician, and the fact that you might be an above-average guitarist, drummer, or vocalist doesn't hold much weight, as there are thousands of skilled musicians in this town. Don't be surprised if you see somebody famous hanging out at a bar or shopping in a local supermarket; Nashville is home to many superstars. If and when you do encounter a celebrity, don't gherm them, as a year or two later you could find yourself auditioning for them and possibly playing in their band. Never lose sight of the fact that there's no such thing as a second first impression.

So welcome to Nashville. Just settle in, work towards becoming comfortable in your new home, and try to enjoy the ride.

Tornado siren on Church Street

Climate

"Don't knock the weather; nine-tenths of the people couldn't start a conversation if it didn't change once in a while." — Kin Hubbard

Nashville has a humid subtropical climate which means we have hot, humid summers and cool to cold winters. Our winters are short, and our summers are long. We are also located in the recently expanded, newly improved tornado alley, (Tennessee is now the deadliest state in the U.S. with regards to tornadoes.)

Winter: Although December and January are typically our coldest months with typical daytime highs in the 30s to 40s and lows in the 20s, it is not uncommon to have a few 60° and 70° days in the middle of winter. It will occasionally snow during this time of year, but more often wintertime precipitation comes in the form of rain, freezing rain, and the occasional ice storm. If and when it does snow, the entire state literally shuts down, as the state and city governments are ill-prepared for it. Snow is so rare that most people have little experience driving in it, and this causes gridlock on the roadways. If it snows, stay home.

Springtime temperatures are mild as well, and by March, daytime temperatures are usually already into the 60s. Accompanied by this warmer air is our primary tornado season. During the months of March, April, and May, the threat of severe weather is at its highest. In addition to the possibility of tornadoes, high winds, hail, flooding, electrical storms, and torrential rainstorms can and will periodically occur. The good news is that the local weather forecasters do a great job predicting the storms. Just be sure to pay attention and watch the local weather forecasts daily, and you won't get caught with your pants down.

Summer in Nashville is hot, humid, and nasty. The stifling summer heat seems to arrive by the beginning of June (if not the middle of May), and usually lasts all the way through September. The daytime highs will remain in the 80s to 90s during this time with most night-time temperatures hanging around 70°. I began living in Nashville in June of 2002, and from the day that I arrived until the end of September the daytime temperatures were

90°F or more, with the nighttime lows never falling below 70°. Although that summer seemed exceptionally hot, those kinds of temperatures are typical for summertime in middle Tennessee. It is noteworthy to mention that most businesses and homes have central air conditioning.

Fall weather in middle Tennessee is a bit more mild and pleasant but seems all too brief. With the summer heat and humidity often still lingering at the end of September, October and November can be among the best months for outdoor activities as the air is dryer and the temperatures are more moderate (daytime averages in the 60s to 70s). Unfortunately this dryer and cooler air also brings with it some occasional bursts of unstable humid systems and with it our secondary tornado season for the month of November. Although the threat is less than that of the primary season, there is still a good chance of a few rounds of severe weather. Again, pay attention to the daily local weather forecasts to avoid injury or death.

Summers In The South Can Be Like Winters In The North

As a native of New England I endured many a harsh winter over the years, as do many northerners. Most people in the north spend the majority of their time during these cold, frigid months indoors, as the weather deems many outdoor activities impractical. No matter how hard I tried, it was never that much fun to sit on the back deck when the temperature was 15°F. As a Northerner now living in the mid-South I find that the excessively hot and humid weather during the summer months can often render outdoor activities impractical, and these are the months in which I tend to spend the majority of my time indoors. No matter how hard I try, it's just not that much fun to sit on the back deck when it's 98°F and humid. The southern summer has replaced my northern winter as a time for indoor life, while fall through spring, now that time is King.

Severe Weather

To live in middle Tennessee it is important to understand the weather patterns in general, the dangers of severe weather, and how to be prepared for extreme weather events. Severe weather in the forms of tornadoes, high winds, electrical storms, torrential rains, localized flooding, and hailstorms, can happen at any time of the year, not just during the two official tornado seasons.

The single most important thing you can to do to be prepared for these hazards is to watch the local weather forecasts on the Nashville news programs regularly. The ability to forecast extreme weather has been greatly improved in recent years, and there is often advanced warnings regarding rounds of storms moving through. You can also go to www.weatherchannel.com and sign up for an inexpensive service that will automatically send a weather alert to your cell phone when severe weather is imminent. I highly recommend doing this and purchasing an inexpensive weather radio for your home.

If there is a threat of severe weather moving in, avoid being out on the roadways and stay indoors if possible. If there is a tornado warning in your area, your basement (if you have one) is usually the safest place to be. Second to the basement would be an interior bathroom on the lowest level of the building. Third would be any interior room without windows on the lowest level of the building. There is a considerable amount of information regarding extreme weather online; just perform a Google search on severe weather safety, educate yourself, and you will be better prepared for these events when they occur.

April 7, 2006

This more than typical Sunday began for me in Denver, Colorado, as a travel day at the end of a couple of West Coast performances with the Honky-Tonk Tailgate Party. Shortly before boarding a plane bound for Nashville, I spoke to my wife, Kelly, on the phone and she informed me that some severe weather had been forecasted for Middle Tennessee. The previous day had already produced a round of severe storms that battered the Midwest, and these storms were working their way eastward. A few hours later, well into the second leg of the flight, we went through some heavy turbulence for an extended period of time. The pilot announced that there was some "rough weather" in the area, and we would have to stay in a holding pattern above the airport for a while. After a tense hour or so of circling the airport we were finally able to land.

It was evident that something dramatic had happened when anxious passengers turned on cell phones, and the plane became filled with excited chatter. I became greatly perplexed upon calling my wife when I learned that several tornadoes had touched down in Middle Tennessee, and that she had been hiding in a crawl space beneath our house with our son for the last hour. She said at times it sounded like a freight train was going over the house, and that she could hear hail hitting the ground and high winds blowing. While still engaged in conversation with my wife, another member of our tour, drummer Cliff Thompson, told me that his wife had just informed him that his neighborhood had been hit hard by a tornado. His family was alright, and while his house was intact, it had sustained damage, and other houses nearby had been completely leveled. Learning all this so quickly put us all in a mild state of shock, and we scattered quickly to find rides home to our families as they were not there to pick us up because of the storms.

We were fortunate. Our loved ones escaped injury, and the damage to Cliff's home was repairable. By the time the dust settled at the end of that historical weekend, 73 tornadoes had touched down across 13 states killing 13 people and causing $1.5 billion worth of damage. Middle Tennessee was the hardest hit area with 12 lives lost and countless homes, neighborhoods, and businesses damaged or destroyed with the total losses at $650 million. Thousands of lives were forever changed.

Over our four previous years of living in Middle Tennessee my family had already experienced some extreme weather events on a few different occasions. While April 7 was certainly the worst, we had already once been close to the path of a tornado when an EF2 touched down 6 miles from our home. The conditions for extreme weather exist at least a handful of times a year in Tennessee. Once you've experienced these kinds of severe weather firsthand, you will forever be aware of some distinct characteristics. The sky becomes enveloped by a dark green hue. A strange rumbling sound can often be heard. The air changes in an indescribable way. Wall clouds form. Time seems to stand still. If this sounds scary, it's because it is. We don't live in constant fear, but when severe weather is in the forecast, we pay attention and take it seriously.

Allergies And Sinus Problems

As Nashville is located in a valley, the combination of stagnant air, long springs and autumns, and a diverse array of trees and grasses can result in many people developing allergy and sinus problems. In 2008, the Asthma and Allergy Foundation of America ranked Nashville as the 18th-worst spring allergy city in the U.S. It is extremely common for people with no history of allergy and sinus problems to develop them within a few years of living in Nashville.

That's about it. Other than the Amazon River basin-like summers, the threat of extreme weather, and the likelihood of developing sinus problems, the weather and climate of middle Tennessee is generally great.

The Tennessee Flood Of 2010

During the writing of this book Tennessee was devastated by a massive flood, a catastrophic event that was barely covered by our mainstream media under the shadow of the Gulf oil spill. This life-changing event was mentally draining and interrupted the writing of this book for several weeks. As it was the single largest disaster to hit the state of Tennessee since the Civil War, I felt it necessary to include this brief documentation of the Tennessee Deluge of 2010, Nashville's "Katrina," and the dawn of the superflood.

Saturday, May 1st, 2010

Saturday morning began for me at 5:30 AM when I was suddenly awoken in my home in Pegram, Tennessee, by a loud crack of thunder. By the time I dragged myself out of bed a short while later, a heavy downpour was underway, and we were beginning to receive a walloping storm. On another day this would have been less significant for me, but on this day Rhett Akins and band were leaving for an outdoor show in Alabama, and it was my job as tour manager to see it through.

Over the next couple of hours my wife and I kept checking the weather, growing more concerned with every passing minute as severe weather and heavy rain was in the forecast for Tennessee and several neighboring states, including Alabama. We left for the bus around 10:00 AM and during the 40 minute drive, which was exceptionally precarious due to the now torrential rain, I received a call from Rhett who informed me he would driving himself to the show. We arrived at the bus, loaded up, and began the 130 mile drive to our destination, the small town of Hartselle, Alabama, just a little ways over the Tennessee/Alabama border.

The rain was relentless for the first half of the drive, and just when it seemed like our show was doomed, it gradually began to subside as we neared the Alabama border. I received my second call from Rhett, now en route and just south of Nashville on Interstate 65, and learned that he saw a car completely submerged underwater on the northbound side of Interstate 65. Our concerns grew as we watched the news now showing video footage of the devastation this storm had just wreaked upon Arkansas in the form of tornadoes and on Memphis by way of flooding.

We safely arrived to our destination, a large open field in the middle of nowhere upon which a local business was throwing a groundbreaking ceremony. As we pulled down the long gravel driveway, I received my third call from Rhett who informed me that the Nashville radio stations were no longer playing music but delivering storm news, and that I-65, I-24, and I-40 around Nashville were now closed due to flooding.

As we sat on the bus, the latest news reports began showing a broader picture of the pending apocalypse that loomed just outside our doorstep. Flipping between the Weather Channel and CNN, we were horrified to see images of Nashville interstates that looked more like lakes filled with half submerged cars and tractor-trailers, viewed through a gloomy mist of grey.

A little while later Rhett safely arrived and told us of his harrowing trip. It seemed surreal that we were getting ready to play a concert while just 100 miles to our north there were more than 70 cars under water on the roadways we had just traveled upon. We played our concert, and afterwards, our bus driver Steve informed us that I-65 was now passable but that another round of storms was on its way. We made a hasty departure to try to beat the next storm. Fortunately, the ride home was uneventful, and we arrived safely back to our cars in a parking lot near the Opryland Hotel. A short while later, as Kelly and I neared our home just west of Nashville, we came upon a city truck blocking the road in front of some standing water and had to take a detour to a secondary entrance to our development. As we pulled into the driveway of our home we were greeted by a cold dark house as the storm had knocked out the power in our area.

Sunday, May 2nd, 2010 - Marooned On Pegram Island

It was just after noon on Sunday, May 1st, and the electricity was still down when we turned on our battery-powered weather radio. Now day two of the heaviest rainstorm we had ever seen, we sat around the living room amidst an ambience of perpetual twilight, and listened to the computer-generated voice of NOAA Weather Radio deliver a frightening and unsettling story. Round two of this marathon downpour had began in the early morning hours and was now causing many rivers across the state to reach flood stage. We were rendered speechless as this digital weatherman went down the list of where the rivers in the different counties were about to, or already cresting, with the Harpeth River, about a half mile from our home, among them. The list of road closures was also statewide and learning all of this while sitting in near darkness made it seem all the more ominous.

After assessing our supplies and taking stock of our situation, I decided to walk next door and talk to my neighbor to see what he knew. He told me that the road at the bottom of our development was under 10 feet of water, and that several houses in the area had been flooded. My mind struggled to comprehend his words which seemed to just hang in the humid spring air. A short drive to the bottom of the hill was now in order.

As we neared the main entrance, the scene that came into focus was beyond words. Still raining heavily, we viewed the entrance to our development and saw the top couple inches of a stop sign poking up out of the brown water from about 40 feet away, which was the closest we could get to the main street, now a lake spanning hundreds of feet across. To the left of the entrance stood two beautiful two-story homes, now submerged in water that almost reached the second floor. To the right of the entrance, "Lake Harpeth" stretched as far as the eye could see, with several homes formerly abutting the road now inaccessible and achieving an unwanted beach front status.

After a few minutes of taking in the eerie site, we retreated to our safe haven on top of the hill. A few hours later the rain finally stopped, and we took a drive to check out another access road. We didn't get too far before we spotted another city truck blocking the road. The impact of this flood was becoming more clear with each passing minute. From this vantage point we could see our community bank completely submerged under six or seven feet of water. We learned that the garage next door was also flooded and that some people had to be rescued by boat from the nearby gas station a little earlier in the day. We also learned that the power substation was under water and would require the floodwaters to recede before it could be repaired. After a few minutes of taking some pictures and video we solemnly returned to our home.

We sat around the living room listening to the radio for news as the darkness of night grew near. We ate a little food, drank a few beers, and played a game of Scrabble to pass the time, but the mood was less than cheerful. By the time we went to bed we still had no idea about the totality of destruction that this flood was having on our state. Meanwhile, safe from the waters below, but cut off from the mystery that lied beyond, we waited, marooned on Pegram Island.

The Aftermath

Eventually the waters receded, the power came back on, and the roadways gradually became accessible, but not before middle and western Tennessee had been decimated by this 1 in a 1000 chance flood. The rain first began falling on the morning of Saturday, May 1st, 2010, and by the time it finished, approximately 36 hours later; it had dumped a record rainfall of between 12 and 20 inches across Middle and Western Tennessee, 28% of our annual rainfall, rendering 46 of Tennessee's 95 counties federal disaster areas. Rivers that normally spanned 100 feet across swelled to a half-mile or more, flooding cities, towns, and roadways, washing away homes and bridges, destroying businesses and infrastructure, and leaving thousands homeless. At least 33 people died across Tennessee, Mississippi, and Kentucky, some while trapped in cars on flooding interstates and others who were swept away from flooding homes by the raging waters. Thousands more were left stranded in remote communities without power or communication for days. Water plants were decimated, historic buildings and icons were damaged or destroyed, and more than $1.9 billion of damage was done to the private sector in Nashville alone.

The Nashville music community suffered a hard hit as well. The Gaylord Opryland hotel and convention center suffered $77 million worth of damage and would remain closed for six months of repairs. The Roy Acuff Theater (home of the Opry House at Gaylord) received extensive damage and the loss of much irreplaceable memorabilia and archives. The Sound Check rehearsal and storage facility was devastated with many artists and bands losing vast collections of instruments and gear, including Brad Paisley, Keith Urban, Vince Gill, Brent Mason, and countless others. Several tractor-trailers full of the touring gear of artists like Toby Keith and Rascal Flats were also flooded, as they were parked on the premises. The Schermerhorn Symphony Center lost a collection of vintage Steinway concert grand pianos and sustained damage to a million-dollar pipe organ. While these are all physical things, many were irreplaceable, and their loss represents yet another dimension to the devastation rendered by this event.

With the help of the federal government and volunteers from around the country, it was ultimately the people of Tennessee who would show great strength and unity during the response and recovery effort. Thousands of volunteers showed up at multiple locations from the onset filling sandbags, assisting with boat rescues, and helping with other relief efforts. Community centers and churches across the state became havens for families who lost homes. Schools became water distribution centers. Some citizens even took it upon themselves to rent excavation equipment to clear roads as the county road crews were overwhelmed. Still, the rebuilding effort is hard and long, and the lives of many will never be the same.

Preparing For The Future

What was perhaps most disturbing about this event was the fact that *no one* saw this coming. Most long-term residents of middle Tennessee are aware of the likelihood of regularly occurring extreme weather, and prior to the flood most had been primarily concerned with tornado outbreaks. We are no strangers to extreme weather disasters. But while significant flooding has occurred here in the past, this Tennessee Deluge of 2010 (Nashville's "Katrina"), might be the dawn of the superflood, for this flood was caused by a rainstorm of epic proportions that was *not* the result of a tropical storm or hurricane.

It is noteworthy to mention that Nashville's News2 weather forecast on Friday, April 30, one day before the rain began, stated the following:

"For the second weekend in a row severe weather and big rains threaten our Saturday and Sunday. Saturday looks a little more random, likely a big round in the morning then just scattered stuff the rest of the day....By Saturday night another big round moves over bringing slight chances of severe weather and heavy rain. What comes in tomorrow evening will likely be what had developed in the afternoon to our west. A significant severe weather outbreak is expected over the deep south and western Tennessee...Sunday a cold front moves over triggering very heavy rain and a chance of severe weather. I think Sunday will be a much more widespread heavy rain event. Flash flooding will be a concern. HPC puts the very heavy rain in the western edge of middle Tennessee on Sunday."

This kind of forecast is not that unusual in the springtime for middle Tennessee. Typically, this kind of storm front passes through much more quickly than this one did. Although no one could have predicted it would stall right over the middle of the state, the forecast did say that "flash flooding will be a concern," and stalling fronts are now happening with more frequency. They correctly forecasted the potential for flooding, just not to what extent it might occur.

With extreme weather events now on the rise I see this flood as a wake-up call. It's not an event I would ever like to live through again, but I feel that I have learned from this experience. I am now watching local *and* national weather forecasts more regularly, and I understand what a simple rainstorm can now do. Be on the lookout and pay attention. Educate yourself about weather patterns and the climate in general. One day, the knowledge thereof could save your life.

Above: Dunlop Lane, Clarksville, TN on May 2nd, 2010 - photo courtesy Logan Moore

Woman stands on rubble in Kingston Springs, TN

Above: Two homes sit under water off of Highway 70, Pegram, TN, May 2nd, 2010

One of several homes totally devastated by the Harpeth River in Shacklett, TN

Twisted tracks in Pegram, TN caused by floodwaters. Similar damage occured statewide.

A family sits on the slab where their home once resided, Harpethview Trail, Kingston Springs, TN. Three homes were washed away from this spot.

"Guitars and groceries" on Third Ave, downtown Nashville.

Cost Of Living

"The art of living easily as to money is to pitch your scale of living one degree below your means." — Sir Henry Taylor

For poor starving artists and musicians planning to relocate to Nashville, there is some good news, and that's the low cost of living found here. The average cost for housing, apartments, and many goods and services are considerably lower than those found in most major US cities. Tennessee is the third most affordable state to live in and has an overall cost of living that is more than 10% below the national average.

Housing And Apartments

According to recent US census data, the average cost of a home in the Nashville area is $110-$135 per square foot. According to the ACCRA Cost of Living Index for the first quarter of 2009, the average apartment rental fee was $740 a month. In some parts of the city or its suburbs even lower prices can be found. At the time of this writing, you can find a two-bedroom apartment in a decent part of town for $600 a month. Even cheaper rents can be found in some areas, but check them out thoroughly in advance if you don't want to wind up living in a bad part of town. Many apartments in Nashville only require your first month's rent and a minimal deposit of around $100.

Here is some general cost-of-living information based on my observations:

» car registration: $65 - $90

» downtown parking garage fee: $10

» nightclub cover charge: most are free

» single public transit ticket: $1.60 - $2.10

» public transportation unlimited monthly pass: $78

» transportation to and from the region: $300 for flights

» set of electric guitar strings: $5

» pair of drumsticks: $7.50

Although Tennessee has a very high sales tax rate, ranging between 7% and 9%, there is no income tax and most other taxes are very low, including property taxes. The utility rates are also considerably lower than those found in many other parts of the country.

If you would like to get a better idea of how the cost of living in Tennessee compares to where you currently live, go to the website www.salary.com.

Top: Second Ave as viewed from the Shelby Street Pedestrian Bridge
Bottom: Shelby Street Pedestrian Bridge

Where To Live

"Mid pleasures and palaces though we may roam, Be it ever so humble, there's no place like home." — John Howard Payne

There are many different communities within Nashville and its suburbs, and choosing the one that's right for you can take a little time and research. Just like any other city, Nashville has some parts of town that are more desirable to live in than others. The desirability of a given area can be greatly subjective and dependent on each individual's needs. There are many factors you should consider when choosing a location for your residence. Ask yourself a few simple questions first:

» Do you want to live in a house or an apartment?

» Do you want to purchase or rent?

» What can you afford per month?

» How close do you want to live to downtown?

» Do you want to be in walking distance of stores and restaurants?

» Will you be commuting to and from the city during rush hour?

If you have children, there may be additional things to consider:

» Is the area safe for children to be playing outside or walking on the street?

» How good is the school system?

Obviously someone with children will desire an area that provides a good school system and a safe neighborhood, whereas a single person might be less affected by those kinds of factors. An Internet search will provide you with a wealth of information regarding school systems, crime rates, etc. Once you have narrowed your search based on your family needs, you will want to take daily commuting into consideration.

Some of the biggest traffic backups occur on the north and east sides of the city, especially during rush hours, and in this respect it is less desirable to live in those areas. Traffic on the south side of the city can be a little better; however that area is generally a more expensive area in which to live. Traffic on the west and northwest part of town is often considerably less congested and many of these suburbs do have reasonably priced housing and apartments.

The further out from the city you go, the more affordable housing becomes. If you don't mind living 30 to 45 minutes from the city, you can find some great deals especially north and west of town. Unlike many other major U.S. cities, in Nashville, you can live 20 miles from downtown and make the commute in 30 minutes or so.

Is it safe...

All cities are going to have certain areas that are more desirable for living in and traveling through than others, and Nashville is no exception. While certain areas might "feel" safer than others, Nashville, and its suburbs, are always working towards improving the quality of life within *all* communities. Still, there are some areas that you might want to avoid moving to or traveling through if you have a choice. Some parts of East Nashville (much of which is actually north of downtown just over the river from the stadium) can be a bit "spotty." Parts of Madison, Antioch, and Nolensville Road could fall into this category as well. Music Row, believe it or not, can be sketchy at times. 70S/Charlotte Pike just west of downtown also falls into this category. Downtown Nashville itself is relatively safe during the daytime, but has some questionable areas after dark. Of course, in all fairness, these things change over time. As all of this is essentially "anecdotal information," the best thing to do would be to speak to some locals within whatever communities you are exploring.

Getting Around

"Thanks to the Interstate Highway System, it is now possible to travel from coast to coast without seeing anything." — Charles Kuralt

Learning how to get around in Nashville can take some time and patience. The city and its surrounding suburbs cover a huge area, and the circular network of roads is not always clearly marked and often confusing. One way to look at the Nashville road system is that of a wagon wheel. Nashville is at the center of the wheel, the spokes are the interstates and roads crossing through it, and the circle of the wheel is the outer loop roadways circling the city.

There are three major interstates that cross through and intersect in Nashville: I-65 runs north to south, I-40 runs east to west, and I-24 runs northwest to southeast. These are the spokes of the wheel. Briley Parkway is a beltway that circles around the north part of the city, and 440 is a beltway that circles around the south part of the city. This is the outer circle of the wheel. Obviously there are more spokes as well as other parts of the wheel, but these are the basics.

One of the problems I have found in getting around Nashville is that there can be more than one road with the same road name. Highway 70 is a perfect example. There is a Highway 70, and a Highway 70S and they both run east to west and are only a couple of miles apart in places (obviously well thought out). Old Hickory (a road with no beginning and no end) is another problem in this respect. There is only one road with that name in Nashville, but that one road seems to show up all over the city in a deceptive and illogical way. Many directions in Nashville start out with "Get on Old Hickory…." Only trial and error and a good GPS will eventually get you straight.

In downtown Nashville, the roads are set up a little more like a grid. There is a series of avenues that runs north to south, parallel with the Cumberland River, and most of these are one-way streets. Broadway runs across these avenues east to west cutting them into two parts. The avenues north of Broadway run 2nd Avenue North, 3rd Avenue North, etc. The avenues south of Broadway run 2nd Avenue South and so on. This can be both helpful and confusing.

Learning how to drive in Nashville and its surrounding areas can involve learning more than just the roadways. There are some hazards that are unique to this place that one can only truly appreciate when experienced firsthand. It is not uncommon for drivers to cross over the center yellow line and drive partially on the wrong side of the road. In most states this is illegal; however, in middle Tennessee the law actually states that the painted road lines are mainly "a suggestion" and that it is not illegal to "weave" on to the wrong side of the road. I've even seen the police do it.

You should also be on your toes when approaching intersections with traffic lights. Although it is illegal to cross the intersection when the light is red, this doesn't stop a lot of drivers. When the light turns yellow many drivers accelerate. Once the light turns red, sometimes three or four more cars might continue speeding through the intersection. Although this problem may potentially improve as a result of the recent implementation of traffic cameras at many busy intersections, it is a problem at the present time.

Another peculiarity to the roadways of Nashville is the misalignment of roads. You might be driving along a road in the middle of the city, and upon crossing through an intersection wind up on the wrong side of the road, even though you never turned the wheel. This is because the entire road shifted over a few feet because the roads were originally built around old buildings. If you look carefully at the pavement through one of these misaligned intersections, you will see a dotted line painted diagonally across the intersection, shifting the road over a lane. If you aren't paying attention and miss this painted line, you *will* wind up driving on the wrong side of the road.

Parking downtown can be a bit of a nuisance depending on the time of day and time of year. There are quite a few metered spots, but these usually go quickly, and may not allow enough time for your work day or gig without taking a break to feed it more quarters. Most metered spots require quarters for daytime business hours and allow free parking at night and on weekends. Parking garages and paid lots are fairly plentiful; however most of these are $10. If you search the avenues around Broadway and other areas of the inner city, you can find some on street parking spots without meters. For some, it is worth driving around for 20 to 30 minutes to save on parking fees. There is a helpful website called parkitdowntown.com that shows many parking locations and the cheapest rates.

When heading into the city for work, appointments, or leisure, allow some extra time to find a parking spot. Also beware that there are annual and seasonal events such as fanfare, the CMA's, sporting events, and conventions that can and will cause gridlock within the city.

Employment

"Nothing is really work unless you would rather be doing something else."
— James M. Barrie

While you are working towards your goals in the music business, you might need to work a day job, and there is a wide variety of employment opportunities within Nashville and its surrounding areas. Although the music industry provides a significant amount of jobs in Music City, health care is actually the largest sector providing approximately 94,000 jobs to the Nashville economy. Other major industries in Nashville include automobile manufacturing, insurance, tourism, finance, printing, and publishing.

Aside from those industries, Nashville offers most of the same kinds of jobs found in other major cities. Along with the lower cost of living, the starting pay at many jobs is also less than found elsewhere. For musicians relocating to Nashville with full-time careers outside of music, there is a wide variety of 9 to 5 type jobs to be found, and the job market for specialized vocations is competitive as well. Have your resume and references ready, and get busy searching the Internet and making calls.

In order to have a schedule that is flexible and conducive to the late hours and erratic schedule that a lot of musicians endure, many try to avoid the stereotypical career-oriented day job. (In other words, we musicians don't like to work real jobs.) In addition to all of the music performance-related jobs described in the first section of this book, Nashville offers a good variety of non-performance industry related jobs that will put you in proximity of the action and offer some flexibility as well. With year-round tourist activity, the Nashville nightclubs provide many musicians with the supplemental income they need. With a high turnover rate, many of these establishments are regularly looking for bartenders, bar backs, kitchen staff, wait staff, bouncers, hawkers, hosts and hostesses, DJs, maintenance people, and assistance with house PA systems. These kinds of jobs can provide a more flexible schedule while putting you in contact with many other musicians and music industry workers.

There are many other music industry related jobs with less flexibility that will still keep you close to the action, such as administrative work for publishing companies, record companies, recording studios, booking agencies, and talent agencies. If you have a CDL, you might be able to find work as a bus driver at one of the many Nashville-based bus companies. There are also many music stores throughout the Nashville area that employee salespersons, music teachers, and repair technicians. While many of these jobs won't always allow a flexible schedule, they will put you in contact with many other music industry types.

Street performer playing for tips on Broadway

Nashville Winter

"If we had no winter, the spring would not be so pleasant: If we did not sometimes taste of adversity, prosperity would not be so welcome."
— Anne Bradstreet

Nashville winters can be especially hard for many music industry workers since much of the regular activity slows down. Many of the country acts tour seasonally, as a big part of the touring work is provided by festivals and outdoors shows. This can mean minimal touring work from November through February for many nationals. In-town nightclub work also slows during this period, as do some aspects of the recording industry.

Although Music City has tourist activity year round, it seems that the numbers are fewer during the cold winter months. As many of the nightclubs pay a minimal base pay, players rely on the tip jar for the majority of their pay. Fewer tourists equal less pay. Many of the nightclubs in town downsize their schedule during the winter months, and this equates into fewer shifts for the players.

Activity on Music Row seems to go at a slower pace during the winter as well, and this can cause a slowdown for some, especially those in the publishing and recording business. It seems there is much less activity from Thanksgiving through the end of the year as many people take time off for the holidays.

Most musicians who are earning a living from their craft in Nashville try to save some money during the busy time of year to prepare for less work in the winter months. If you are making a living as a professional musician and get paid over the table, such as many touring musicians and some session players do, collecting unemployment benefits during these months can be an option. It probably won't add up to enough income to pay all the bills, but for some it can help supplement. Learn to adapt, and save your per diem.

at&t

Land of the Permanent Job Interview

"Opportunity is missed by most people because it is dressed in overalls and looks like work" — Thomas Edison

Living and working in Nashville can cause many musicians and music industry workers to feel like they are on a permanent job interview. This holds especially true when working or hanging out in the Nashville nightclubs and bars. With such a large number of people living and working in Nashville that are connected to virtually every facet of the music industry, you never know who might be hanging around. You could be playing a seemingly unimportant gig on Broadway to a small audience, but that audience might contain someone who could be influential to your career, someone you don't yet know who may be in a position to hire you for a road gig, recording session, or publishing deal. Perhaps someone could be watching you that might not need to hire you until a couple years down the road, and you are unknowingly making an impression at that moment. You never know who's watching, so assume that you are always being auditioned.

This holds true whether you are working as a player in a band, *or* just hanging out. If you hang out or network in the clubs and bars around town on a regular basis, you will meet many people. As they aren't handing out nametags at the door, it would be wise to assume that at least *sometimes* some of the other patrons might be important songwriters, musicians, producers, etc. You might wind up in a conversation with one of them and not even know it. In a casual conversation, they might take an interest in you without volunteering their credentials. Maybe you're a player, and they saw you perform at another club. Maybe they're a big-time songwriter. Maybe they're in a position to hire you for something important, but not ready to show their hand yet. Never write off anybody, and always assume that even your smallest actions are important.

This atmosphere can exist outside of the nightclubs as well, as many of these same music industry people go to coffee shops, grocery stores, restaurants, malls, parks, etc. Some of the biggest connections you might ever make can happen completely by accident in the least obvious places.

In Nashville you're always building a reputation whether you know it or not. Your musical performances, your body language, the things you say and how you say them, the clothes you wear, and the people you associate with are all representative of your inner character. How you perform on stage, and how you act off stage, can and will be evaluated by your peers. It can take a long time to build a great reputation for yourself, but only a brief minute to destroy it.

Here are a couple of true short stories to illustrate these points:

Opening Doors

A few years ago, there was a talented guitar player performing regularly at nightclubs on Broadway. He had already been in town for several years at this point and had not done much else outside of the nightclub gigs. One day out of the blue, he received a phone call from a producer. The producer told him he wanted to hire him for some recording projects. Although they had never previously met, the producer told him that he had watched him perform at Roberts on Broadway about a year before. When the bandleader at that show announced the guitarist's name, the producer made a mental note and eventually tracked him down. Unbeknownst to the guitarist, that one arbitrary $40 gig at Roberts was actually the beginning of a door opening to a career as a session player.

Secret Auditions

During my years working as tour manager, bandleader, and guitarist for Rhett Akins, I have been responsible for the hiring and firing of band members. Like many music professionals in Nashville, I have a big list of musicians and phone numbers that I've accumulated over the years. When someone leaves the band, I began to go down the list in search of a replacement.

A few years ago, I needed to hire a new musician. I began to go down my list and narrowed it down to four of five players that I thought could fit the bill. While all of these players were musically competent, some had very likable personalities, and some had reputations for being difficult to work with. I went downtown to watch these players perform in clubs and chatted with them briefly, never mentioning my intentions. They were auditioned and interviewed and they never even knew it. This was also the case for the player we eventually hired. Although I had previously met a couple of the players that I didn't hire and had never had any problem with them, their reputations for being difficult to work with is what ultimately scratched them from the list.

It is important to carry yourself confidently but not arrogantly. Don't be overly aggressive but don't feel you need to walk on eggshells either. Always put your best foot forward and show some respect and courtesy for others. A seemingly unimportant conversation with a stranger might help you get a job someday, or it could prevent you from getting one. You never know who's watching.

Band playing at Legends Corner on Broadway

I-65 just south of downtown Nashville, Tennessee

All Roads Go Through Nashville

"I've always felt that blues, rock 'n' roll and country are just about a beat apart." — Waylon Jennings

Nashville is known to many musicians and music enthusiasts as the country music capital of the world. And while this label might be correct, there is much more to be found here than just country music. While it's true that Nashville is essentially the birthplace of the country music recording and touring industries, and a majority of what is currently going on here is still centered on that element, there are many other musical roads that intersect here. We have both kinds of music, country *and* western (sorry, I couldn't resist). Actually, it goes far beyond that.

Many musicians and artists outside of the country genre have chosen to make Middle Tennessee their home base, some of them working within the industry here, and others who aren't but simply enjoy living here and use Nashville as a home base for their touring entities.

Among the great talent pool of non-country artists who have homes in middle Tennessee are legends like Kid Rock, Peter Frampton, Sheryl Crow, Leon Russell, Ben Folds, Dan Seals, Jack White of the White Stripes, Steve Cropper, Larry Carlton, Wayne Jackson of the original Memphis Horns, Reese Wyans from Stevie Ray Vaughan and Double Trouble, Billy Cox from Jimi Hendrix's Band of Gypsies, Leo Lyons from Ten Years After, guitar virtuoso Phil Keaggy, Charlie Wayne of the Bullet Boys, guitar ace Jack Pearson formerly of the Allman Brothers, and members of Bela Fleck and the Flecktones.

While some of these artists have little or nothing to do with the Nashville music industry, some of them do and have previously employed or currently employ Nashville musicians and/or studios for their musical endeavors. Bassist Randy Smith has toured with Larry Carlton. Steel guitarist Rusty Rhoades has toured with Kid Rock. Leon Russell has used Nashville based musicians for his touring over the years as well. These are just a few of many similar examples.

There are also some artists outside of the country genre who don't live in Nashville but do hire Nashville based players for their tours and/or recordings. Keyboardist Will Doughty worked on several country music tours before being offered a job with the 80's rock band Poison. Sound engineer Penn Robertson has been recently working with Susan Tedeschi. Viktor Krauss has been bassist for Lyle Lovett for many years. The list goes on.

Some of the recording studios in Nashville are among the finest in the world and a regular destination for many of the biggest recording artists of our time. Robert Plant and Alison Krauss recorded a critically acclaimed, Grammy-winning album here in 2009. Neil Young's "career" album *Harvest* was recorded in Nashville in 1971, and Young has returned to Nashville many times over the years for his recording projects including his critically acclaimed 2006 release *Living with War*. The list of recording giants who regularly record in Nashville includes literally all styles and genres of popular music. Although this fact does not directly help most of the regular working musicians in town, it does impact many studios, engineers, session players, and others who work in the Nashville recording industry.

Over the years, many artists and bands that are based elsewhere and not a part of the country genre have also used the Nashville rehearsal halls like Soundcheck and SIR for their pre-tour rehearsals. I'll never forget the day that I was on a break while rehearsing at Soundcheck and walked down the hall to hear the band Journey running through their hits for an upcoming tour. I was fortunate to engage in a brief conversation with Neil Schonn when they took a break. I've met Peter Frampton there on a couple of occasions as well. It's funny how they both looked so much taller in concert.

Many superstars like to visit Nashville regularly. As many famous musicians and artists live and work here, the locals are accustomed to seeing celebrities out and about on a regular basis, and for the most part don't bother them in public. I myself have seen heavy hitters Hank Williams Jr., Neil Young, Brent Mason, and Ricky Rockett sitting in the audience at different nightclub gigs I've played in town. It's almost a surreal experience to be on stage performing for the people who usually do the entertaining.

Making connections with artists and bands on this level is not attainable for most in Music City. However, this place *is* an intersection of a greatly varying array of artists, bands, and musical styles. And Nashville's heritage has been at least partly defined by the great legacy of American roots music that has passed through this place over the years. All roads go through Nashville.

Jamming With Oteil

During the summer of 2008 when the Rhett Akins band was between bass players, our sound engineer Penn Robertson threw out the idea of calling his friend Oteil Burbridge to sub a few gigs, as he was currently on hiatus from his regular gig with the Allman Brothers. Apparently the brothers were on an extended break that summer and Oteil happened to be available and interested in coming out with us. The next thing I knew we were doing a handful of gigs with him and riding around on a bus listening to first-hand stories about my childhood idols.

While the gigs and stories were great fun, it was the sound checks that were most memorable. As Rhett and band are well-versed in the Allman Brothers classic material, our sound checks during this time period contained several songs from their repertoire; Blue Sky, Statesboro Blues, Don't Keep Me Wonderin', and Aint Wastin' Time No More. These moments contained some great improvised jams propelled by Oteil's masterful groove and melodic sensibility. It was almost as if a little piece of one of America's greatest bands fell from the sky and landed on our doorstep, to be shared only in the moment with a few appreciative friends. Eventually our stint with Oteil came to an end, but it was an inspired road to travel on while it lasted. One I will always remember with fondness and never forget. Thanks Oteil!

Oteil & Rhett Akins band at The Georgia Theater, 2008

Left to right:
Scott Tweten
Cliff Thompson
Oteil Burbridge
Penn Robertson
Eric Normand

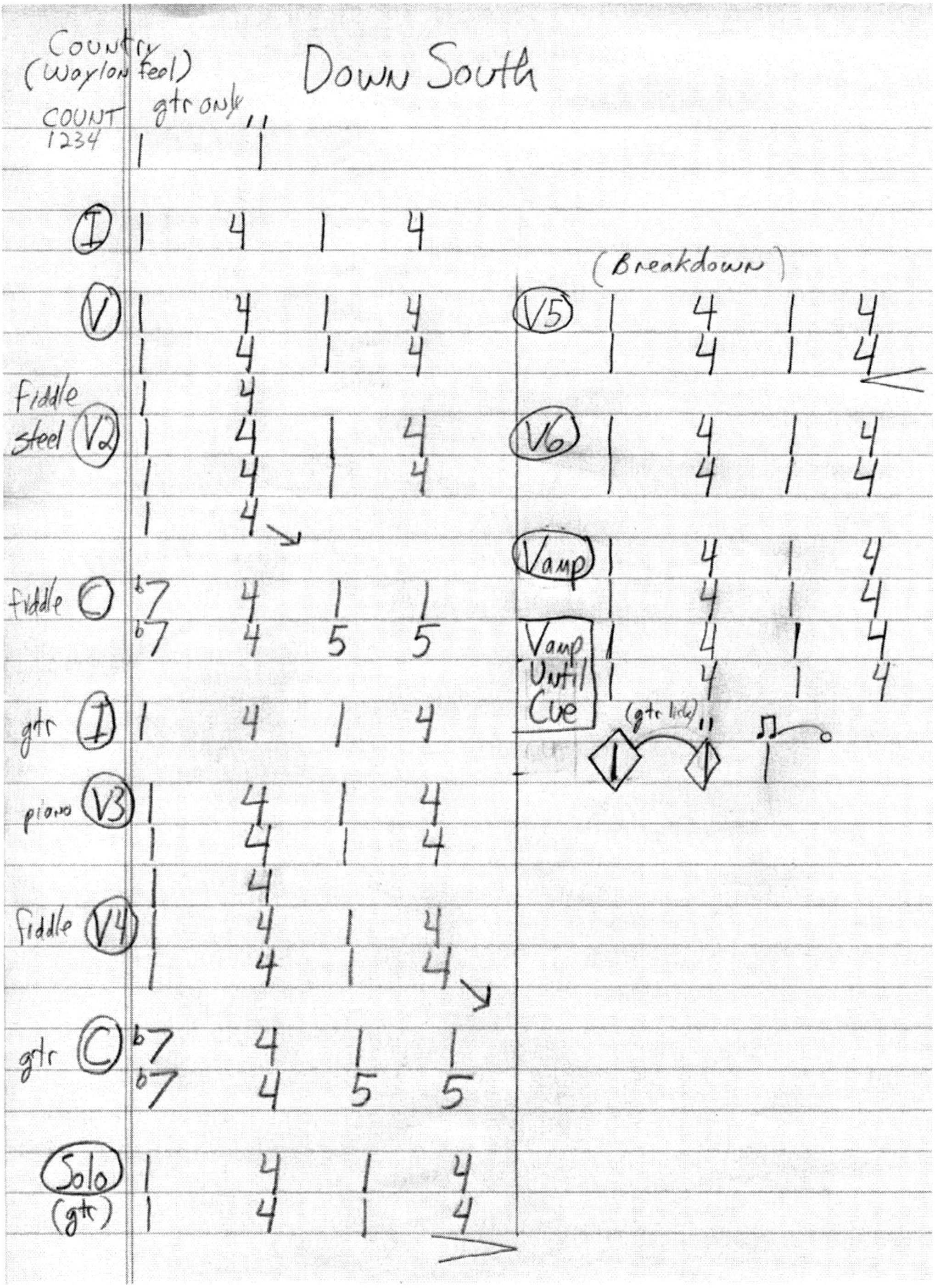

Country
(Waylon feel)

Down South

COUNT 1234 | gtr only: 1 | 1

I: 1 | 4 | 1 | 4

V: 1 | 4 | 1 | 4
1 | 4 | 1 | 4
fiddle: 1 | 4

steel V2: 1 | 4 | 1 | 4
1 | 4 | 1 | 4
1 | 4

fiddle C: b7 | 4 | 1 | 1
b7 | 4 | 5 | 5

gtr I: 1 | 4 | 1 | 4

piano V3: 1 | 4 | 1 | 4
1 | 4 | 1 | 4
1 | 4

fiddle V4: 1 | 4 | 1 | 4
1 | 4 | 1 | 4

gtr C: b7 | 4 | 1 | 1
b7 | 4 | 5 | 5

Solo (gtr): 1 | 4 | 1 | 4
1 | 4 | 1 | 4

(Breakdown)

V5: 1 | 4 | 1 | 4
1 | 4 | 1 | 4

V6: 1 | 4 | 1 | 4
1 | 4 | 1 | 4

Vamp: 1 | 4 | 1 | 4
1 | 4 | 1 | 4

Vamp Until Cue: 1 | 4 | 1 | 4
1 | 4 | 1 | 4

(gtr lick) ◇1◇ ◇1◇ 1

Nashville Proficiency

"Only one who devotes himself to a cause with his whole strength and soul can be a true master. For this reason mastery demands all of a person."
— Albert Einstein

Whether you sing, play the drums, play the guitar, engineer, or write songs, being highly proficient at your craft will greatly improve your chances of success. As music is subjective, so is musicianship. There is no minimum standard for being a professional musician, no test to be taken, and no license to be issued. Therefore, the overall competence of a musician is determined by each individual's efforts. Working hard to hone your skills can give you a competitive edge. Aside from just being good at what you do, there are some things you'll need to do in Nashville that will require some skills specific to this scene.

The Nashville Number System is a system of musical shorthand that is used throughout Nashville. Whether you are working nightclub gigs or recording sessions, at some point you will probably need to read a chord chart that was written using this system. At nightclub gigs, this system is often used to help quickly convey the chords of a song through the use of hand signals and verbal communication. There's a great book by Chas Williams called "The Nashville Number System" that can help you gain a basic understanding.

Chart Writing: Knowing how to write chord charts using the Nashville Number system can be a valuable asset for studio and live performance, as well as for songwriting and arranging. Not everyone can do this, so if you can, it's just one more thing you have to offer. Whenever I learn a new song, I write a chart to help me understand the arrangement. I've found that it also helps the memorization process as it allows me to visualize the entire song form. Some people are able to earn extra income by writing charts for songwriters and singers who need them for showcases, etc. $10 per song would be a loose standard.

Keys and Tempos: Knowing the correct keys and tempos of the standard cover material played in Nashville will come in handy if you're doing in-town nightclub gigs, and it can also be helpful in some touring situations. It is especially important for singers to know this information, as quite often they perform cover material in a key or tempo that is different from the original. It's just as important for the other players to know this information too, as many singers don't know the keys or tempos of the songs they sing.

Signature Licks: This applies to players who play melodic instruments like the piano, fiddle, steel guitar, and especially electric guitar. When singers call out tunes they expect you to know the signature licks that set up these tunes. If you wind up in a situation where you don't know the signature lick to a tune, ask one of the other players to hum it, and then try to copy their phrasing. Nothing can be more embarrassing than blowing the intro to a tune. Even if the audience doesn't notice the mistake, I guarantee everyone on stage will.

Count Offs: This especially applies to drummers, as many of the standards require a unique count off to set up the signature lick intro to the song (example 2, 3, 4, 1 to set up a 3 beat guitar lick intro). If the drummer doesn't know the correct count off, the player playing the signature lick or the bandleader should be able to count off the tune. If a wrong count off is given at the beginning of a tune, it might prevent the signature lick from being played at all, or possibly cause a train wreck before the song even starts.

Trading Fills and Solos: In traditional country music, melodic instrument players took turns playing fills throughout the songs. For instance: fiddle on the first verse, steel on the chorus, electric guitar on the second verse, etc. If the solo section is eight bars, the piano might take the first four, and the electric might take the second four. This approach is still used today. For recording sessions, this is usually decided in advance while the song is being arranged. For live performances, this might be decided in advance or it might be done on the fly while the song is being played, with the decisions being made by either the band members or the bandleader and conveyed through eye contact.

Laying Out: There are many performance situations in Nashville, both in the studio and live, that might employ a large band with five or six players or more. A typical instrumentation might be drums, bass, electric guitar, second electric guitar, keyboards, and fiddle. This many instruments playing rhythm all at once can be too busy for certain sections of a song. In these situations it is not uncommon for some of the instruments to completely lay out for some sections, especially verses and other sections that require a lighter dynamic. When in doubt, lay out.

Multiple Styles: Just because it's Nashville doesn't mean we only play country music. Freelance musicians working in music city should be prepared to play a wide variety of styles ranging from; Traditional and Modern Country, Pop, Hard Rock, Southern Rock, Blues, R&B, Motown, Western Swing, Reggae, Funk, etc. Being proficient at a wide variety of styles will help you in many live performance situations and can be especially useful in many recording situations.

Chicken Pickin': This applies specifically to guitar players and refers to an alternate picking technique. Holding a flat pick between your thumb and first finger, you play the first note of a phrase with the pick, and then alternately pluck with either the middle finger or middle and ring fingers combined. This technique is often used for rhythm and soloing and is essential to traditional and modern country guitar playing.

Guitar World

"The time I burned my guitar it was like a sacrifice. You sacrifice the things you love. I love my guitar." — Jimi Hendrix

Regardless of what instrument you play, you will need a reliable and good sounding rig. Being a guitar player first and foremost, I would like to share what I know about developing a happening Nashville-style guitar rig. While I do believe that great tone comes from the hands, understanding some of the commonalities among modern-day Nashville guitarists will help give you an edge.

Guitars: The Telecaster is by far the most common electric guitar played in Nashville, as its unique character is a big part of the Nashville sound. Many guitar manufacturers now build a good Tele; just own a decent one and make sure it's well intonated. Strat style guitars are less commonly used but do have their place. Beyond that - Gibson SGs, Les Pauls, and 335s; Paul Reed Smiths, and Gretsch style guitars are also used, especially on recording sessions. For live playing in Nashville and on country tours based out of Nashville, guitars with single coil pickups win the shootout, with the Tele being most common.

Amps: "Vox" style amplifiers are the first choice of many guitarists in Nashville and perhaps a cornerstone of the modern-day Nashville electric guitar sound. The Vox AC30 circuitry developed in the 50s has inspired a plethora of modern-day boutique versions that all strive to achieve that bell-like "Vox" sound. Amps made by Vox, Matchless, Dr Z, Badcat, Crate and other manufacturers are commonly found in the Nashville clubs and on Nashville-based tours. These amps have a unique character, and combined with the right guitar, create a tone that could be described as "spanky" with a vowel-like quality to the midrange. While many players also use amps made by Fender, Mesa Boogie, Peavey, etc., in general, the "Vox-style" amps are the ones that tend to turn heads in most live applications. For recording sessions, many in demand session players have rigs consisting of two or three heads with extension speaker cabinets. A typical setup might consist of one Vox-style head, one Marshall-style head, and maybe one Fender-style head.

Why "Vox-style" amps are an essential part of the modern Nashville guitar sound.

The original Vox amps, designed by Dick Denny in the late '50s, were specifically engineered to sound good with the Telecaster, the most popular mass production electric guitar of that era (and the most commonly used guitar in Nashville today.) The fact that Dick was a guitarist also helped to give the amps a different sensibility – *"If it sounded good to Dick, it sounded good to everybody."* Dick and the other engineers at JMI felt that an electric guitar and a guitar amp were each half of one musical instrument.

Contrary to popular belief, these amps are not actually a "Class A" design; they are "Class AB-1". They are, however, vastly different in design and tonality than Fender and Marshall, the other major amp manufacturers from the era in which they were born.

Vox amps were the sound of the "British Invasion" of the 1960's, an age where the quest for treble was big, and as luck would have it, this extra dose of top end also happens to be a natural fit for modern country twang. In 1989 the birth of "Matchless" amplifiers (a design based on the original AC30) started a boutique amp craze which helped introduce a whole new generation of guitar players to the "Vox" sound, in Nashville and beyond.

Pedal Boards and Effects: For most live playing situations, whether in town or on tours, most players will use one or two combo amplifiers set to a clean sound, and use stomp boxes for overdrive. Many players will use a clean boost such as the Keeley Katana boost or the Xotic RC booster to help add sustain and sparkle to a clean sound. Compressors like the Boss CS-3 or the Keeley compressor are also commonly used for this purpose and greatly aid the chicken pickin' technique. Having two overdrive pedals on your board, one set for a light grit and the other one set for a heavier overdrive, is also standard practice. A good delay pedal with tap tempo, such as the Boss DD-5 or the Line 6 DM-4, is also very practical. Boss tuners are still very popular, but the recent introduction of the Peterson Strobostomp allows players to now tune on the fly with the accuracy of 1000th of a cent.

Beyond these basic essentials, many players also use a volume pedal, a wah-wah, and various modulation effects. If you begin to get beyond three or four pedals in a chain, you might want to consider running some pedals through a true bypass loop pedal to eliminate some signal loss and to give you an emergency bypass in case a pedal goes down in the middle of a show. Hardwire all of these pedals together in an anvil-style pedal board case with good cables and a reliable power supply and you're ready to rock.

Make it foolproof. A good guitar rig should be able to be set up or torn down in seconds. Whether you are playing nightclub gigs or touring with a national act, having your amp in a professional road case with wheels and a pedal board setup in which everything is hardwired will help keep your expensive gear protected, make it easier to transport, and make your rig more likely to work correctly every time you set it up.

What I use and why I like it

Many guitarists, regardless of skill level, develop a personal connection to their guitar gear. Even though some of my gear holds a certain sentimental value, it's all simply tools of the trade. I mean, I don't actually sleep with these instruments. It's not the gear I love; it's the sounds I can make with this gear that I love. For most guitar players, it boils down to whatever gets the job done, or whatever works for you. The following is a review of what works for me. And by the way, I'm not getting paid to say nice things about all these manufacturers. I have accumulated this collection very slowly, over a long period time, and genuinely appreciate the guitars and equipment made by these companies.

G&L Telecaster ASAT Special: A gift from D, this late 90s maple necked beauty, nicknamed "whitey", has been my main axe since I first moved to Nashville. There are a few things that make this instrument unique, setting it apart from the traditional telecaster. First, it didn't come with the standard bridge pickup base plate, and instead of the usual two single coil pickup configuration, it sports three alnico P-90's. These two factors give it a meatier sound than a traditional tele, and although it can produce a fairly "spanky" country twang, with the right overdrive, it can also deliver a pretty convincing Gibson-like tone. I've replaced the tone knob with a "blend" knob which acts like an EQ, combining and blending different increments of the neck and bridge pickups. I've also added locking tuners and a dropped D tuner on the low E string. Put that all together, and you've got one extremely versatile, bad-ass tele!

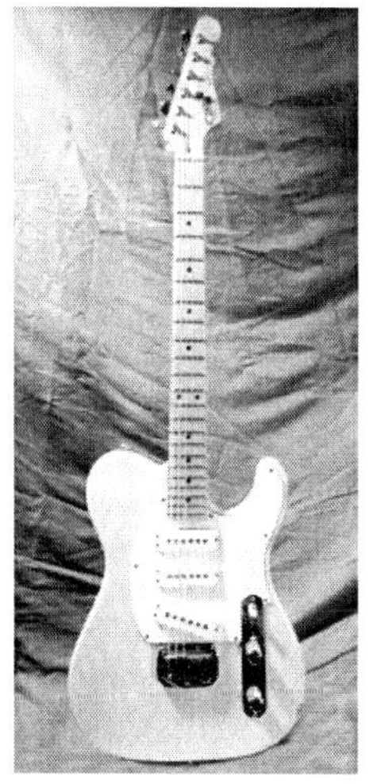

Fender Stratocaster: My American-made 79 Strat, nicknamed "the first wife" by my real wife Kelly, was brand-new when my dad bought it for me in 1981. After trading in my previous starter guitar, I worked off the $300 balance by mowing the lawn for free for the next two years. In the years since, it's seen seven or eight re-frets, as many pickup changes, and even a Floyd Rose bridge at one point. (I paid a small fortune to add the Floyd Rose during the height of the 80s shredder movement, and then paid another small fortune to have it put back to normal some years later.) Currently, it has medium jumbo frets, locking tuners, Fender "Tex Mex" pickups, and a blend knob which replaced one of the tone knobs. The paint job is custom, the result of years of systematic abuse. If anything ever happened to this guitar, there would be a brief 10 minute period in which I would be inconsolable, but then I would probably move on.

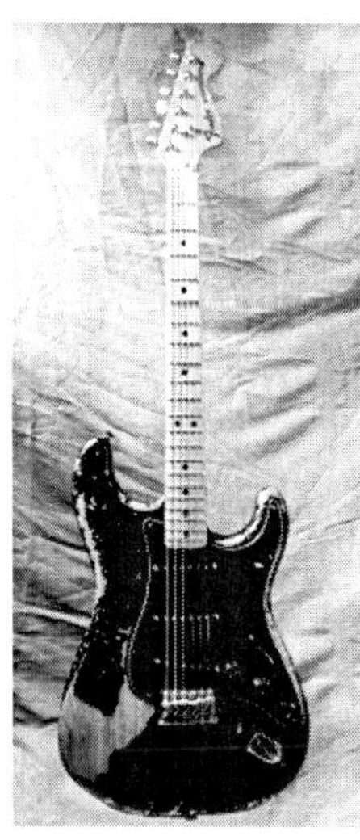

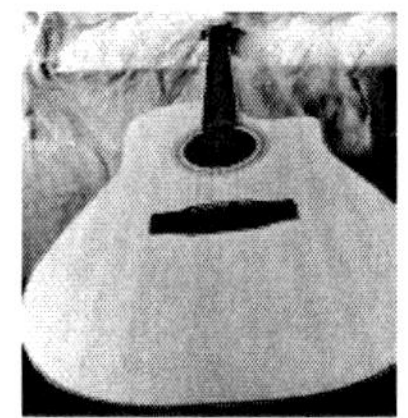

Larrivee Acoustic: Every Nashville guitarist needs a good acoustic, and my acoustic happens to be a Larrivee DV-03R. This solid spruce top has state-of-the-art electronics for live applications, and also sounds great on studio recordings, "acoustically" speaking. Fairly durable as far as acoustics go, this well-made instrument has a warm, woody tone (but not too dark), stays in tune, and plays exceptionally well.

Vox AC30: I bought my 2003 British-made AC30 in 2005 when I was working on the HTTP tour. We were playing some big stages, and I needed something that would throw a little more heat than the smaller amp I had been using. If you want to fill a stage with sound, this puppy will do it! I use the "brilliant" input, which delivers a sparkly, clean tone, and use overdrive pedals for grit. It's a bit heavy, weighing in at 70 pounds, but well worth it as its tone is to die for. It's extremely versatile and easily the most powerful combo I've ever owned, which can make it a little hard to control in smaller rooms. In those situations where I need to "tame the beast" a little, I use it in conjunction with a "Weber Mini-mass" speaker attenuator, allowing for a singing sustain at lower volumes. It also records quite well and is an essential part of my session work in Nashville.

Marshall JMP50: I bought this 1978, 50 watt gem back in the late 80s, and for years this was my main amp when I was gigging regularly in the New England nightclub scene. While it can rock with the best of them, it also delivers a wonderful clean tone. It has a preamp and a master volume, and I run it without using much preamp, allowing for a relatively clean sound with a slight bit of grit. Using the Marshall set to a clean sound allows me to run modulation and delay before the amps input, something you can't do when an old Marshall is set to a dirty sound. When I want to rock, I just kick on my tube screamer or rat pedal. In recent years, I've been using my Prosonic amp as a speaker cabinet, its single "Celestion Vintage 30" 12 inch speaker being a great matchup. In my earlier club years back in New England, I used this head with my 1968 Marshall 4X12 Cabinet. This not only delivered that classic, woody Marshall tone, but it looked cool as hell!

Fender Prosonic: When I first arrived in Nashville, I was using my old style Fender combos for gigging: a '64 Vibrolux and a '70 Deluxe. D told me I needed to lose the "frying pan tone" and that he had just checked out a Prosonic that he thought would fit the bill. Only made for a couple of years in the late 90s, this was Fender's attempt at a Vox-style design, and although the Prosonic never really caught on, it is an undiscovered

gem, perhaps one of Fender's best sounding amps ever. It came with two 10 inch Celestion speakers which I replaced with a single 12 inch Vintage 30. Relatively lightweight, it packs quite a punch, and although a little darker than my Vox, it achieves similar tonal characteristics, kind of a "mini-Vox." I had an airbrush artist paint a custom design on some T-shirt material stretched over the speaker baffle (back when I had too much free time).

Pedal Board and Effects: "We've got to build you a rig" was the suggestion D made after he first saw the 'milk crate' set up I was using when I first moved to Nashville. "You need a good pedal board set-up that can cover all the bases," he continued. His suggestion was the only excuse I needed to begin buying and experimenting with different effects pedals. Nine years later and my custom pedal board setup, one that some might consider overkill, is versatile, fairly foolproof, and (thanks to my "Loop Master" switcher) quite transparent.

First, I plug my guitar directly into an "Xotic RC Booster," essentially a clean boost that I leave on most of the time. The signal then enters my custom "Loop Master" pedal - a series of six switchable loops with a master bypass and tuner out. My first three loops go to a Keeley-modded Rat, a Keeley-modded Tube Screamer, and an HBE Power Screamer. The next loop is for modulation effects – a Fulltone Deja Vibe, which I leave on most of the time set to a very slow sweep, and a Keeley-modded Boss CE-2, which, thanks to the mod, does an amazing 'fast Leslie' sound. Next is a Keeley-modded Boss TR-2 Tremolo.

You've probably realized by now that I'm a big fan of "Keeley mods," If you're not familiar with them, Keeley Electronics is an Oklahoma-based, boutique guitar effects company that, in addition to building some great guitar effects, does some amazing modifications to stock effects pedals, greatly enhancing the tone and transparency of many popular effects. If you have never played through a Keeley effect or heard one of their mods, you owe it to yourself to check them out. www.robertkeeley.com

The final loop is reserved for a pair of delays – a Boss DD-6 with a tempo tap set to triplets and a Keeley-modded Line6 DM-4. I have three delay models set on the DM-4 - a tape echo set to slap back, a low-res delay set to a couple of repeats, and the 'analog with mod' set to heavy repeats. By doing the same tap tempo on both delays, I can achieve a wonderful 'galloping' type delay, similar to some of the guitar sounds produced by David Gilmour and "The Edge." A Peterson Strobostomp helps me quickly tune down to 1/1000th of a cent, and a Voodoo Labs Pedal Power II provides the AC. Everything is hardwired together with George L cables and housed in a sturdy anvil style case with room for cable storage underneath the board.

So that's about it - my guitars, gear, and gizmos. I hope you enjoyed the tour!

How To Run A Good Tip Jar

"Tipping – it's not just for cows anymore." — Anonymous

Many newcomers to Nashville are surprised to discover that most of the nightclubs in and around the city pay performers either by a system of "base pay" plus tips, and in many cases, tips only. Most of the venues that offer a base pay will guarantee the artist or band anywhere between $20 and $50 per player (typically closer to $20), making it necessary for the performers to work the tip jar to earn a decent wage. Many of the patrons in these clubs don't know this and will likely assume the band is getting paid some kind of a normal wage, and therefore, in many cases, will be reluctant to part with their money when the jar is passed around. Giving your audience a subtle and humorous tip jar education throughout your show can help change that greatly. Here are several factors that can contribute to a successful tip jar operation.

1. **Have it going on**. A band that is enjoying what they are doing is always more fun to experience. The positive energy of a group of players getting into their performance is contagious and can permeate a crowd. Give your audience a reason to tip you.

2. **Connect with the audience.** The singer needs to be a strong front person and entertain the audience. Just simply singing well won't necessarily make a crowd throw money at you. The front people that seem to command the best tips are the ones that are great at leading a party, not just the band. If the singer can help create an atmosphere that is fun and engaging by being entertaining, funny, personable, making eye contact, etc., patrons will be more likely to tip.

3. **Play fun songs.** Most of the audience members in a typical nightclub setting want to hear familiar, up-tempo songs, so play the biggest hits from the biggest artists and bands as well as some cult classics. Playing this kind of material also makes it easy for people to sing along which allows them to feel like they're part of the show.

4. **Read the crowd.** If it's a slow night, nobody's dancing, or the crowd is not engaging, don't just keep pounding out a set list verbatim. Try playing a couple of ballads back to back, perhaps some songs that are more geared towards listening than dancing, start taking requests, tell a joke, etc. Don't just accept that the night will be a dud; do what you must to try to get the party going.

5. **Ask for requests.** This is a great way to engage the audience, and done correctly, can get a good tip every time. Make a slightly humorous announcement, such as "If there's a particular song you want to hear, just write it down on a $20 or a $100 bill and pass it on up to the stage." Another approach is, when somebody requests a really worn out standard like "Mustang Sally " reply by lightheartedly saying, "That song is usually at least a $20 request." This will usually at least get some laughs, and quite often a $20 bill, especially if you hold out for a little while.

6. **Announce birthdays and special occasions.** If someone comes up to the stage and asks you to announce someone's birthday, anniversary, engagement etc., make it an event. Ask them if there is a special song they would like to hear. Use it as an opportunity to bring others into the moment by asking, "Is it anybody else's birthday today?" A few subtle moments like these throughout a performance will help create a closeness between the audience and band and can go a long way in regards to the tip jar.

7. **Make sure the jar is visible and accessible.** The tip jar should be placed somewhere on the front of the stage where it is clearly visible and accessible to both the audience and the band. If it's out of sight, it's out of mind.

8. **Jumpstart the jar.** What does an empty tip jar sitting on the front of the stage look like? An empty jar sitting on the front of the stage. Before you begin your show, put a couple of one dollar bills in the empty tip jar to make it obvious that it's a tip jar. That will help draw some attention to it and keep it from going potentially unnoticed.

9. **Work the tip jar.** Make periodic references over the mic, again, in a half joking manner, saying things like "We play for tips, so if you like what you hear, don't be afraid to throw in a dollar, or 10", or "Don't forget folks, for every dollar you throw in the tip jar, we each make a quarter." One singer I worked with used to regularly say "Diane's coming around with the tip jar, and this is how we make our living in Nashville. If you could just spare a few dollars, I'll be able to pick up some Krystal burgers for my daughter on the way home. Please throw in some money so I can feed her, she hasn't eaten all day." This often produced tips, made the audience laugh, and made the band laugh even harder, as we knew that he didn't even have a daughter.

10. **Send the jar around regularly.** The frequency that you send around the jar can vary depending on how quick your audience is turning over. At a club like Tootsies, where there is a fast turnover, the tip jar might go around every 30 to 45 minutes. If you're not getting any turnover, once an hour is probably plenty.

11. **Announce the tip jar.** When the time comes during your performance to pass the tip jar around the room, make an announcement like "Suzy's going to be coming around with our tip jar. This is how we make our living, so please be kind." The deliberate action of walking a tip jar around the room is something that many people outside of Nashville have never seen. Making this announcement is a vital part of making your audience receptive and prepared for this action.

12. **Choose a personable, but assertive person to take the jar around the room.** The person walking the tip jar needs to say something like "Would you like to tip the band?" Ask with authority, but with a friendly tone. Expect that some people will tip, some won't, and a few will give you an attitude. Use subtleties like raising an eyebrow or saying things like "Do you realize this is the only pay these guys are getting tonight?" This one task in particular can be the make or break it part of the night, so If possible, the person taking the jar around should be someone who is close to the band like a spouse or friend, as they will have a vested interest and be more likely to understand the importance of this action.

13. **Walk the jar slowly and efficiently.** The person walking the jar needs to slowly work their way from one end of the room to the other literally addressing each individual person if possible. They need to make sure they don't miss anybody, but avoid asking people twice. If you walk by people too quickly without looking at them, they will be much less likely to tip. Making eye contact while stating your cause is essential.

14. **Play a good song for the tip jar walk.** When it's time to send the jar around, make the announcement, and then play one of your biggest crowd pleasers. The more fun the audience is having when the tip jar appears in front of their face, the more likely they will be to give a good tip. This also makes the point that you should always send the jar around while the band is still playing, and not on a break if possible. When the band stops playing, the party goes into a lull. Hit em' up, while they're up.

15. **Squash the money**. If and when the jar starts to fill up with money, reach in and squash it down so it looks like less. A full jar reeks of "Yee-ha, we're getting rich," a near empty jar reeks of "Please help, we're going broke."

16. **Watch the tip jar**. A tip jar full of money sitting on the front of a stage can be vulnerable. Most people won't steal from it, but there is always the occasional thief lurking in the shadows. Always be aware of the jar's presence.

17. **Count the money using the buddy system.** Having two people count the money isn't always necessary, but it will help keep the honest, honest. If your band or group is comprised of friends or coworkers with a high level of trust, this probably isn't necessary. However, I have heard some stories in which one player was left to count the tip jar money and got caught stealing. Having two people count the money will virtually guarantee that this will never happen.

18. **Band spouses, girlfriends, and boyfriends, don't tip.** If your significant other is hanging out at your show, there is no need for him or her to tip. You are probably not getting paid particularly well in the first place, so why give up your hard earned money and there is no need for your family to give.

Learning how to run an effective tip jar operation is an art form and can be an exact science. Just hang out nightly at different clubs on Broadway and observe how artists and bands work it (or don't work it). Learning how to maximize the tip jars potential can be the difference between making $100 or $25. In Nashville, the conscious and aggressive working of a tip jar is most prevalent on Broadway; however it does exist to varying degrees in other clubs throughout the city. If you are working outside of Broadway, be aware of the different clubs tendencies, as some situations won't allow for a Broadway style operation. In general, over-working the tip jar, by either passing it around too often or making too many references to it on the mic, can be just as ineffective as under-working it. Every situation is different, and you need to learn the right balance. It's a fine line and almost requires a sixth sense. In the end, if you play the right tunes, play them well, enjoy what you are doing, and make your audience the priority, most people will gladly toss a dollar or more into the tip jar when the time comes.

A Tip Jar Gallery

See if you can find the tip jars in these Nashville bar room scenarios. Notice any similarities? And by the way, even if you can't find the tip jar you still have to tip the band!

Painting of the original Country Outlaws at the Stage on Broadway; Willie, Waylon, Kris and Johnny

The Nashville 100

"Bob Dylan, Neil Young, Merle Haggard, Hank Williams ... all of them are different styles, but those are the songs that make the times. They're the songs that last through time" — Dolly Parton

When I first arrived in Nashville I frequented the clubs on lower Broadway almost nightly. Growing up on classic rock and blues rendered me a bit unprepared for gigging in this town, so I had some catching up to do. In the months prior to my move, I watched CMT daily to start learning what I expected they would be playing here, but quickly found this was not the case. Instead, the songs of choice were classic country standards, the biggest hits from the biggest stars of the golden era of Country, interspersed with classic rock, pop, and occasional current radio hits. I began writing down song titles on napkins, acquiring recordings, and learning material. During that first year I had learned about 150 songs which proved essential for gigging in Nashville.

A few years later some of my friends interested in gigging on Broadway asked what they play down there which prompted me to organize "the Nashville 100". Obviously these are not the only songs played in town, but they're a good starting point and make up the bulk of what is commonly referred to in Nashville as standards.

If you grew up playing classic country you probably already know most of these. However, if you didn't, the list is a great starting point. If you are planning on moving here to be a player or an artist you will need to perform some of these songs at some point. If you are new to town and trying to sit in to get gigs, some of these tunes will definitely be called. Guitarists need to know the signature licks. Drummers are expected to know the tempos and count offs. Bassists need to be able to lead arrangements with the proper root motion. Singers need to know some easy standards if they expect to sit in or gig regularly.

Beyond all of that, if you don't know country music but want to succeed in that side of the business, it is essential to know these chord progressions, melodies, feels, and signatures as they are at the core of this style. This list of songs is like Country Music 101. If you know all the intros, chord progressions and arrangements of these tunes you will be prepared for much of what you will be doing in Nashville as a working musician whether you play clubs, road gigs, or work as a session player.

The Nashville 100: Classic and New Country - Male

Dixieland Delight	Alabama
Mountain Music	Alabama
Chattahoochee	Alan Jackson
Don't Rock The Jukebox	Alan Jackson
Save a Horse Ride a Cowboy	Big and Rich
My Maria	Brooks & Dunn
Neon Moon	Brooks & Dunn
Devil Went Down To Georgia	Charlie Daniels
Long Haired Country Boy	Charlie Daniels
The South's Gonna Do It Again	Charlie Daniels
Killin' Time	Clint Black
Tight Fittin' Jeans	Conway Twitty
You Never Even Call Me By My Name	David Allen Coe
Every Time I Roll The Dice	Delbert Mcclinton
Standin On Shaky Ground	Delbert Mcclinton
Super Duper Love	Delbert Mcclinton
Fast As You	Dwight Yoakam
Guitars and Cadillacs	Dwight Yoakam
Tulsa Time	Eric Clapton
Thunder Rolls	Garth Brooks
He Stopped Loving Her Today	George Jones
Hotter Than A Two Dollar Pistol	George Jones
I Don't Need Your Rockin' Chair	George Jones
She Thinks I Still Care	George Jones
The Race Is On	George Jones
White Lightening	George Jones
All My Ex's	George Strait
Amarillo By Morning	George Strait
Fool Hearted Memory	George Strait
Right or Wrong	George Strait
The Chair	George Strait
The Fireman	George Strait
Unwound	George Strait

Bluesman	Hank Williams, Jr.
Born To Boogie	Hank Williams, Jr.
Country Boy Can Survive	Hank Williams, Jr.
Dinosaur	Hank Williams, Jr.
Family Tradition	Hank Williams, Jr.
Kawliga	Hank Williams, Jr.
Whiskey Bent & Hell Bound	Hank Williams, Jr.
Hey Good Lookin’	Hank Williams, Sr.
Jambalaya	Hank Williams, Sr.
Lovesick Blues	Hank Williams, Sr.
So Lonesome I Could Cry	Hank Williams, Sr.
Statue Of A Fool	Jack Green
Be My Baby Tonight	John Michael Montgomery
Folsom Prison Blues	Johnny Cash
Ring Of Fire	Johnny Cash
Slide Off Your Satin Sheets	Johnny Paycheck
I Want to Love Somebody	Keith Urban
Don’t Close Your Eyes	Keith Whitley
Never Go Around Mirrors	Keith Whitley
When You Say Nothing	Keith Whitley
Walk Softly	Kentucky Headhunters
Bluest Eyes In Texas	Little Texas
Too Cold At Home	Mark Chestnut
Big City	Merle Haggard
Chase Each Other	Merle Haggard
Dukes of Hazzard	Merle Haggard
Great Afternoon	Merle Haggard
Make Up And Faded Blue Jeans	Merle Haggard
Mama Tried	Merle Haggard
Okie From Muskogee	Merle Haggard
Pancho & Lefty	Merle Haggard
Ramblin’ Fever	Merle Haggard
Silver Wings	Merle Haggard

Classic and New Country - Male (Continued)

Sing Me Back Home	Merle Haggard
Stay Here and Drink	Merle Haggard
Swinging Doors	Merle Haggard
Take Me For Granted	Merle Haggard
That's the Way Love Goes	Merle Haggard
The Fugitive	Merle Haggard
The Way I Am	Merle Haggard
Today I Started Loving You Again	Merle Haggard
Workin' Man Blues	Merle Haggard
Bandy the Rodeo Clown	Moe Bandy
Rocky Top	Osborne Brothers
King Of The Road	Roger Miller
Lonely Women Make Good Lovers	Steve Wariner
Should Have Been A Cowboy	Toby Keith
Who's Your Daddy	Toby Keith
Anymore	Travis Tritt
T.R.O.U.B.L.E.	Travis Tritt
Go Rest High On That Mountain	Vince Gill
Liza Jane	Vince Gill
One More Last Chance	Vince Gill
Whenever You Come Around	Vince Gill
Good Hearted Woman	Waylon Jennings
I Don't Think Hank	Waylon Jennings
I'm A Ramblin' Man	Waylon Jennings
Mama Don't Let Your Babies	Waylon Jennings
Only Daddy That'll Walk The Line	Waylon Jennings
Blue Eyes Cryin' In The Rain	Willie Nelson
Georgia	Willie Nelson
Nightlilfe	Willie Nelson
On The Road Again	Willie Nelson
Whiskey River	Willie Nelson

Classic and New Country - Female

Could I Have This Dance	Anne Murray
I Was Country When Country Wasn't Cool	Barbara Mandrell
I Don't Want You To Go	Carolyn Dawn Johnson
Don't Touch Me	Connie Smith
Strawberry Wine	Deana Carter
Let'r Rip	Dixie Chicks
Some Days You Gotta Dance	Dixie Chicks
There's Your Trouble	Dixie Chicks
Tonight The Heartaches On Me	Dixie Chicks
Coat Of Many Colors	Dolly Parton
Jolene	Dolly Parton
It Matters To Me	Faith Hill
Here for the Party	Gretchen Wilson
Redneck Girl	Gretchen Wilson
There is No Arizona	Jamie O'Neal
Harper Valley P.T.A.	Jeannie C. Riley
Heads Carolina, Tails California	Jo Dee Messina
Lesson In Leavin'	Jo Dee Messina
It Wasn't God Who Made Honky Tonk Angels	Kitty Wells
You Ain't Woman Enough	Loretta Lynn
Satin Sheets	Loretta Lynn
Broken Wing	Martina McBride
Independence Day	Martina McBride
My Baby Loves Me Just The Way I Am	Martina McBride
Blue Moon Of Kentucky	Patsy Cline
Crazy	Patsy Cline
I Fall To Pieces	Patsy Cline
Leaving On Your Mind	Patsy Cline
She's Got You	Patsy Cline
Walkin' After Midnight	Patsy Cline
Your Cheatin' Heart	Patsy Cline
Blame It On Your Heart	Patty Loveless
Suds in the Bucket	Sara Evans

Rock, Blues, and Pop

One Way Out	Allman Brothers
Ramblin Man	Allman Brothers
Can't Get Enough	Bad Company
Old Time Rock and Roll	Bob Seger
Wanted Dead or Alive	Bon Jovi
Summer of 69	Bryan Adams
Already Gone	Eagles
Hotel California	Eagles
Peaceful Easy Feeling	Eagles
Tulsa Time	Eric Clapton
Drift Away	Dobie Gray
Long Train Runnin'	Doobie Brothers
Tore Down	Freddie King
Keep Your Hands To Yourself	Georgia Sattelites
Pink Houses	John Mellencamp
Feelin Allright	Joe Cocker
Margaritaville	Jimmy Buffet
Sweet Home Alabama	Lynyrd Skynyrd
Gimme Three Steps	Lynyrd Skynyrd
Hit Me With Your Best Shot	Pat Benatar
Every Rose Has Its Thorn	Poison
Honky Tonk Woman	Rolling Stones
Pride and Joy	Stevie Ray Vaughan
Mary Jane's Last Dance	Tom Petty
Brown Eyed Girl	Van Morrison
Mustang Sally	Wilson Pickett
Signed Sealed Delivered	Stevie Wonder
Give Me One Reason	Tracy Chapman
Hold on Loosely	Thirty Eight Special

Chapter 6

Sustainability

"Life is not a problem to be solved, but a reality to be experienced."
— Soren Kierkegaard

For most of us musicians, the decision to learn how to play a musical instrument was made at an early age, long before we would ever consider choosing it for a possible career. In the early stages of musical development, most beginners are not thinking about anything other than the task at hand. During this period, you are not concerned with technique and play with reckless abandon, living in the moment and unconcerned with consequence. As the years pass and you slowly improve your craft, other factors often come into play. You might realize that performing music can gain you attention, popularity, and/or income. The moment you made those realizations was the inevitable moment you began considering music for your career.

Before you know it, you've been playing music for 10 or 20 years, making some money doing it, and are now trying to figure out how to take your career to the next level. The decisions you make about performing music can become guided by a host of external factors. You start to ask yourself questions like: Will joining this band help my career? Are these clothes appropriate for this gig? Do I write songs that people want to hear? How do I get a meeting with somebody at a management company? How do I achieve a bigger following? If you're not careful, it is easy to become consumed by your career aspirations and lose perspective. Meanwhile, the years are churning past. Your goals change, your tastes in music change, your body changes, your persona changes, your life situation changes. Sustainability becomes an issue.

The road for many musicians is a lifelong journey. Whether you play music for the fun of it, or professionally for income, there are a lot of variables that will impact your ability to be able to perform music for the rest of your life. Do you hope to still be able to play music when you are 50 or 60? Are you enjoying your musical activities right now? Will you be able to earn enough money from your craft to support yourself and your family for the rest of your life? Will you still be able to earn money from your craft in 20 or 30 years? Will you still want to? Do you have a fallback plan?

This last section of the book focuses on building a musician with a sustainable future. Your skills, your inner character and mindset, your goals, and your friendships and relationships will shape that future. Being proficient at your craft and maintaining your body and mind will help allow you to play the music you want to play, effortlessly and with less susceptibility to injury for the rest of your life. Making the right decisions today will help ensure your ability to enjoy your career, your life, and your musical endeavors later on. You are living your future each and every day so try to live life in the moment. With the right outlook, you'll always be able to enjoy your musical life, regardless of what you achieve with your career. Educate yourself and excel with music and life, and there will be many rewards along the way. Build a good ship, and it will sail for a long time.

New recruits in downtown Nashville

Aspiring Artists

"I met someone the other night who's 28 years old, and he hasn't worked a day since he left college because he's pursuing a dream he'll never, ever realize: He thinks he's a great singer. Actually, he's crap." — Simon Cowell

The term "artist" is used loosely in today's music world, and the origins of this word in a musical setting are vague, at best. When I first moved to Nashville, I heard references to "artist gigs" quite often, and I remember thinking, why would a musician move here to get a job with someone who makes paintings? Of course I quickly came to understand that "artist" was short for recording artist, touring artist, or performing artist. In my mind, an artist is, simply, one who makes art. Perhaps the definition of an artist in the music world is a combination of all of the above: someone who makes art, in the form of music, records their art, and then performs it for audiences across the land by way of touring, usually, with the goal of selling their art to earn money to sustain their artistry.

So let's assume that most people in the music biz' who call themselves artists are looking at their career in this way. How do you get from point A to point B? What different approaches can you take to turn your aspirations into a real and practical living? While there is no quick or easy answer to this, here are some concepts and theories that should apply to most.

Define your success. You need to come up with your own definition of success and then build your plan of small incremental steps that might lead to that success. Do you want to write and record your own music? Build a sustainable fan base? Tour the country? These are lofty goals that take time, money, commitments, and patience. You need to know where you're heading before you jump in the ocean.

Don't expect the "Music Industry" to provide a clear path to success; it won't. The old music business model created a mirage in which the music industry would "discover" obscure struggling artists, "sign them" to "record deals," put them on tour, and launch them into superstardom to forever enjoy a fruitful career of fame and fortune for the rest of their days. In reality, it didn't work out that way for most artists, and in this new era, even less so. That old mirage is waning.

Be prepared to go it alone. No one is going to care about your music, your art, and your career as much as you do. Once you get the train rolling, people will want to jump aboard, but initially, you'll have to do most of the work yourself. If someone presents you with an offer that sounds too good to be true, in this business, it most definitely is. Be prepared to dig in, get your hands dirty, and work hard.

Wear a lot of hats. We are living in the age of the do-it-yourselfer, and this holds especially true for musical artists. You should work towards being a good songwriter, singer, showman, engineer, producer, bandleader, instrumentalist, tour manager, merchandise person, booking agent, publicist, and any other position that might apply to your situation. The more you can do yourself, the less you'll rely on others.

Don't confuse music with the business of music. These are two separate entities and need to be treated as such. Building a career in the music business involves more business, than music. If you don't like the idea of being a business person, this might not be the best career for you.

Be a real artist. The last decade has brought forth millions of amateur bands and artists, many of whom perform and record poorly written music that they put forth into the world on MySpace and small local venues. This has created an oversaturation of mediocre music. Work hard to improve your songwriting, musicianship, stage presence, and you will be more likely to stand out in this ever-increasing market. Try to connect with the inner artist in you and create music that contains real depth and emotion. Have something to say and learn how to say it.

Just because you moved to Nashville doesn't mean none of this applies. Because of the extreme level of competition found here, and the sheer numbers of people getting into the game, you'll have to work extra hard if you expect to stand out in the crowd. What Nashville does have to offer the aspiring artist is a wide array of music related resources combined with a low cost of living. Compared with much of the country, Nashville is an inexpensive place to live, and this makes it a cost effective place to launch a career for some. As far as resources, the city has an abundance of great musicians, songwriters, engineers, recording studios, live music venues, publishing companies, songpluggers, record labels, publicists, music stores, rehearsal studios, bus companies, and any other useful entity you can think of that would apply to a career in music.

It's all here; you just have to figure out how to make it work for you.

Wearing A Lot Of Hats

"I just hate to be in one corner. I hate to be put as only a guitar player, or either only as a songwriter, or only as a tap dancer. I like to move around."
— Jimi Hendrix

With the music industry rebuilding from the ground up, we are now living in the age of the do-it-yourselfer. This means that to succeed at a career in music you will need to wear a lot of hats. Not cowboy hats; those are for the artists. I'm talking about multiple job roles. The more music business-related skills you have, the better you will be equipped to survive and thrive in the unknown future that lies ahead.

Here are a few hats you might learn to wear:

If you play an instrument but don't sing, learn how to sing. Players who can sing harmony are more in demand than players who don't. Players who can sing harmony *and* lead are usually more in demand than players who can only sing harmony. Being able to lead sing makes you a stronger harmony singer *and* puts you in the unique position of being able to offer the main vocalist of your group a mid-set break. Being a strong singer can also aid in the writing of original music and allow you to sing on your own demos and recordings.

If you sing but don't play a second instrument, learn how to play a second instrument. Singers that can play a second instrument, such as guitar or piano for instance, have the added option of working for bands or artists that need harmony singers who can also play a rhythm instrument. Singers who can accompany themselves have the option of working as a solo performer. You will also be less dependent on other musicians for things like writing original songs and recording your own demos.

Learn how to think like a band leader. Whether you are practicing with a band, recording, or playing live, most band situations have a band leader. Learn from the good ones you work with. How do they go about organizing a rehearsal? What sort of visual cues do they provide the band during recording or performance? Learn how to hear *and* see the big picture of a great performing band and understand the organization that helps make them great. Someday you might be working for a band or artist when the band leader quits. When that happens, that role is usually delegated to whatever remaining person within the group is the most obviously qualified. Be ready to step up to the plate when the time comes. Your value to the artists will be increased.

Learn how to make a good recording. There has been a recent explosion in the number of home studios in Nashville and beyond, so by building your own and learning the recording process you will have more options than those who don't. If you are a songwriter you will save thousands of dollars by being able to record your own demos. If you can make a good recording you also give yourself the option of recording other projects for additional income. Not to mention, learning how to record will make you a better musician.

Be a manager. Maybe your band or career situation doesn't require being one at this moment, but most professionals that earn a living from music are freelancers. A freelance "gun for hire" is in many ways similar to an independent artist. Ultimately, you need to take full responsibility for your career if you expect to do well, and this requires managing skills. To be a good manager, you need to see the big picture, organize schedules, anticipate problems, solve problems, have good social skills, and be good at marketing, etc. If you are good at managing your own career, your managing skills might also be of use to whatever artist or band you are working for at any given moment. When I first began playing guitar for Rhett Akins, there was no dedicated tour manager, as the last one had just quit. Although I had no prior experience in this position, I volunteered to give it a try. I ended up getting pretty good at it, and this increased my value to the organization. Along with the added responsibility came a pay raise and that didn't hurt either.

Be a booking agent. This doesn't mean you have to set up a booking agency, and this doesn't apply to everyone. If most of your musical activity consists of nightclub performances, learn how to talk to club owners and try to help create more work for whatever projects you are involved with. If you are working for a touring artist or band, learn to be on the lookout for venues that might be appropriate and pass tips along to the group's manager or leader. If you are a singer or an aspiring artist, it will be in your best interest to learn how to book yourself, with or without the help of booking agencies. The more you can book yourself, the less reliant you will be on others. A booking agency might also represent other interests, but *you* will always be your biggest priority.

Be a tech. Learn as much as you can about your own equipment and develop the ability to perform minor repairs. Depending on your career, some common tasks that need to be done regularly might be things like soldering a broken instrument or microphone cable, intonating guitars and basses, replacing a blown speaker or tubes in an amplifier, fixing broken drum hardware, building or fixing a recording computer, troubleshooting software problems, etc. Home studios require maintenance. On many tours, a sound engineer or member of the band will also act as the guitar tech for the artist. In the long run, having these kinds of skills will not only improve your value to your employer, they will save you money.

Everybody is different. Some of us are better at certain things than others, so learn to build on your strengths. If you are good at graphic design, you might be able to use those skills to design logos, flyers, or merchandise. If you have some knowledge about web design, you might be able to build your own website, offer those services to your employer, or build websites for other entities for hire. If you have some background driving commercial vehicles, you might be able to be a relief driver on your tour. Being good at more than one thing and having the ability to wear a lot of hats at the same time makes you more valuable to potential employers than those who don't. It also makes you less reliant on others for your own endeavors. While many musical situations rely on collaborations and teamwork, the reality is that most of us working in the music industry are working for ourselves. You may have an employer, but in most cases, at the end of the day, you are essentially a freelance "gun for hire." Be able to wear a lot of hats, and your options will become more limitless.

Marketing And Communications

"Everyone lives by selling something." — Robert Louis Stevenson

Every person who desires a career in the music business is signing up for a career in sales whether they realize it or not. If you're a songwriter, you're trying to sell your songs. If you're a musician, you're trying to sell your music performing services. If you're an engineer, you're selling your engineering skills. You are offering either services or commodities, and if you want to be paid for what you do, you need to be good at selling your product. This means you need to become good at selling yourself. Understanding exactly what products you have to offer and honing your marketing and communication skills is essential.

Networking: Effective networking takes time, effort, and awareness. Aside from the meeting of new players while out on the town, I have found that everyday life outside of its obvious musical situations can offer more subtle, yet still effective networking opportunities. Simply be receptive and open to the possibilities within each existing or new relationship you have.

Maybe you own a home recording studio, and the Terminix man you hired happens to be working towards a career as a songwriter. How would you ever know that he's looking for a new studio to record his songs at if you don't at least have a brief conversation with him? Maybe you're working towards becoming a session player and your mailman's brother owns a recording studio and is looking for new players. You'll never know if you don't engage in conversation.

Being good at networking requires a specific mindset, and you must make a conscious effort to develop these skills in a way that is effective and natural for you. You don't want to come off like your hustling everybody, but being overly passive won't get you anywhere. Find a middle ground that you're comfortable with. Most importantly, be sincere. If you're just out to build friendships to serve your own needs, many people will figure that out pretty quickly.

Name dropping: There is an art to using name dropping in an effective way. In the right context, it can enhance your position in a way that seems like you're not bragging. Poorly executed, you will come across like an attention starved dufus with low self-esteem. If you live and work in Nashville long enough, you will probably meet some famous people. You might also wind up working for some of them. There's nothing wrong with using these connections in your resumes and mentioning them in conversation; everybody does. Just be honest about your relationships or it could backfire on you. Also, a little goes a long way. If you are throwing a few big names into a conversation and somebody cuts you off midsentence and says, "Whoops, you dropped something," you know you've gone too far.

Web Presence: For career-minded musicians, having an Internet presence can help increase visibility. Musicians are in the service industry as we are offering our musical services, typically for a fee. If nothing else, having a real website creates a central point of contact. 10 or 20 years ago, people used the phone book or the yellow pages to look up a service. Not anymore. Internet searches are now the norm. If you are trying to obtain work as a freelance player, having the ability to direct potential employers to a website that contains audio clips, a bio, and pictures can help improve your chances. A good website could also demonstrate the mixing abilities of an engineer, the appeal of an aspiring artist, the credentials of a producer, or the skills of a songwriter.

Many musicians and artists use MySpace to create an internet profile as it is free and fairly easy to set up with a minimal knowledge of computers. The plus side of MySpace is that you can do this yourself and use your "space" to network with other "friends" in your related genre of music. This approach has worked well for a number of successful indie artists such as Corey Smith and Colt Ford who have built large followings using MySpace as one of their main marketing tools. There are a couple of downsides to MySpace. It's not entirely secure and can provide easy access to your network for spammers and scammers while increasing your chances of downloading a virus. It's also often slow and cumbersome and flooded with mediocrity.

If you are a serious music professional, a real domain website can look far more professional, navigate more effectively, and ultimately give you a more professional and impressive internet presence. Many artists choose to use a combination of their domain site with their MySpace and Facebook sites for marketing. If you have a real domain website, it is a good idea to have a MySpace page that contains a similar look, similar information, and links to your real site and vice versa.

Social Networking: This especially applies to artists and bands who are trying to build and sustain a long-term fan base, but ultimately applies to any music entrepreneur. Use any and all forms of social networking websites as a launch pad for your projects, services, or products. Learn how to connect with your target audience by blogging, twittering, messaging on Facebook etc and use your domain website as a central hub to connect all of these social platforms. There is no right or wrong approach, but a consistent, continuous effort over a long period of time is needed to see any tangible results. When you regularly engage with your fans and customers online for free, they will be more likely to purchase your services or products when that time comes.

The Internet is a powerful tool and offers many possibilities for today's music professionals providing marketing options, career insight and perspective, as well as specific knowledge about almost anything you could think of.

For many musicians, bands and artists, there are many ways to promote your shows and events online ranging from advertising your show on free club listings, sending instant messages using Twitter or Facebook, sending out bulletin's on MySpace, or linking your site to other related sites. For those looking to sell their music online, websites like iTunes and Amazon offer the ability for songs and ring tones to be sold in the form of digital downloads.There are also online referral services that might help you find work. Just perform a Google search and you will find many, such as www.musicians-in-your-city.us or www.roadie.net.

If you are looking for information about musical equipment or recording techniques, there are hundreds of sites offering free and useful information. HarmonyCentral.com has extensive product reviews and many forums that could provide answers to just about any question you might have about music equipment and recording. Many print publications also have great websites that contain archives of past publications such as Guitar Player, Modern Drummer, Mix Magazine, Electronic Musician, etc. If you can become good at performing Internet searches, you can educate yourself and gain perspective about many things pertaining to your career.

Craigslist is a truly unique Internet site that can provide some interesting perspective to the Nashville music scene as well as music scenes around the world. The "For Sale" section can be a good place to find deals on musical instruments and can also be a good place to sell gear you're trying to liquidate. Under "community," the musicians section contains some occasionally useful, but almost always entertaining ads. While some people post ads looking for players for band projects or freelance musicians for studio projects, a majority of the ads are for people selling their services or promoting their projects. There are also occasional rants about almost anything pertaining to the music business, and these rants, which often go back and forth for days, can offer a unique perspective into some musicians' perceptions of their local music scenes. One of my favorites is a long running debate about playing for free, as there is a fair amount of that in Nashville.

Bulletin boards, like the ones found at local music stores and coffee shops, can be a good place to post flyers or business cards promoting your services. However, you will seldom find any paying gigs advertised on them. You're not likely to ever see a bulletin board ad that says "Kenny Chesney is looking for a bass player" or "Dark Horse recording seeks session players."

Communications: Being good at communicating is an essential part of being a successful working musician in Nashville or anywhere. In the post-digital era in which we live and work, there are many new trends. Texting has become more popular than phone conversations and e-mailing for many. For musicians working in Nashville, it is simply important to be consistent with all forms of communications with others. If someone calls you for a gig and leaves a voicemail, call them back even if you aren't available. A simple "I'm already booked on that night, but thanks for thinking of me" will show them that you appreciate the offer, and make it more likely for them to call you again. Not returning calls or answering e-mails puts forth a message that you're either too busy or don't care.

Grammar: In the rapidly expanding digital world in which we live, Pour gramar and 'punctuation' are increasingly becoming the norm. As many people are now communicating through texting or e-mails, and often doing it quickly on-the-fly, a certain kind of laziness has crept in to our society. Taking the few extra seconds it will take to add a couple of commas or periods to your message will not only put forth the notion that you made it past the third grade, it makes the statement that you actually care about how you are perceived. A little spell check here and there can also go a long way.

Technology: A good basic understanding of computers can greatly aid the modern career minded musician. You don't need to be able to write code, but having a good working knowledge about file management, how to install software, how to use e-mail programs and other word processing programs, virus protection software, and basic audio recording software is essential for a musicians survival in this post internet era, and will greatly aid your communication efficiency.

An Error In Communication

A few years ago, a Nashville based songwriter was financing his own recording project. Instead of going with the usual A-Team session player approach he opted to hire some of his friends, most of whom were touring musicians. He had almost all the players lined up for the project, but there was one player in particular he couldn't seem to get a hold of, despite leaving multiple voicemails over a period of weeks. Ultimately, none of the phone calls were ever returned, and the songwriter eventually went with another player. The all-day recording sessions lasted for two or three weeks, and all of the players were paid union scale. The one fellow who missed out, despite having an impeccable reputation as a player, was notorious for not returning phone calls. I wonder how many other career opportunities he missed out on over the years?

Networking Truths: by Dan Kimpel

» Effective networking has to benefit both parties. Why should someone give you the time of day, if there is no potential benefit for them?

» Everyone wants to get on the train that's up and running, so it is imperative that a project appears to have momentum.

» Often, we meet music people in non-musical settings: church, AA meetings, the medical marijuana dispensary, the dog park. So before someone buys you as an artist, songwriter, or musician, they must first trust and appreciate you as a person.

» Finding common ground is a networking key: people like to do business with those who are like themselves.

» Nashville is the most cordial of the music cities. In New York people reject and say no emphatically. In L.A. they never say no, they just don't call back.

» Name dropping can be a bit hazardous because we never know the relationship between the person we're talking to and the name we're dropping. Folks exaggerate their relationships, too.

» Meeting someone more than once is imperative to build credibility. For that reason I encourage songwriters and artists to attend a variety of events in diverse locales to give the impression of a national presence.

» Not taking yourself too seriously is an excellent tool for maintaining equilibrium in a social setting.

» Always wear a little pin, a music t-shirt, or something to identify yourself as a music industry professional when traveling, shopping, etc. It allows others access to you.

» No networking can ever happen if someone is on a cell phone or texting. These are death to effective social interaction.

Author and speaker Dan Kimpel is one of the American media's foremost authorities on popular music and songwriters. To learn more about Dan you can visit his website at www.dankimpel.com.

RECORDING CONTRACT

Avoiding Scams

"Caveat emptor"

Nashville is overflowing with musicians, songwriters, artists, producers, and just about every type of aspiring music entrepreneur imaginable. Unfortunately, this massive talent pool also attracts a fair share of scammers and fakes, many who actively seek out the unsuspecting, attempting to extract as much money as possible in exchange for their less than honorable services. Many may claim to have extensive industry contacts, often boasting a long list of seemingly impressive professional credits.

The best sharks will come off as being genuinely interested in you, your music, and your potential, often stating that they have all the connections needed to evolve your career quickly and efficiently. They may not even ask for money on the first several encounters or phone calls. Some of these shady characters could be unsuspecting patrons circulating the local nightclubs, while others advertise their illegitimate operations on the Internet.

Although most of these scammers are primarily interested in your money, some might be interested in sex, companionship, or other favors, and will work towards these ends through a series of music career related manipulations that initially, on the surface, might seem to have your best interests at heart. To avoid getting ripped off, here are some things to be on the lookout for:

Shady Internet Ads

» **Lack of a real domain website**. Most, but not all, legitimate businesses have a real domain website, for example www.justduckydesigns.com. Be wary of companies that don't. If a company only has a MySpace page, or a freebie site (if you scroll down to the bottom of the home page it might say something like "free site by Go Daddy") that usually implies they are on a low budget. Granted, some companies may be just getting started, but if you expect them to have the resources to make a difference in your career, it is only logical to expect them to have enough of a budget for their own advertising.

» **Requiring payment for an initial consultation**. In this day and age, literally any legitimate business will offer at least one free consultation. If an individual or company is truly interested in helping further your career, they should be willing to at least have an initial conversation with you (if not several) free of charge.

» **Lack of contact info**. If you find a music business-related advertisement on the Internet and it doesn't have a business address or phone number, that's usually not a good sign. Most honest businesses are easily accessible.

E-mail Solicitation

» **How an e-mail is worded.** If you get an e-mail from somebody stating they are interested in you as an artist, or your music, pay close attention to the wording. Realize that much of your information is easily available to everyone on the Internet (especially if you have a MySpace or Facebook page) and it's not hard for spammers to inject some personal information to their message. Read between the lines. Are they speaking about your music in general terms, using descriptions that could apply to any song, or is it obvious they've researched beyond that?

» **Lack of a domain e-mail.** As noted above, most legitimate businesses will have a real website, usually accompanied with an e-mail address that has the same domain. Be wary of e-mail solicitors whose address end with generic e-mail hosts like @ gmail.com or @yahoo.com. Once again this is not always the case, but this can be a flag.

» **Solicitation of songs for a compilation CD.** If you get an e-mail or MySpace message from some organization claiming they want to put your music on a compilation CD, for a fee of course, delete the e-mail. You should never have to pay to have your music placed anywhere. A legitimate organization will pay *you* for the use of your songs.

In-person Solicitation

» **Fast talkers**. When you are performing in a nightclub or other music venue, whether it's a full performance with a band or just a quick sit-in, you have inadvertently opened the door to any scammers that might be present. While some legitimate entities may be interested in talking with you, be wary of the ones that begin making big promises early on in the conversation. If they seem like they might be legit, don't be afraid to ask questions about their business and background.

» **Read between the lines**. Often, a person's body language and how they say something can be just as revealing as the content they put forth in a conversation. If they avoid eye contact, seem nervous, or lack focus when you are speaking, that could mean they're less than honorable. Of course it could also mean that they are simply shy and that you are boring them to tears. Try to be as objective as you can.

» **Learn how to research**. If you meet someone in public who shows in interest in helping your career, ask for a business card, or jot down their name and contact info if they don't have one. Visit their website and review their info. Perform a Google search and read up on as much background information as possible. If they are a plausible entity, it should quickly become obvious. If you can't find any information about them at all, that should be a flag. This also applies to companies that contact you through the Internet and e-mail solicitations as well.

In General

If it sounds too good to be true, it probably is. There are more musicians and artists trying to get ahead than there are opportunities or work for them. In reality, as the supply far outweighs the demand, our services aren't really essential to society. So when somebody says, *"You've got what it takes to be a star, and I want to help make it happen for you,"* then there's a good chance this is BS. Never lose sight of the fact that no one will ever care as much about your music and your career as you will.

Whether you realize it or not, when you signed on for a career as a musician or artist, you became a salesperson. You are trying to sell your songs, your craft, and ultimately yourself. Depending on your goals, you might need some help along the way, and some of this help will cost money. Ultimately, the key to avoid getting ripped off is a combination of common sense and research. Thoroughly research all individuals and companies before you fork over your hard-earned cash, especially before you ever sign anything. If you're still unsure after your research efforts are exhausted, ask for references and don't be afraid to call them. And if you're still not sure, always refer to rule number one - "If it smells like BS, it's probably BS!"

JACK
LALANNE
P90X

Maintenance

"Every human being is the author of his own health or disease."
— the Buddha

At some point during their life, many musicians experience a rude awakening upon the discovery that their lifelong pursuit of mastering their craft has resulted in bodily injury. The performance of many instruments can require musicians to stand, sit, and hold their bodies in some unnatural positions, often under less than desirable circumstances, for hours on end. This can cause a host of performance-related injuries and discomfort such as carpel tunnel, tendonitis, back pain, joint pain, and muscle fatigue.

As a lot of musical situations can require excessive volume, hearing loss and tinnitus are also potential hazards. Whereas much live music performance takes place in nightclubs, secondhand smoke resulting in respiratory illness is a potential danger as well. And for some, a lifetime of poor lifestyle choices can lead to battles with heart disease, diabetes and other chronic life-threatening illnesses, all which can greatly hamper or end a career. Most of these problems take years to develop, and in some cases there are no warning signs until after most of the damage is done. The good news is that many of these injuries are preventable and treatable.

Repetitive motion injuries, like tendonitis, carpal tunnel, and inflammation affect many musicians, especially, but not limited to guitarists, bassists, drummers, and keyboardists. Recording engineers and people who work desk jobs within the industry also suffer from these kinds of injuries as their jobs require them to sit in a chair for long periods of time, often using a mouse or typing while staring at a computer screen. The daily activities of many musicians are in some ways similar to that of a construction worker. You perform the same kind of hand and arm motions every time you play your instrument, which is probably daily, for decades just like a carpenter swings a hammer or an electrician pulls wires. Over a lifetime of performing the same kind of repetitive arm motions, muscles can become tight and weak resulting in damage to soft tissue causing pain and possibly restricting use. You can play your instrument for many years with literally no signs that this damage is being done, until suddenly the problem reveals itself. What seems like a problem that developed overnight was actually years in the making.

Once you have tendonitis, or other forms of muscle inflammation, stretching and icing regularly can help to get it under control. There are several different stretching techniques that, when performed regularly, will loosen the tendons and reduce pain. Just perform a Google search on tendinitis stretching exercises and you will find a wealth of information available.

The muscles in your arms are actually a series of overlapping interconnected muscles, tendons, and ligaments that run from your fingers all the way to your shoulder. It is because of this fact that it important to also stretch areas of the arm that might not have any pain or problems. Performing stretches that work your wrists, triceps, and shoulders will ultimately help stretch all the muscles and tendons in between.

Stretching an arm with tendonitis is not the same as stretching a healthy arm and requires some caution. Listen to your body. The stretching should cause some sensation, but should not be painful. The more you stretch, the more results you will experience. Stretch at regular intervals throughout the day, always making it a point to warm up with some light cardio before your first stretching sequence. (Stretching cold muscles can cause further injury.) If you are gigging, try to stretch before the performance, after the performance, and even in between songs if you have a chance.

Icing morning and night will also help reduce the inflammation. Apply the ice by holding some ice in a washcloth and rubbing it firmly on the inflamed area for about 10 minutes. It is best to do about 10 minutes on and 10 minutes off, 2 to 3 times at each icing. Once the tendonitis is under control it is absolutely essential to continue with your regular stretching. If you don't, these problems will likely reoccur.

Back, neck, and shoulder pain can cause discomfort and restrictions for potentially any musician or technician. Any job that requires you to sit in a chair or stand while performing a repetitive task will put long-term stress on your back. From my experience the best remedies for chronic back or shoulder pain are regular exercise and stretching combined with good nutrition. Much of the back pain that people experience is the result of weak stomach muscles, therefore, engaging in core strengthening exercises (walking, jogging, hiking, yoga, Pilates, martial arts, etc.) on a regular basis will strengthen your core and provide more support to your spinal column. Everything is connected.

Joint pain, like back pain, is also more often the result of a lifetime of repetitive muscle use combined with a lack of regular exercise and poor lifestyle choices. Strengthening the muscles around a joint will help take some of the stress off of the joint. Recent studies have concluded that smoking and diabetes tend to make circulation less efficient and help perpetuate the cycle of these kinds of chronic injuries.

Tinnitus is nerve damage that causes a permanent ringing in the ears from the result of long-term exposure to excessive SPLs (Sound Pressure Levels). If you have ever gone to a loud concert and woke up the next day with your ears still ringing, this is what it is like to have tinnitus, except with tinnitus the ringing never goes away.

Tinnitus is irreversible nerve damage to your ears. Once you have it, it *can* get worse, so the use of earplugs is essential to stop its progression. For musicians, the use of molded, fitted, noise reducing earplugs can reduce excessive volume while still retaining a fairly realistic perception of the performance. If tinnitus goes unchecked, the ringing can eventually become so loud that it will eventually overcome most of the sounds you hear, and this can lead to a host of physical and mental problems ranging from headaches to nausea, and even insanity, in some cases.

Some musicians have tinnitus and don't even know it, as the early stages produce the ringing at a barely audible level. Many musicians that perform regularly never spend enough time away from performing to realize they have this permanent ringing. Next time you have a week off, listen carefully. Are your ears still ringing a week after your last performance?

Hearing loss can also be the result of years of overexposure to music played at excessively loud volumes. You can have hearing loss in one or both ears, and it can be an overall reduction across the frequency spectrum, or a dip in certain frequencies. Hearing loss can be gradual, so you may not notice this as its happening. An inexpensive hearing test with an audiologist will help you assess how well you hear.

Overall fitness including cardio, strength, and flexibility training will greatly help you maintain your music performance skills and reduce your susceptibility to repetitive muscle injuries. The better aerobic condition you are in, the better your circulation will be, and your muscles need this constant supply of oxygen to avoid fatigue. By strength training (i.e. push-ups, pull-ups, weightlifting) your muscles will be stronger and better able to endure the long hours you will spend playing your instrument. Flexibility exercises such as yoga, Pilates, and basic stretching will make your body more flexible and keep your muscles loose, furthering your ability to withstand the rigors of performing music.

Good nutrition can also have an impact on your overall health. If you want to improve your overall health and condition, it would also be wise to examine your nutritional intake. You need to put good gas in the car if you want it to run well. To learn more about nutrition and healthy eating concepts visit the website www.doitthehardway.com.

Nonstop Whining

Many years ago I knew a guitar player who had been playing professionally in nightclubs for many years. He kept a busy schedule, teaching music during the daytime, and playing music in nightclub bands about three to four nights a week, year-round. The bands he was involved with played aggressively, everybody dug in. Around the year 2000, he had an extremely busy summer, playing gigs 6 to 7 nights per week. Right at the tail end of that busy season, he played an afternoon gig with a blues band that was exceptionally loud, and then went on to play another show that night. When he woke up the next morning his ears were ringing loudly, much louder than he had ever noticed before. Three days later, the ringing was still there. A week later, it was still there, and had not decreased in volume as it had in the past. Now that he finally had a week off, the inability for the ringing to subside was finally noticeable. This was the beginning of his new life wherein his ears would never again stop ringing.

A couple of weeks into this new life of permanent ringing he began to play some more gigs. He quickly realized that the volume of the ringing was increasing, so he began to wear foam earplugs. This unnatural reduction in volume made it difficult to play music. He went to an audiologist, who after some testing, explained that he had tinnitus and suggested using custom musician earplugs. He found that the musician earplugs worked far better than foam plugs. At first it was a struggle getting used to playing with ear plugs, as even the custom musician's plugs still did not sound as realistic as hearing with no protection, but it was better than the alternative.

10 years later, I still have tinnitus. The ringing never went away. It's still there, and it will always be there. I sleep with a white noise generator next to my bed to cover-up the ringing. I wear my earplugs religiously in any circumstance where there is excessive volume, because if I don't, the ringing gets louder! This includes virtually all live music situations whether I am performing or in the audience. I also wear them while operating a power saw, flying in an airplane, or mowing the lawn. The level of the ringing in my ears is manageable, but the thought of it becoming permanently louder is terrifying. Having tinnitus has definitely taken some of the fun out of performing and experiencing music.

Looking back at that long, loud summer, the tinnitus was probably already there for a while. But I probably didn't notice it because my busy schedule never gave me enough time to notice. It took 10 years of performing with loud bands for it to show itself, but it was obviously beginning to develop long before that one loud summer. Along the way there were some warning signs. I did notice my ears ringing after some shows.

A few friends and family members had suggested wearing earplugs as they thought my bands were too loud. During performances I often found myself turning up to find my guitar amps' sweet spot and to hear myself above the roar of the drummer. I don't have many regrets in life, but if I could go back and do it all over again, learning how to control the volume of my music, and the use of hearing protection would definitely be explored.

Musicians with Tinitus include Neil Young, Pete Townsend, Paul Schaffer, Jeff Beck, Eric Clapton, Eric Johnson, James Hetfield, Lars Ulrich, The Edge, Cher, Ozzy Osbourne, Huey Lewis, Mick Fleetwood, Al Di Meola, Trent Reznor, Steve Lukather, Anthony Kiedis, Todd Rundgren, and many more.

Down and Out

A couple of years after I moved to Nashville, I began to play some weekly shows with a female singer at a club on Broadway. She had some great players in her band, and I really hit it off with the rhythm section. The drummer was in his early 50s and an exceptional musician. One day in between sets, I was chatting with him, and he told me a little bit of his story. For most of his career he had worked as an A-Team session player. He had played on many big album projects over the years and earned a more than modest living doing it. About a year before this point in time, he suffered a stroke and was forced to take some time off from his session work. A couple of months later he had recovered and was ready for work again, only to find that his work had all dried up.

Every studio situation and account that had been employing him had found other drummers, and his spot no longer existed. Now he was playing low-paying gigs on Broadway for the first time in his life just to try to get back in the loop. It wasn't that his old session buddies didn't want to help him; many of them did try. But in the end, his absence created a void that needed to be instantly filled, and once it was filled, his spot was gone.

These stories demonstrate how the "show must go on" attitude inherent to the career musician can result in preventable illnesses and avoidable problems being ignored or unnoticed until it is too late. They also underscore the important role that health plays in your career and life.

Why Not Record Yourself

"Making records is like making sausages, the end result is palatable but you don't want to see how it's done." — Bob Powers

Are you hoping to find work as a session player? Or planning to record your original music on a long term basis? Rather than spending your money at someone else's studio or waiting years for your first session call, why not put that time and money into building your own studio and learning how to record yourself? With computers and technology now affordable to the masses, it is now possible to produce recordings in your own home studio that are competitive with the rest of the music industry. All you need is a good computer, some studio monitors, a couple of microphones, and an inexpensive interface to get started. Other than the computer, the rest of this can be had for under $1000 if you shop wisely (there's nothing wrong with buying used equipment). It won't take very many trips to someone else's studio to spend $1000, and you might be waiting the rest of your life for your first session call.

When I first moved to Nashville, I, like many, wanted to work towards being a professional recording musician. I figured to gain some experience and connections, recording my originals was a good place to start. I found a great studio on music row and spent roughly $3000 (80 hours at $40 an hour over a 2 week period) recording this project. I tried to take my time to get it right, but in the end I always found myself watching the clock as it was all on my dime. This fact, always in my subconscious, seemed to get in the way, sometimes restricting the overall creativity and vibe. Although the final product turned out good, I felt I could have spent more time on it, but simply could not afford to.

This experience prompted me to buy some gear and learn how to do it myself. It was the best investment of time and money I have made since my move to Nashville. Now I record myself and others on a regular basis, both for money and enjoyment. I can put as much time into my projects as I need or choose, work at my own pace, and really get deep inside of the recordings I make. I have found that by learning how to make a good recording, I have learned a great deal about how a great song is constructed, the importance of good parts and the space they need, and the art of capturing a strong performance plus much more. I have no doubt improved my overall musicianship throughout this process and learned a great deal about engineering, producing, arranging, composition, and the importance of these roles in the recording process.

So, if you are thinking about going to a studio to record your own music on any kind of regular basis, just do a little math. How many trips to a studio at $30 to $40 per hour or more will it take to add up to the cost of some recording gear? How much time will you spend in the years to come earning the money for those sessions? How much more effective could you be if you had the freedom to record whenever you want without punching the time clock? And for those who want to be paid for playing on sessions, understand that paid sessions in this town (and in general) are hard to come by. There are a lot of people that already have those jobs sewn up. If you create your own home recording environment, you will be one step ahead of all the players that don't.

Home recording is an art form that isn't right for everyone. In today's DIY world, millions of amateurs are flooding cyberspace with millions of amateur-sounding home recordings. To make an exceptional-sounding home recording takes time, money, perseverance, and dedication, but, then again, so does a career in music. The Internet contains a wealth of knowledge about how to build a home studio as well as recording and mixing techniques. If you have some friends who are home recording savvy, they will initially be your best teachers. In the end you will become a better musician and have a better understanding about what makes a great song by learning the recording process. If you hope to ever get paid for your studio performances, or plan on writing and recording your music for a long time to come, learning to record yourself may be the only viable option.

Mindset And Character

"Character cannot be developed in ease and quiet. Only through experience of trial and suffering can the soul be strengthened, vision cleared, ambition inspired, and success achieved." — Helen Keller

Being a part of the Nashville music industry is like belonging to a club - a unique club for musicians, singers, songwriters and other various technicians that attracts all kinds of people, from all walks of life from all over the world. These musical immigrants can vary greatly in regards to the personal and social character traits they each possess. The extremely high level of competition found in this community requires a person to have a strong character, one that can survive the pitfalls of an industry that eats its young. This fact is true of the music business in general. If you want to succeed, it is to your advantage to know your inner strengths and weaknesses and always strive to improve on them.

Many people earning a living from music today built their careers slowly over a long period of time and endured a lot of tough times along the way. A lot of them started with very little and worked hard to establish good reputations, and their reputations ultimately led to work.

As I mentioned at the beginning of this book, when I first arrived in Nashville in the summer of 2002, I was most fortunate to already have a great friend here - someone I had known and shared music with many years before that moved here for a career in music, accomplished many of his goals, and built a solid reputation for himself along the way. He took me under his wing and offered me advice and insight that could only come from someone who had put years of sweat and hard work into a music career in Nashville. This advice rang true, and I took it to heart. His words became part of my being, and I slowly implemented many of his messages and ideas into my daily life.

Over the years I also received some great advice from many other talented people and have adopted some of their ideals as well. The following pages puts forth some of my favorite quotes and many key concepts I always try to keep in mind. Some are from D, a few are from me, and the rest are from the best.

The people you are meeting today and the relationships you build with them are what is going to give you work 5 years from now

You're not going to come to this town and take over in 6 months

When in doubt, lay out

Your tone will get you work

Don't join a band here, bands starve

Don't play over the vocals

We're the country music commandos; when the call comes, you gotta go

Good news travels slowly, but if you fart on stage they'll immediately hear it all over town

The janitor said we rocked!

Remember the three P's - Professionalism, Persistence, and Patience

Remember the three T's - Timing, Tone, and Taste

Listen for the silence in between the notes

Play for the song; it's the only thing the audience cares about

Less is usually more, but occasionally less is less

Play every note as if it were the last note you will ever play

Try to find ways to continually challenge yourself

Flash might get you noticed, but taste will get you the gig

Your performance is your business card

Your appearance is part of your advertising

Have a strong work ethic

Be a team player

Don't fear your competition; learn from it

Have a lot of irons in the fire

Be a one-stop shop and be prepared to wear a lot of hats

Observe and assess each situation before you act

Choose your friends carefully

Choose your words even more carefully

Be objective about your abilities

Be realistic about your goals

Be cautiously optimistic about life

Don't wear your heart on your sleeve

Don't ask for somebody's opinion if you aren't prepared for harsh criticism

Take criticism in stride and use it for self-improvement

Show respect for your peers and others around you

Don't count somebody out just because they're down

Every gig you play is an audition

Every night on the town is a job interview

You never know who's watching, so always assume somebody's watching

Don't lose sight of your own dreams and aspirations

Have a good balancc between your career and the rest of your life

Have a good balance between your music and your career

Have a good back-up plan

Keep it fun

Life is short, so make it count!

Like everything else in the music business and life in general, it comes down to relationships with people to provide the right path needed for you to reach your goals. These people are everywhere, in all walks of your daily life; you must simply be receptive and open to the possibilities. Most people who are in a position to help your career have busy careers themselves and don't have time for insincerity or game players. Your sincerity and ability to form genuine, long term relationships with the people around you is ultimately going to determine the level of success you achieve.

My old rock band "Shockwave" rocking out in a New England nightclub, 1995

Define "Making It"

Hey, I don't have all the answers, in life, to be honest, I've failed as much as I've succeeded, but I love my wife, I love my life, and I wish you my kind of success." — Dicky Fox from the movie Jerry McGuire

So, that's it. If you have read the entirety of this work, you now know much of what I have learned about the Nashville music industry. It is now up to you to decide what to do with this information. Now that you know a little about what goes on behind the curtain, do you still desire a career in music? If you do, this might be a good time to define your vision of success.

What are you trying to accomplish, and why is this important to you? Sometimes it's easy to determine what your goals are, but much harder to understand why you have them. Ask most musicians and aspiring artists what they are working towards and answers are usually quickly forthcoming. *"I want to play on a tour." "I want to land a record deal." "I want to be a session player." "I want to be a hit songwriter." "I want to make my living from music."* These are all common responses.

When I was 12 years old I heard the music of Jimi Hendrix for the first time and I was deeply moved. At that moment, all I knew was that the sound of his music was pure magic, and that connection instilled in me the desire to also one day make music that was magic. I didn't know or care about the realities of touring, playing concerts, recording, or music careers in general; all I understood was the electrifying experience I got when I listened to this music. As the years churned past I worked at my abilities as a guitarist, enjoying each musical milestone as it occurred. At some point in high school I thought it might be a good idea to explore becoming a career musician, even though I didn't know what that entailed. By the time I was in my early 20s, I had already attended Berklee College of Music and was playing music professionally in nightclub bands. By this point in time, I was determined to "make it" in the music business. I was driven, literally obsessed, with this goal. But when one of my best friends would periodically say to me, *"You say you want to make it in the music business, what do you mean by "make it? And why do you want to make it?"* I couldn't answer him. I would say things like, *"I want to be a rockstar," "I want to be on tour,"* and even, *"Because I feel like I was meant to."* The truth is I didn't have a clue. I didn't know what it meant to be on a tour, and I didn't really even know why this was important to me.

Regardless of *what* you're trying to do, take a brief moment and think about the why. If your goal is to land a record deal, *why* do you want to land a record deal? Is it because you think that's the best way to become a popular touring and recording artist? If that's the case, *why* do you want to become a popular touring and recording artist? Is it because you feel so strongly about your music that it must be shared with the world? Is it for the money, the fame, or maybe the recognition of your peers? Are you sure that a record deal is the best way to accomplish your goals? If it is your goal to simply earn a living from music, again, ask yourself *why* this is so important to you? Is it because you've heard that it is a lucrative and rewarding profession? Is it because you think it will be fun to play in front of 10,000 people or work in a recording studio? If you begin to understand the *why,* it becomes easier to figure out the *how*. Understanding why you have the goals you have can also help determine if the business of music can even deliver the success you envision. In other words, is your definition of success a reality in the real world?

Music is a powerful force. It possesses the ability to inspire, heal, teach, transcend, and liberate people. Music is life's all-encompassing communicator, crossing over ethnic, social, and language barriers. But the business of music rarely has any of these aspirations at its core. It is all too often driven by a less noble set of principles.

So the bottom line is - do what you love. If you love playing music, play. If you love singing, sing. If you love writing songs, write. If it is your desire to turn these talents into a career, arm yourself with knowledge. Work towards understanding the path on which you proceed and put your best foot forward. Do your best to understand *why* you're doing what you're doing, so you will be less likely to wind up on the wrong path. Maybe a music career is right for you, but maybe you could be just as happy, or even happier, doing something else for a career and keeping your musical life separated from the business world. A good day job can create a regular schedule and financial stability that can, at times, be *more* conducive to setting the stage for rewarding musical experiences. On the other hand, even working as a sideman on a tour will take you places that you might never otherwise explore, and teach you about life in a whole new way.

For me, I wouldn't trade in my musical journey for anything. It was through performing music that I met my beloved wife, Kelly. My path as a career musician has introduced me to many wonderful friends. It was also through music that I discovered my hidden talent of writing, which ultimately has led to the writing of this book and a whole new alternate career. Music has taught me about life, and life has taught me about music.

So decide for yourself. What's *really* important is *your* definition of success. The music industry's definition of success, or society's definition, ultimately means nothing. You must be happy with the choices you make.

To me, success is good times with my friends and family, being able to pay the bills on time, and getting to make some magical music once in a while. As long as I can continue doing this, I've made it.

When I was living in New England in the 1990s, I frequently attended some shows of a great local cover rock band. Most of the guys in this band worked day jobs and primarily played on the weekends. They were a fun, energetic, talented party band that played classic and modern rock. Over time, they built a large following, eventually packing every venue they played and getting paid well to do so. Every show they played was an event, with people showing up early, dancing and partying all night, and at the end of the night nobody wanted to leave. These guys were doing well enough to hire a production company that not only set up and ran a PA and light show, they actually carted around and set up the band's personal gear, allowing them to show up minutes before downbeat, making a rock star entrance every time. They even had girls falling all over themselves to make their acquaintances.

While they never wrote a song, made a recording, or even ventured outside of their region, they were kings of the New England night club circuit for over 10 years. During that same time, I played in a rival band on the same circuit. Although we didn't have quite as large a success, we also did pretty well. Looking back, none of the bands that played on this circuit, mine included, really viewed themselves as achieving the kind of success we envisioned, everybody was still trying to "make it." Flash forward another decade to Nashville Tennessee, and I've now played on concert stages in front of tens of thousands of people, in every state in the country. I've played in Canada, Europe, and on the Grand Ole' Opry. By everybody's definition back home, I have "made it." While the numbers might be bigger, the concept is still the same. I'm still playing music with a good band to receptive audiences and getting paid to do it. But now that it's a career, while there are many high points, there's also more pressure and less stability. To me, the reality is that there is very little difference between these two worlds. It's all just music and life, only the scenery has changed. Now when I look back to my nightclubbing days in New England, it is with fondness and pride. I had already made it long before I moved to Nashville.

Have you already made it but just don't know it yet?

miles
miles
Pearl

About The Author

By the time Eric Normand relocated from New England to Nashville in the summer of 2002 he had already invested a lifetime into music. Beginning at a very early age, many years before he would ever see the countryside from a tour bus window or set foot upon the stage of the Grand Ole Opry, he found himself surrounded by music. With dad on the bass and mom on guitar and vocals, Eric found himself soaking in their regular performances at churches, nursing homes, and family gatherings. Although much of what they played was folk music, it was dad's record collection of old school blues and rock that that seemed to be of most interest to a young and impressionable Eric.

Eric showed a desire to be different with his first two forays into playing an instrument, the banjo at age eight, and the piano at age ten. But it wasn't until hearing a recording of Jimi Hendrix at the age of twelve that he would discover the electric guitar as his true calling. With a little help from mom and a couple of other young guitar buddies, he would spend his high school years learning riffs and songs from records, jamming with friends, and exploring the world in the way only a teenager can.

At age 15 with his new Fender Stratocaster

By his junior year of high school, he was taking music pretty seriously and became interested in attending the world renowned Berklee College of Music in Boston, Massachusetts. After a few unsuccessful attempts to gain admission followed by a couple of years of formal training he was accepted and began his studies as a performance major.

Berklee
COLLEGE OF MUSIC

GRADE REPORT

1140 Boylston Street, Boston, Massachusetts 02215 · (617) 266-1400

NORMAND ERIC J. 60112 TERM 1/89

COURSE NO.	COURSE TITLE	GRADE	CREDIT
AR101 008	CHORD SCALE VOICINGS FOR ARR	A-	2.0
EN108 021	RHYTHM SECTION & VOCAL ENS	A	1.0
ET014 012	EAR TRAINING 4	A-	2.0
HR014 025	HARMONY 4	B+	2.0
IL168 002	BLDING GTR TECH THROUGH TRIADS	W	0.0
IS015 212	PRIVATE INSTRUCTION - GUITAR	B+	2.0
PS207 001	PERFORMING HARMONY WORKSHOP I	A	2.0
SW120 001	LYRIC WRITING 1	W	0.0

ERIC J. NORMAND 203
KINGSTON NH
03848000000

CODE: 3DXX
INST: GUIT
DATE: 5/12/89

NOT AN OFFICIAL TRANSCRIPT

G.P.A.	LETTER GRADE	C.G.P.A.
3.64	B+	3.47

In the fall of 1989 he began what would be a 14 year adventure into the world of the nightclub performer, playing throughout the Northeast in several successful top 40, rock, and blues bands. It was during this time period that he discovered his knack for organizing and problem-solving and wound up as the bandleader in many of these groups, eventually owning a box truck full of state-of-the-art PA and lighting equipment.

Along the way, the combination of an inquisitive mind with a desire to share his knowledge would lead to an alternate career, that of the music teacher. By the time he headed for Nashville, he had built up a roster of 35 private students, teaching guitar and bass out of his home and several music stores. Always interested in helping others develop musically, Eric encouraged his students to be involved with band activities and would often invite students to sit in with his own band.

For Eric, moving to Nashville was just the next step in the lifelong quest of a professional musician, and he arrived eager to learn. With the full support of his wife and son, and some advice from a friend, he began his freshman year in Nashville with the same wide-eyed wonder and openness he had when he attended his first year at Berklee, some 14 years before.

Growing up on a diet of classic rock, blues, and jazz, he would now have to dig in hard to get up to speed with country music. Financing his first year in Nashville with a combination of credit cards and his new career of selling off musical equipment on eBay, he spent many long hours working on his chicken pickin' technique and learning country standards while going out on the town nightly to network.

In addition to some sporadic gigs around town, that first year found Eric working a handful of tour dates as guitarist and bandleader for country music legend Vern Gosdin. Also within that first year, he spent a few months working as the house guitarist at the weekly variety show, Libby's, in Daysville Kentucky, once famous for its live radio show and the launching of several major Nashville artists.

About a year into this new life of a country commando he landed his first road gig as a guitar tech on the Toby Keith tour. Going from gigs on Broadway and Printers Alley to the biggest tour in country music was another eye-opener, and the experience would provide him with a wealth of knowledge and new experiences. Working as a tech on a tour of this magnitude would grant a birdseye perspective into the daily activities of an artist, band, and crew on this level, as well as what has to go on behind the scenes to make a large scale concert and tour happen. The tour was a whirlwind playing 90 concerts in as many major cities across all lower 48 states in about a six-month period, as well as making several appearances on the popular late-night shows.

The following year would grant Eric an opportunity to work as a guitar player on the Honky-Tonk Tailgate Party, a package tour in which one band backed four artists nightly: Rhett Akins, Daryle Singletary, Chad Brock, and Jeff Carson. It was during this time that Eric enjoyed his first experiences performing on the Grand Ole' Opry, backing Singletary and Akins on numerous occasions. By the fall of 2005, this tour disbanded, and Eric stayed on with Rhett. This transitional point would create a void in the position of tour manager within Rhett's new organization, and Eric seized this opportunity, seeing it as another opportunity for learning and advancement.

Continuing some in-town nightclub work along the way, it was during this period that Eric began playing on some paid recording sessions, experiences which would lead him to build his own recording studio, Music on a Hill. On one memorable session in a major recording studio in town, Eric found himself playing guitar behind Hank Williams Jr. when the legend made a cameo appearance for the recording of the Rhett Akins hit "Kiss My Country Ass."

Photo courtesy Bart Busch

Adventuring deep into the world of composition, Eric began recording a vast library of instrumental music which led to the licensing of his music to the television shows "Realtrees Road Trips with Michael Waddell," "the Tommy Wilcox Show," and the documentary Chef Da Riz by award winning filmmaker Jeremy Campbell. Along the way he also learned how to record and mix songwriter demos.

For Eric, this second half of his life, a life which was born in Nashville, has peeled back the curtain of mystery that had previously cloaked the music biz, as it has, and continues to do for most musicians not working within it. While his story is unique, the experiences he has had are similar to many working in this industry, and while attainable for some who desire a career within it, this world remains a mystery to most.

Always searching for answers and often feeling compelled to share the gifts of knowledge, Eric' first major work as an author,"The Nashville Musician's Survival Guide," is a useful guide and perspective about the music industry. More importantly, it is a story about people, music, and the intersecting roads they travel. And it is perhaps the teacher within Eric that has brought him to put forth what he has learned along those roads in the hopes of helping others achieve their dreams.